DISCARD

Making Money in Technical Writing

Peter Kent

MACMILLAN • USA

Macmillan General Reference USA
A Simon & Schuster Macmillan Company
1633 Broadway
New York, NY 10019-6785

An Arco Book

ARCO, MACMILLAN and colophons are registered trademarks
of Simon & Schuster, Inc.

Manufactured in the United States of America

10 9 8 7 6 5 4 3 2

Library of Congress Number: 97-071470

ISBN: 0-02-861883-1

Raves for the First Edition of This Book

"I took your advice and doubled my income overnight! I made $150,000 last year."

—*Technical Writer BR, Texas*

"What a treasure trove of information! It was truly inspiring and encouraging to a tech-writer wannabe."

—*Evelyn Barker, Coppell, Texas*

"Your book has been an inspiration . . . And it's working! Your book gave me solid practical pointers, good advice and ego boosting, too . . . I'm working because I followed your advice."

—*Nancy McDonald-Kenworthy, Athena's Pen, Columbus, Ohio*

"I have never worked as a tech writer before this . . . I read your book. I created a business plan. I followed it. I've been lucky, but part of that luck was running into a copy of your book."

—*Jeff DeLeeuw, Woodinville, Washington*

"I thought your advice on pros and cons of freelancing was better than any I've encountered in 16 years of putting up with corporate entrapment or 10 years of academia . . . Your [book] is sound information, pithy, extensive, and (best of all in my mind) it's well-written."

—*Julia Ripley, Denver, Colorado*

"Your book is very practical and covers every aspect of freelancing . . . It's obviously written by a successful, experienced professional, and now I can't imagine striking out on my own without a copy on my bookshelf."

—*TE, Colorado*

"I started to search for a book to help me, as I didn't have a clue how to get started. I found about a squillion books telling me how to write, how to interview techies, how to prepare manuals, etc. but only one (YOURS) that told me how to get started in the business of writing."

—*Sharilyn Mildon, San Pedro, California*

"I've been a successful freelance writer for over 20 years and I still learned quite a bit from this book. Peter Kent covers all the bases in the freelancing writing trade . . . He speaks to every level of writer from rank novice to the highly experienced and shows you how to increase both your skills and your income exponentially."

—*Ryan Bernard, Wordmark . Com, Houston, Texas*

"I was determined to be a successful freelancer and now I am. Thanks for the guidance."

—*DSS*

"I found your book very helpful in my budding freelancer career . . . a very well-written book with some very practical advice."

—*H. Frank Harper, HIDS, Inc., Kennesaw, GA*

"I found your approach to be realistic and right on target."

> —*Karen Steele, Manager of the Society for Technical Communication's Consultant's and Independent Contractor's Professional Interest Committee*

"Your book definitely made the difference and all the advice was right on the money . . . I'm still getting calls even though it was over a year ago that I first sent out résumés to agencies per your plan."

> —*JHS, Simpson NC*

"Anyone in this business who doesn't have Peter Kent's book, or doesn't refer to it, is flying blind!"

> —*Jim Bersie, Editors Unlimited, Chicago, IL*

"Thanks so much for your book, which steered me in the right direction. It was the right information at the right time."

> —*Greg Davis, Kissimmee, FL*

"I've been freelancing for about four years, and [your book] has been very helpful. I'm really looking forward to the new edition."

> —*JL*

"I've worn out two copies of [your] first book!"

> —*KN*

"I'm looking forward to the second edition. I have the first edition and it's been the most-used book on my freelance business shelf the last few years!"

> —*CT*

"This book is filled with good information about setting rates, networking, negotiating with agencies, the IRS, and taxes . . . a must for any technical writer's bookshelf."

> —*John Eldard, in the STC (Society for Technical Communication) Intermountain Update*

"It covers its topic extremely well."

> —*Maine Regional Library System*

"A comprehensive primer for the aspiring technical writer."

> —*The Bookshelf, a syndicated book review column*

"The book is well organized in sequential steps to help readers make intelligent decisions about how they will make the change from direct employment to contracting . . . the book has plenty to offer the aspiring contractor . . . this book should be a useful addition to the library of the beginning freelancer and the person considering independence."

> —*Paul T. Foote, in Technical Communication, the Journal of the Society for Technical Communication*

Contents

Introduction   *vii*

Part I: Getting Started

Chapter 1: Technical Writers: "Just Passing Through"?   3

Chapter 2: How to Get Started in Technical Writing   13

Chapter 3: Teach Yourself Technical Writing   23

Chapter 4: What Is Freelancing?   31

Chapter 5: The Advantages of Freelancing   43

Chapter 6: The Disadvantages of Freelancing   49

Chapter 7: How Much Do You Currently Earn?   57

Part II: Step One: Using the Agencies

Chapter 8: Finding the Technical Service Agencies   71

Chapter 9: Negotiating with the Agencies   81

Chapter 10: Unethical Agencies   91

Chapter 11: The Interview   99

Chapter 12: Contracts   103

Chapter 13: Buying Your Benefits   105

Chapter 14: Work Habits and Overtime   117

Part III: Step Two: Cut Out the Middleman

Chapter 15: Preparing for Step Two   129

Chapter 16: Networking   133

Chapter 17: Looking for Work   141

Chapter 18: Taxes for the Freelancer   149

Chapter 19: Are You Really an Independent Contractor?   163

Chapter 20: More on Contracts   171

Part IV: Step Three: Consulting

Chapter 21: Step Three—Technical Writing Consultant   185

Chapter 22: Sales Basics   197

Chapter 23: Should You Incorporate?   207

Chapter 24: Working Online   219

Chapter 25: Writing Magazine Articles and Books   231

Epilogue   245

Appendix A: Contractor's Checklist   247
Appendix B: Contractors' Publications   251
Appendix C: Technical Service Firms   253
Appendix D: Associations   258
Appendix E: Correspondence Courses, Training Courses, and Seminars   264
Appendix F: Other Resources   268

Bibliography   269

Index   273

Introduction

A few years ago I attended a writer's conference, where I met a woman who had once been a reporter. She'd left journalism and was looking for another way to make a living, so when I told her that I was a technical writer, she wanted to know how much money technical writers could make. I responded that it depended on a few factors, but that in most North American cities, "It's fairly easy for a freelance technical writer to make $70,000 a year." I'd hardly finished my sentence when a man close by laughed. He'd been eavesdropping, and was eager to explain that he was a technical writer, and none of *his* colleagues made $70,000 a year!

And now here I am telling you that technical writers can actually make *$100,000* a year. Am I serious? Or just trying to hype a book? In fact, as you'll learn in Chapter 1, technical writers really can make that sort of money. I'll even explain how you can confirm for yourself that this figure is not merely pie-in-the-sky nonsense. Will *you* make $100,000 a year if you read this book? Perhaps not—or perhaps you'll make a lot more. I've met technical writers earning $150,000 and up. In Chapter 1 I'll present the evidence, and in the rest of the book I'll explain how you can tap into a lucrative market and boost your income.

Why are you reading this book? Maybe you're already a technical writer—or technical author, as the profession is known in some countries—and want to find out how you can leave your job and work freelance. Perhaps you have worked with other freelancers or contractors, have heard about the money they make, and envied their freedom and detachment from office politics. Maybe you are already a freelancer (or contractor, job-shopper, or consultant) and are just looking for ways to improve business. Or maybe you are a journalist who is tired of the low wages and long hours, a copywriter who needs a change of pace, or just someone who wants to be a writer and is looking for a way to make a living. Whatever your reason for wanting to know more about freelance technical writing, I'll tell you how to get where you want to go.

The main topic of this book is how to use your technical writing skills to build a freelance career, but I will also explain how to get those skills in the first place. You will find out how much money technical writers make, what they do, and how they came to be technical writers (it's remarkably easy for a determined newcomer to enter the profession). If you are not already a technical writer, you will learn how to become one. If you are a technical writer, you will learn how to double or triple your income.

This is not a "quit work/risk everything/work freelance/make loads of money" book, however. I will tell you how to become a freelancer, and I will tell you how to make a good living. But I'm not going to tell you to risk everything, because you don't need to.

The systems described in most freelancing books have two major problems. The first is that you need a lot of money to get started. And if you don't have the money? Wait until you have saved enough, says the author of one of these books, or get a bank loan. How long will it take to save enough money to survive without an income for five or six months, for example? And how many people want to go into hock on a gamble?

The second problem is the risk involved. Leaving a steady job and using your own marketing skills to find contracts is dangerous. If you are not successful, you lose not only the money you saved (or borrowed) but also the money you would have earned had you been fully employed.

I'm going to explain why you don't have to start with large sums of money, and why you don't need to take any risks. In fact, your job security will actually increase—real job security, that is, not the illusion of security that so many of us have.

I will describe a Three-Step Method that makes it safe and easy to become a freelance writer. In Step One you will use the technical-service agencies to find work for you. You can go straight to a high-paying job, without any time out of work. Follow my advice on how to deal with the agencies and you can increase your income 50, 60, or 70 percent, perhaps more.

Step One helps you save money and build the network you need for Step Two. In Step Two you'll move out on your own, make your own contracts, and cut out the middleman.

If you reach Step Three you will have a different form of relationship with your clients, more of a consulting relationship. No longer considered just "a "warm body," the consultant gets work because the client is looking for someone with a reputation for being the best in the business. Some writers in this third group make an income in the $100,000s.

I'll be explaining more than this Three-Step Method, though. I'll talk about how you can use your writing skills to get published in technical magazines and books. You'll gain the satisfaction and pleasure that comes from seeing your work in print, and a little more respect from your clients that translates directly into a higher income. If you are lucky you may also find a *very* lucrative occupation; some computer-book writers make several hundred thousand dollars a year.

Many books on freelancing try to cover everything, including the details of setting up a business—accounting, getting a business name, setting up your office, and so on. One book even tells you in which desk drawer you should place your most-used items (the top-right one, apparently)! My book, however, concentrates on finding work. Where I have digressed into taxes and the law, I have done so to discuss issues of particular concern to freelancers. If you want a *general* business book, look elsewhere; there are many excellent ones in your local bookstore.

But if you want to freelance, and don't know where to start, you've come to the right place. Read on!

Part I

Getting Started

Technical Writers:

"Just Passing

Through"?

A feast is made for laughter, and wine maketh merry: but money answereth all things.

Hebrew Bible. Ecclesiastes 10:19.

There is a common theme in technical writing humor (yes, there is such a thing): Technical writing is boring, technical writers get no respect, and everyone would rather be doing something else. A friend of mine once published a small newsletter called *Dull Way (A Publication for Tech Writers & Dullards)*. Another friend claims he was dancing with a girl one evening when she asked what he did for a living; when he said he was a technical writer, she walked away. And the following poem by Roger L. Deen satirizes a widespread feeling among technical writers.

Just Passin' Thru

He claimed to be one of those few
Who detested what tech writers do,
So as the years rolled by,
He continued to cry
"I'll be gone soon—I'm just passin' thru."

Quoth he to all who would hear:
"Tech writin's for chumps, that's clear.
I'm smarter than you,
'Cause I'm just passin' thru."
He's been saying that now seven year.

When Judgment Day finally comes true,
And Saint Peter asks, "What'd you do?"
He'll answer with pride,
As he swaggers inside,
"I'm a tech writer, and I'm just passin' thru."

There's no smoke without fire, of course (I'll discuss the "fire" later in this chapter), but there's another way to look at technical writing. For all the complaints about technical writing, most technical writers stick around. I don't know why the jokes circulate—maybe it's simply black humor common to all professions, or maybe it's just the people I hang around with—but if the Society for Technical Communication (STC) is right, most technical writers are quite happy. In a 1988 survey, the society found that 87 percent of its members were "very satisfied" or "satisfied" with the profession, while only 10 percent were "dissatisfied." And the money can be good, too. But before we get to that, let's talk about what technical writers actually do.

What Do Technical Writers Do?

Technical writers explain things. They explain how to use VCRs, how to use computer programs, how to install telecommunications switches, how to operate blood-testing instruments. Sometimes the technology they are explaining is very complex; it may take a team of 60 writers several years to document a telecommunications switch, for example. Other times what is being explained is fairly simple: how to operate an iron, for instance, or a telephone.

Sometimes they migrate to slightly different tasks. They might produce public relations brochures, company reports, or even advertisements, or help prepare articles for professional journals. They sometimes end up designing computer program "user interfaces," or even computer-based training courses. Sometimes they write proposals—documents used by a company to sell its products. These days many technical writers produce online help systems (such as Windows Help), World Wide Web pages, and multimedia presentations. In fact these last three areas are the "hot" new technologies that can provide a lucrative niche for the ambitious writer.

How Much Money Do They Make?

So how much do technical writers make? From $10,000 a year to $250,000, sometimes more. That's not a very useful range, so let me elaborate. Let's start by looking at the 1995 Salary Review published by the STC. (You can find a summary of the latest salary survey information on the Internet, at the STC's Web site at http://www.stc-va.org/ or http://stc.org/; you'll learn more about working on the Internet in Chapter 24.)

According to this survey, the median salary for a technical writer in the United States—or rather, a technical writer who also happens to be a member of the STC—was $41,078 (that is, 50 percent earn that much or less, while 50 percent earn more). The average salary was $42,469. In Canada the median salary was $44,550 and the average $44,322. In both nations, one writer in four was earning over $50,000. Let's look at the average salary related to years of experience (U. S. figures):

Years of Experience	Average Salary
Less than two years	36,714
Two to five years	36,062
Six to ten years	42,223
Eleven years and more	49,444

To me, those figures sound a little low. Of course, averages hide a lot. The 1995 STC survey found that one writer in 10 with less than two years experience was making $59,000 or above. (There must be a shortage of entry-level writers, because the survey found that many of these new writers were making more than writers in the two-to-five-year and six-to-ten-year groups. This just goes to show that surveys often raise as many questions as they answer.)

Location has a big effect, too: The median salary ranges from $36,000 in the Montana to Wisconsin region, to $44,000 in New England. The Pacific coast (California, Oregon, and Washington) is almost as high, at $43,000. Of course, breaking it down by geographical region doesn't give a perfect picture. Rates in Milwaukee, Wisconsin are probably higher than in Billings, Montana, though they are both in the same region in this study. In general, though, rates are higher on the coasts. And even in low-rate areas, there are probably pockets of high rates. Also, remember that you are not limited to finding work only where you live. Thanks to the wonders of electronic communications and overnight shipping services, you can live one place and work in another. I'll discuss that in Chapter 24.

Freelance Rates

This book is about freelancing. Salaries are all very well, but how much do *freelance* technical writers make? The 1995 STC survey doesn't contain information about freelancers. The 1990 survey did, though. Back then the average gross income for a consultant/independent contractor was $50,300, and 25 percent of freelancers were making $58,000 or more. These were the percentages of freelancers in several hourly-rate groups:

Hourly Rate (Dollars per Hour)	Percent
Less than 20	6
20 to 29	22
30 to 39	40
40 to 49	18
50 to 60	7
Over 60	4
No set fee	3

So 72 percent of the freelancers surveyed were making over $30 an hour, and 32 percent were making over $40 an hour. Bear in mind that "consultant/independent contractor" covers a lot of ground: people working through technical service agencies, people working on hourly-rate contracts, genuine consultants, and so on.

The 1995 STC Rocky Mountain Chapter Salary Survey found that the median income for freelancers was $52,500. The survey also found that the median experience for freelancers in that area is 11.4 years. Now, the salaried writers in the 11- to 15-years-experience category earn a median income of almost $47,000, so the freelancers are making more. However, even allowing for the fact that the "median" freelancer is at the bottom of that experience category, freelancers don't seem to be making a whole lot more.

The shame is that these freelancers are working for much less than they need to. With the right knowledge and effort, these writers could be making $80,000, $100,000, or more. I spoke with the person coordinating the Rocky Mountain survey; she told me that the respondents claimed hourly rates of from $6 to $110 an hour, with the lower rates being earned by the more inexperienced writers and some writers who had full-time work but were doing a little moonlighting. Six dollars an hour is a totally ridiculous rate, usually earned by people who don't understand the value of their skills; I sometimes run across writers who have no idea that anyone's making $50 an hour, let alone $100 or $110. In fact more than half of the freelancers were making $35 an hour or less—either because they were inexperienced or because they didn't know how to sell their services.

These surveys don't show the highest rates, of course, because they get merged in with all the other numbers. Unfortunately some of these salary surveys have been designed in such a manner that they either don't collect information about really high incomes, or fail to report any such collected data. In some cases respondents are asked to check a box next to the salary category they are in. In one STC survey the form had a category of "$40,000 and above." That covers a lot of ground! Some of the people checking that box might have been earning $40,001, while others might have been earning $150,000. Yet they all appeared in the same category!

I called the Dallas chapter of the STC to find out what the range was, and was told that there were several "six-figure incomes." At the top was a man in his mid-30s—with 11 years in technical writing—making $110,000. Next were two more men, each making $100,000, one in his mid-60s and one in his mid-50s, both with a lot of experience. All three were independents, of course. (To be fair, I should mention that at the other end of the range were two people who said they made only $12,000, and neither was entry-level; I can only assume these people were unable to work—because of sickness or inability to find a job—or didn't need to work.)

I've run into a few more big earners since then. One writer who read the first edition of this book wrote to tell me that he'd taken my advice "and doubled his income overnight," and that he was making around $150,000 a year. We've kept in touch, and he told me later that his income had almost reached $200,000 a year. A writer I met in Denver told me he'd made $150,000 during his best year.

When I called the Rocky Mountain chapter of the STC I was told that it had, indeed, received surveys from members making over $100,000. Four, I was told, were making between $100,000 and $124,999. One was making between $125,000 and $149,999. About 7 percent of the freelancers were making over $100,000. When you consider that some of the freelancers were making $6 an hour, and that over half were making less than $35 an hour, it's clear that many freelancers don't know how to sell themselves. Of the "serious" freelancers—those making $40 an hour and above—about 16 percent were making over $100,000. (Oh, but that's not fair, I can hear some of you saying, you're skewing the figures by ignoring the lower-paid writers. But I don't care to be lumped in with the lower-paid writers. This book is not called *"How to Barely Make a Living as a Technical Writer."* I'm concerned with showing you the true potential, not how little uninformed writers make.)

By the way, you might like to refer to the STC's Consulting & Independent Contracting Special Interest Group Survey Results page on the World Wide Web, which you can find at http://english.ttu.edu/cicsig/Salary.htm. This provides an idea of the sorts of hourly rates freelancers are making. With luck this page will be regularly updated, so you'll be able to find the latest information.

Writing Computer Books

Those incomes are pretty good, but they go higher for some technical writers who write computer books. These books can be huge sellers: just take a look at any large computer-book publisher's catalog (publisher's such as Que, IDG, Sams, and many others). As you flick through, you will notice little signs saying "75,000 Sold," "Over 75,000," "Over 125,000," and "Over 500,000," even "1,500,000 in Print."

In general computer-book authors are paid a royalty—a share of the profit—on each book that's sold. Here's a quick way to figure out what an author made on a book that has an *xxx copies sold* sign on it. Take the price of the book and divide by two. If the book costs $25, you end up with $12.50. That's about the amount that the publisher sold the book for, on average. Now, take 10 percent of that sum; that's probably an average percentage that the author would make (so we're down to $1.25). Now multiply by the *xxx copies sold* value. If the book sold 250,000, multiply $1.25 by 250,000—we end up with $312,500. Not bad for a book that took 6 to 10 weeks to write! (Computer books have to be written very quickly, in order to keep up with a rapidly changing software market.) The numbers will vary a little, of course; royalties tend to range from 8 to 15 percent, sometimes higher, and some authors have agents, so they lose 15 percent of everything they earn in commissions. Still not bad, though.

These are not average technical writers, of course; very few reach these heights. In fact, some of the really high incomes are earned by writers who entered the computer book market at just the right time. When they began writing, there were few other computer book authors, few computer book publishers, but a rapidly growing market. While some of the early computer-book authors quickly became millionaires, such success is far more difficult today. Still, one computer book agent told me that his agency had "lots" of writers making $100,000 a year (but lots more writing part-time and making only $20,000). If you'd like to see a completely unscientific (yet interesting nonetheless) poll of computer-book writers, see http://www2.studiob.com/studiob/resources/articles/polls/comp.html on the World Wide Web.

While most computer-book authors write a book or two—perhaps make a little money, and never write more—some get lucky. Some just happen to write a best-seller the first or second time around. And others keep plugging away until they get a best-seller, or until they have enough books on the market to make a healthy income. (I had to plug away for a while—I got a best seller on my 11th book, and again somewhere around my 20th.) I'll talk about the computer-book business in Chapter 25.

Well, that's a lot of money talk. Money's not everything, though. To me, the great advantage of freelance technical writing is that it gave me the time I needed to pursue my book-writing career. I could earn in a few months enough to live for a year—and spend the rest of the year working on my books. Yes, I've broken the magic $100,000 mark. But I could have made much more money if I'd concentrated purely on my freelancing or consulting career. Instead I used freelance technical writing to fund my foray into the book business.

Will You Make $100,000 a Year?

You probably *won't* make $100,000 a year—at least not right away. Statistically, the average reader of this book is not going to run out and go straight to the top of the technical writing payscale. (On the other hand, some readers may be able to do this; one reader of the first edition of this book increased his income from an annual rate of $75,000 to $150,000 within a few months.) And remember, too, that even if you are capable of making this sort of money, it may take a few years to build your business, skills, and reputation to the degree that a six-figure income is possible.

It is relatively easy in many parts of North America to make $70,000 or $80,000 a year as a technical writer, though. Not everywhere—in some areas you'll have to work much harder to make that sort of money than in others. However, in many cities, agency technical-writing rates are high enough (all it takes is $35 an hour or so through a technical-writing agency, plus a little overtime now and again) that it really is easy to make this sort of money without any great effort. (Of course you'll have to know the ropes, but that's what this book is about.)

There's a problem with these rates, though; many experienced writers don't believe they exist. Writers who have never worked as freelancers may be unaware of just how much freelancers can make, through agencies or on their own. Even somewhat experienced freelancers may not sell their services well, and may settle for rates that are far too low. And many writers won't publicly admit how much they make. As one writer told me, "I don't discuss salary information, because 'captive' writers at my client might hear, and that would pose some discomfort all the way around!"

It's certainly true that many writers cannot become successful freelancers; it's just not for everyone. In Chapter 6, in fact, I list a variety of reasons for *not* becoming a freelance writer. But I'm sometimes accused of being too "optimistic," as if this is something bad! (Is it optimistic to tell people that they can do what thousands of others are doing, make a good living as a freelance technical writer?) It's usually people who don't know the freelance market, and so find the rates hard to believe, or people who haven't been able to make as much as other writers and so dismiss my claims as optimistic. Well, I am optimistic, and I believe a little positive thinking goes a long way. Pessimists rarely succeed; they always see the problems, not the potential. The money's there, after all. I'm not saying everybody can succeed, only that many people are making great incomes from technical writing, and *you may* be able to become one of them.

Talk to as many freelance writers as you can, read the technical writing mailings lists on the Internet (see Chapter 24), keep your eyes and ears open, and you'll learn that high rates really are possible. After that, it's up to you to do what it takes to get a share of the pie, or to decide that freelancing is not for you.

Is There a Gender Gap?

Incidentally, the STC reports that most of its members are women. Over 57 percent of the Dallas respondents were women, and almost 62 percent of the respondents to the national survey were women. Does this mean most technical writers are women? I don't think so. Most of the writers I know are men, though it seems that many of the younger writers are women. The national survey found a "larger number of women in the lower-paying, entry-level range."

Anyway, the fact that there are so many young women writers in the STC would tend to skew the median incomes a little, making the numbers look lower than they are in the real world. Do women writers get paid less than the men? Yes and no; in general, yes, because they are more likely to be in entry-level positions. But the 1990 STC survey found that when salaries are broken down by experience and age, women get paid about the same.

The 1995 survey was structured differently; it contained no experience categories broken down by sex. It did report, however, that in the last 10 years the "gender gap" in the technical communication profession has decreased from 19 to 4.5 percent." I suspect this is mainly because until recently there simply weren't many women in the profession. As more women entered, the salary figures tended to show a large gender gap—because most women in the business were entry level or slightly above. Now many women have been in the profession longer, and are gaining the seniority that brings them higher salaries. Technical writing is a profession in which women are doing well, taking many management positions, and, it seems to me—a mere male, admittedly—competing on an equal footing with men.

The Rest of the World

Technical writing is not limited to North America, of course. There are technical writers throughout the world (or technical authors, as they're called in many places). The STC has members in Australia, Austria, Belgium, Bermuda, Denmark, Finland, France, Germany, Hong Kong, Iceland, India, Ireland, Israel, Italy, Japan, South Korea, Kuwait, Namibia, New Zealand, Norway, Portugal, Saudi Arabia, Singapore, South Africa, Spain, Sweden, Switzerland, Taiwan, the Netherlands, and the United Kingdom. It has active chapters in France, Israel, Japan, New Zealand, Singapore, and Taiwan. There are other technical writing organizations throughout the world, too (see Appendix D for more information about the STC and other organizations).

The Drawbacks of Technical Writing

Now for the fire behind the smoke that I mentioned earlier. There are many problems in technical writing (though most can be cured by moving to another company—one of the beauties of freelancing). It is true that technical writing can be very boring; some technical writing is boring, that is, while some can be very interesting. Some jobs are very dry. One job I did for a telecommunications company consisted of "translating" computer printouts—pages and pages of numbers—into words. It was probably the most boring job I've ever had, almost matched by the time I worked for a Japanese telecommunications company translating "Jinglish" (English written by a Japanese person) into English.

But I've also had some very interesting jobs, like the "Windows application builder" I documented, a program that uses simple commands to build programs for Microsoft Windows, or the Windows Help authoring tool for which I wrote a user's manual. If you like playing with computers, there's a job waiting for you somewhere in technical writing; you get paid to play with the computer program and then write about it. Yes, some technical writing jobs are boring, just as some jobs in any profession are boring. The secret is being able to pick the jobs you want, something you can do after gaining experience and building a reputation.

Another oft-mentioned problem is the lack of respect accorded to technical writers. Again, some companies respect their writers, some don't. There are three reasons for this lack of respect. The first is that many companies don't like the idea of paying for documentation. Products are becoming intrinsically more complicated: CD players and VCRs are more difficult to use than gramophones, today's telephones are more complicated than those of just 10 years ago, and the rise of the personal computer has created a whole new field of "stuff" to learn. Explaining these products is expensive, and many companies resent this.

Some companies, however, have learned that documentation is as much of the product these days as the hardware (or software) itself; after all, if the buyer can't use the product, it's no good. In fact, the 1990 STC survey I mentioned earlier found that 60 percent of its members believe their employers are placing more importance on technical writing than they had previously. But many companies are still stuck in the old way of thinking and look on documentation as a necessary evil, to be produced as quickly and cheaply as possible.

Second, many managers don't respect their writers because they don't realize how difficult it can be to write a manual; just getting the information out of the developers can be like pulling teeth from a pit bull. Other companies do realize how difficult writing can be. Some expect their writers to produce just half a page a day, for instance.

The last reason for lack of respect can be thrown back at the writers themselves. Sad to say, standards in technical writing are very low. Technical writing is one of the few writing jobs in which the ability to write is not really essential—it helps, but it's not absolutely required. That's not just my impression, incidentally, but that of many other writers and managers I have spoken to. After *Software Maintenance News* published an article I wrote about the problems with technical writers, I received a call from a computer training company in New York. "We've had so many problems with our writers," the manager said. "I could have written that article myself!" In fact, to save rewriting, here's that article.

The Trouble with Technical Writers . . .

In 1988 I had the privilege of witnessing a "literary" disaster at a small telecommunications company (okay, so I used literary in the broadest possible sense). This company used the services of an international "consulting" firm; the firm provided six technical writers, at $37 per hour per writer—almost $250,000 by the end of the project.

The result? A few good books, but not $250,000 worth. In fact over $100,000 worth of writing time was wasted; much of the time didn't result in anything, and the rest resulted in books that the company had to trash.

Unfortunately, such disasters are not uncommon. Perhaps something similar has happened in your company, or maybe you've heard of similar cases, situations in which a company spends a lot of money on its writers, only to receive substandard documents—or nothing at all.

What went wrong at this telecommunications company? The first mistake they made was to place too much trust in the technical services agency (or "consulting firm" as they like to be called). For example, one of the writers really wasn't. "His résumé said he was a writer," the documentation manager told me, "but they exaggerated his experience."

Most agencies rewrite résumés to stress items they know the client will be looking for, and sometimes "putting the best face forward" turns into outright misrepresentation. In this case the agency took some minor writing work the employee had done while at college, and blew it up into a full-scale writing job. That "writer" was the first of the group to go.

Agencies are clearly not to blame for all of technical writing's problems, though; most of the problems lie with the writers themselves. In general, technical writers are either not technical or not writers, and often are neither technical nor writers.

Many writers have little technical experience—they may be graduates of journalism or English, for example. This isn't a problem if the person can learn quickly and pick up the technical knowledge necessary to write about a product, but in most cases such writers write beautiful prose with little substance. It sounds good, but it doesn't contain the needed information.

Three of the writers at the telecom company fitted this mold. One, for example, was a graduate of a technical writing course, but had no real-world technical experience. All three had difficulties understanding the technology with which they were working.

But all the technical knowledge in the world doesn't do any good if the writer is unable to get the information onto paper in a form that is understandable. Many writers have strong technical backgrounds—especially the ex-military writers who are so common in some industries—but many of these people write poorly, and are often used to writing in the stodgy milspecs (military specifications) style. (You've seen this type of writing: "See paragraph 2.3.4.1.5-A, Utilizing Functionality/Operationality Testing.") They may include all the information, but users won't want to dig through the garbage to find what they need.

Another major problem with writers is one that is probably common in many occupations: laziness. Maybe that's an unkind word. How about "lack of initiative" or "procrastination"? Writers have a tendency to "shoot the breeze" a lot; this was a serious problem with the group at the telecom company. One writer, for example, worked for about three hours, and talked on the phone or with co-workers the rest of the day. And the rest of the group suffered from the same problem to varying degrees.

Now, everyone needs a break now and again, and I won't pretend that I stare at my terminal all day without a rest, but there's a tendency among writers to slip into what the CEO at another telecom company called "a country-club atmosphere." (At that company, by the way, a group of eleven contract writers produced, at enormous cost, documents that the company's clients refused to accept.)

This laid-back attitude expresses itself in another way: Many writers avoid research and fact checking. They use only the information they have been given (which is often inaccurate or out of date), and rely on the product's developers to "catch mistakes in the reviews." (As you know, few developers have the time to review technical manuals thoroughly.)

The last major weakness suffered by writers is that of poor organizational skills. More than most work, writing demands sensible organization. A book may have all the required information and may be written by a Pulitzer Prize winner, but if it isn't organized well, it's wasted. How often have you looked in a document and been unable to find something where you know it should be? How often have you used (or given up using) a manual that forces you to jump from page to page, section to section, or even to another book? Many writers are unable to

continues

continued

organize their thoughts, and unable to put themselves in the reader's place and figure out at which point in a procedure the reader will need certain facts.

Having criticized writers (and risked upsetting friends and colleagues!), let me point out what may have become obvious: that technical writing requires such varied skills that it is actually quite difficult. There are few people who are technically proficient, write well, and can organize their work. (Incidentally, the best writers I know are programmers who can write well, but the worst writers I know are also programmers.)

It's always easy to criticize someone else—writers complain about programmers and programmers about writers—but it's not so easy to understand the problems that others face. As one writer friend told me, "You can't criticize another writer's work until you've been in the shoes he wore when he was writing." There's a lot to that, because many writing problems begin with the company, not the writers.

There are unrealistic deadlines, for example, and an unwillingness to provide the writers with the information and resources needed to do the job. And writers often suffer from a lack of respect within their companies (okay, it's often justified, but which came first, the chicken or the egg?), being regarded as a necessary evil, on the same level as the product's packaging or shipping label—you've got to have it, but you want to spend as little as possible. These attitudes lead to low morale and a lackadaisical attitude among a company's writers. (I remember the comment of one product manager to a documentation manager: "My 12-year-old daughter could write these books!")

Don't despair, though: It is possible to find good writers, and it is possible to produce good documentation. It just takes a little effort. Just remember this: Pick your writers carefully, and treat them well!

When I put this article into the first edition of this book, I expected to receive a lot of criticism. I thought that other technical writers would complain that I didn't respect them, that I didn't respect the "profession," that I was being unfair. I was surprised that most writers I talked with tended to agree with me. For instance, one writer sent me an e-mail complimenting me on the book, but commenting that I seemed to have a very low opinion of technical writers. I e-mailed back, and asked his opinion of most user manuals he received with equipment he bought. The manuals with VCRs, TVs, computers, digital watches, microwaves, computer programs . . . were they good? No, in most cases, they're pretty awful, he responded. As our correspondence progressed, it became clear that he believed *most* technical documentation was awful. Well, who's writing that stuff? Technical writers!

This person wasn't alone. One STC chapter president told me that he was depressed with the standard of technical documentation. Here he was, one of the leaders of an organization founded to promote technical writing as a "profession," yet he felt that few writers did a good job.

There's a real advantage to low standards, though. It's easy to rise to the top. If you are a good writer and know how to sell yourself (which is what this book is about), you can do well in technical writing . . . because you are way ahead of the competition.

How to Get Started

in Technical Writing

All professions are conspiracies against the laity.

George Bernard Shaw (1856–1950)

There's a perennial question in the technical writing world: "Is technical writing a profession or a trade?" (Some would answer, "Neither, it's a racket.") Many in the business like to think of it as a profession, but in many ways it really isn't—which is lucky for anyone trying to become a technical writer. (Okay, I use the term *profession* elsewhere in this book, but I've used it in a general way.) Why do we care whether it's a profession or not? Because it has a bearing on how easy it is to get into technical writing.

What is a profession? (This is really not a question of semantics, by the way; bear with me and you will find out why.) My *Oxford English Dictionary* calls it a "vocation or calling, especially one that involves some branch of advanced learning or science." I suppose technical writing could be called a vocation, but what about the learning? No one really knows what it takes to be a technical writer, what advanced learning or science is required. Yes, there are colleges that teach technical writing, and one day you may need a technical writing degree to enter the profession, but that day is a long way off. I know technical writers who have never even been to college; a 1988 Society for Technical Communication (STC) survey found that 12 percent of its members had no degree, and a survey by the Lone Star chapter of the STC showed that 18 percent of its members had no degree.

A friend suggested to me that technical writing is in the position that computer programming used to be. A few years ago almost anyone could become a programmer without a programming degree; there weren't any degree courses. People transferred into programming from various professions. But newcomers are now expected to have some kind of degree in computing. Perhaps eventually new technical writers will need a technical-writing degree. Perhaps, but not for a while yet.

Quick, name a profession. Doctors and dentists are professionals, right? Lawyers (jokes aside) are professionals. Psychiatrists and accountants are professionals. All these professions have set standards. You can't decide to be a dentist today and start tomorrow. There are specific courses of learning you must undertake, and tests you must pass. But not for technical writers. There are no specific requirements to be a technical writer, and if you ask 10 technical writers what it takes to be one, you will probably get 10 answers.

One reason for this is that the term "technical writing" covers so much ground. Writing a troubleshooting guide for a telephone company's central office switch is very different from writing a user guide for a word processing program, or a maintenance manual for a tape recorder. And there are so many ways to produce technical manuals. A few writers still use typewriters, as absurd as that sounds, while others are working on Sun workstations. The range of software used to write the books is enormous, and the production methods vary, from photocopying typed pages to professional full-color printing.

If you are a newcomer, the great thing about technical writing is that all this diversity means that there's a good chance someone somewhere will hire you, if you just keep looking. If you have a journalism degree, there's a manager somewhere who used to work on a newspaper and will hire you. If you are fresh out of the military, there's a military writer somewhere who will hire you. If you are an English major or worked as a field technician for a few years, there's someone who will hire you. This doesn't mean just anyone can walk in off the street and get a technical writing job, of course, but it does mean that it is possible for many reasonably educated people to enter the field, if they are prepared to spend a little time gaining some extra skills and then looking for work.

How do most technical writers get into the business? Through the back door—by being in the right place at the right time. Most writers seem to drift into it. A technician is out of work and a friend tells him of a company that needs someone with a technical background to document a new product. A secretary is told to write a user manual because no one else is available. A geologist is temporarily without a project, so his company keeps him busy writing a user guide. These days, many writers are actually choosing the career in college, but it's still possible to break into the business by being in the right place at the right time.

Were Do Tech Writers Come From?

What sort of people are technical writers? I think you can break writers down into several groups. Here are the basic groups I've seen:

The Ex-Military

There are many technical writers, mainly men, who got into the field thanks to their military careers. They were writing procedures or teaching while in the military, and often got jobs with military contractors when they left.

The Journalist

Lots of journalists move over to technical writing. They like the reasonable hours, and they've had enough of the poverty that seems to go with most newspaper jobs. The 1988 STC survey showed that 10 percent of its members were ex-journalists. Writers from other fields often gravitate to technical writing, too. One writer put it this way:

> I lost all my money in the mid-70s and early 80s, when I was trying to determine whether I would be a magazine writer, ad copywriter, marketing communications expert, or tech writer. I ended up writing cookie-cutter software

manuals because I could do it with both hands tied behind my back and not have people nit-pick me to death.

Hey, call me a hack . . . I'm a well-off hack. My more artistic friends live in hovels and drive beat-up old wrecks.

The English Graduate

A lot of people leave college with English degrees and then discover that there are few ways to make a good living with such a degree. Technical writing is an obvious choice, and one that can lead to a decent income. The 1988 STC survey found that 32 percent of its members had English degrees.

The Recent College Grad

There's a new breed of technical writer appearing: young people who took technical communication courses at college, as a minor or even a degree course, and make technical writing their first job. There aren't many of them around just yet, but the group is growing, and some companies like to stock up on them.

The Secretary

Some secretaries manage to make the leap from typing the boss's letters to writing technical manuals. It's a matter of being at the right place at the right time, and having a little technical ability. It doesn't happen often, but some secretaries have managed to quadruple or quintuple their incomes by becoming technical writers. I can think of three writers I've met who entered the business this way.

The Techie

A lot of people cross over from technical professions to technical writing. There are computer programmers, engineers, geologists, chemists, and so on—people who used their technical skills to get work writing.

How Other People Started

So how do you get into technical writing? I talked to a few writers and found out how they got into the business. You will find that, in most cases, these people don't have anything to show they are technical writers: no degrees, no diplomas, no licenses. No one ever said, "You are now a technical writer." The main thing these people have in common—except for the one "college kid" in the group—is that they simply decided they would become technical writers, in some cases even when they were told they didn't have the skills or education necessary.

Most people get into technical writing by being in the right place at the right time, or by making sure they are in the right place at the right time. These examples may give you an idea of how you can use your skills to find a technical writing job, or how you can gain the skills to do so.

Peter (That's Me)

I was an oil-field geologist at the wrong time, the early 1980s. I was promoted to manage my employer's Mexico City office and decided to take a vacation before assuming the position . . . when I got back the position had gone! The Mexican government had canceled our contracts, so I returned to Dallas to the company headquarters, where I was given a make-work position. "Write these manuals for the new computer system we are introducing," my employer said, "and in six months we'll send you overseas again." I spent the next six years writing manuals, training users, and installing and fixing computer equipment. Then I got laid off.

I spent about a year running my own import business, and then working in sales jobs to make ends meet. (This was great training, incidentally. If you want hands-on training in selling your technical writing services, spend a few months selling encyclopedias.) At that point, by the way, I didn't realize I was a technical writer. I was an oil-field geologist who had been sidetracked—along with thousands of other people—by the decline in the oil business. I didn't think of myself as a technical writer, that was just one of the things my employer made me do "until the business got better." But eventually I had to decide what I was going to do with the rest of my life. I sat down and thought for a while and decided that I wanted to be a writer. I had considered a journalism career eight years before, but never quite got around to it, and now, analyzing what I really liked to do, I realized that I should be a writer. But there was a problem. Writing doesn't pay much, I was to be a father in a few months, and I had a mortgage.

How, then, to make money writing? I knew journalism didn't pay well, at least in the United States, and didn't feel that I was at a stage in life at which I could start at the bottom of the financial ladder. I took a trip to my local library and started going through the career books. Then I found the *American Almanac of Jobs and Salaries*. Looking up *writers*, I found some interesting stuff. I noticed the section on technical writers. "Experienced technical writers in the private sector usually earn from $30,000 to $35,000," the book said (this was in 1987). It went on to discuss technical writers making $250,000 a year, and I realized that I had found a potential profession.

I was lucky, of course, because I had done some technical writing. Working for my oil-field employer, I had produced and maintained a book on a computer system. It was by no means my full-time job, though—I was also training users and installing computers—and my title was Systems Analyst, not Technical Writer. But I reformatted my résumé to stress the writing and started looking.

I was lucky in that some of my other experiences would give prospective employers more confidence in my technical abilities, not just my writing. I had trained computer users. I had designed computer-program user interfaces. I had installed and maintained computer equipment. I had used computer equipment in a "real-world" environment.

So, I began looking for technical-writing work, mainly in classified ads. Some of those ads were from agencies, some from employers. Luckily, the first couple of interviews *didn't* get me work. One was for a medical technology company that would have paid $25,000 a year, another was for a $16 per hour contract. When I discovered the agencies—I had no idea that working through the agencies was so common—I started trying to track down as many as I could. I used the Yellow Pages, the classified ads, and word of mouth (you will learn how to build your own list of agencies in Chapter 8). The more agencies I spoke to, the more I learned. I discovered, for example, that $16 per hour was way too low.

This is how I found out. After the $16 per hour offer, I spoke to another agency. This agency asked me how much I could work for. I said "around $20 an hour." "Yeah, that sounds okay," they said, so I figured I was asking too little. When I spoke to the next agency, I said "in the low $20s," and they said, "That sounds about right." So I knew I was nowhere near the maximum. But I was running out of money fast, and the contracts were taking too long to appear. I finally took a salaried position with an agency for $32,000 a year—though I later discovered the agency probably would have paid $35,000 if I'd pushed.

So there I was, on a "contract" but paid a salary (you'll learn about that sort of relationship in Chapter 4). I was making enough to get by, but still receiving calls from the dozens of agencies I had sent my résumé to. It's always easier to negotiate when you don't need a job, and I soon found that contract rates in my area were really in the high $20s, sometimes higher. When my first contract ran out seven months later, I found another at $27 an hour. And when that one ran out, I cut out the middleman and got a direct contract at $38 an hour. So in about a year I had gone from thinking that a salary in the mid-20s would be okay, to making $38 an hour, and it didn't stop there. A year and a half after that I was making $41 an hour, and then I began a more lucrative way to work—the "per-project" contract. I began making $100 an hour, sometimes much more.

When I decided to become a writer, I told myself that I would become a best-selling author. It wasn't a matter of "wouldn't it be neat to be a best-selling author." Rather, it was "I will become a best-selling author." The hours are good, I figured, the money great. Someone's got to do it, why not me? My only problem was that I could find no "best-selling-author" ads in the classifieds; I had to find another route to best-sellerdom. And in the meantime, I had to find a way to clothe and feed my family. So I decided to go into technical writing as a stepping stone, a way to become a best-selling author.

Since that time I've had my successes. My work has appeared in dozens of periodicals, from *Internet World* to *The Manchester Guardian*, *Computerworld* to the *Dallas Times Herald*. I wrote *The Complete Idiot's Guide to the Internet* (Que), a computer-book best-seller. Since then I've seen a couple more of my books— *Using Netscape 2 for Windows 95* (Que) and *Discover Windows NT Workstation* (IDG)—hit the computer-book best-seller charts. Now, these are best-sellers on the computer-book charts, of course, and it's really the *New York Times* best-seller list that I want. I'm still working on that.

I feel very fortunate that I found freelance technical writing. It gave me the time and money I needed to pursue my book-writing ambitions.

Now, let's hear some other people's experiences. Names have been changed for reasons of privacy.

Randy

"I was in college, studying advertising and marketing. I was almost finished—all I had left was an internship I needed to do, a couple of months in an advertising agency. I left it kind of late. By the time I got around to it, only one internship was left, a job in an advertising department.

"I really didn't fit in. You had to punch a clock, and people who were late more than two or three times in, say, a year, were in real trouble. It was real bogus, you know. Of course, I was late five times in the first two weeks. The work was really structured, too. We had a list of words we were supposed to use: We could write *"sale," "reduced"* and *"percentage off"* but not much else. After a couple of weeks, I'd had enough.

"I called my professor and told him I was going to quit and get a job; I didn't need the degree that bad, I'd just tell people that I had almost finished my degree. He calmed me down, though, and told me to wait a few days. It turned out he had a friend who ran the Software Technical Writing group at the company where I had my internship. I'd never heard of this—this was in 1982, right at the beginning of personal computing, really. Anyway, she offered me a job, so long as I agreed to leave marketing behind; she didn't want any of that garbage in her manuals.

"I worked there for a couple of years, and then tried to escape. A couple of colleagues and I started a rock band. Anyway, after a while, I went broke and got a job as a technical writer in Denver, and I've been writing ever since."

George

"I did a two-year engineering course provided by my employer, consisting of both classes and on-the-job training. One of my courses was technical writing; I had classes and worked in the service department for a while. When I finished the course I decided to be a technical writer. In engineering you work on just one small part of a product, but with technical writing, you can get involved with the whole thing. In technical writing I could use all my skills."

Marilyn

Marilyn went to a small technical institute in Louisiana, to become a computer technician. When she got out of school she found that the course really hadn't qualified her for anything. She worked in the oil business for a while—on the rigs— and then moved to Dallas, where she worked as a secretary for a temporary agency.

On one assignment she worked for a man who had to produce technical reports now and again. She kept finding and fixing mistakes in the reports, so he finally decided that she could do some of the company's technical writing. After a couple of weeks, another technical writer, working on contract, suggested that she work with one of the technical service agencies. She got a technical-writing contract, and saw her income jump from $8 or $10 an hour to $20 to $25 an hour. A few years later she was finding contracts paying $40 an hour.

Joe

"I was a technical instructor in the Air Force. When I got out, I discovered technical writing was one of the best jobs offered to people with my skills, so I took a job on the Titan missile project."

Steve

"I was a history major, but I worked with computers for five years. I joined the Army and worked as a weatherman for three years. I also had to compile documents and produce various reports. When I got out of the Army, I had a job as a night-shift supervisor for computer operators. A friend said that with my technical experience, I could get a job with his employer (a large computer manufacturer) as a writer, so I tried and got a job."

Carla

"My father was a famous engineer, at least in my home town. He told me to get an engineering degree or change my name! So I studied civil engineering at college . I did really badly in all my classes except for technical writing—in which I got an A. My professor tried to recruit me, and I spoke to a few people who told me that yes, you can make a living as a technical writer, so I changed my major.

"I did change my name in the end—I married an engineer. I make more money than my husband does, so I think my father's forgiven me."

Louise

"I was married at 16, so I didn't go to college. I started going at night, doing a business degree. During the day, I worked in my small town's newspaper as the gofer—I made the coffee, did the typing, did some reporting, did the layout. I got tired of that and took a part-time job supervising a group of composition specialists. We did page layout, graphics, and so on. But I had to correct the writers' work! They were technical people, and a lot of these technical guys can't write to save their lives.

"I knew they were earning more than me, and I knew I could do their job, so six months after starting the job I asked my boss to make me a technical writer. He told me he couldn't because I didn't have a writing background. So I changed my major to journalism—the company paid—and they let me start as an "associate" writer. I also took computer courses at college, because I knew I'd need them, and lots of courses at work. They eventually made me a full writer, and I've worked as a technical writer ever since."

Chuck

"I was taking calculus in college, but I did real well in English, so I decided against engineering. After a year in college my dad stopped the money and I dropped out. I joined the Air Force as a mechanic, and when I left I got a job as an editor and later as a writer at a large aviation company. I spent seven years there. The most unusual technical-writing job I've ever had was for a company that makes hay bailers. My first day on the job was in a small country town in Utah, examining a potato harvester on an airfield near the mountains."

Tom

"I was into poetry when I was young, and joined a small poetry and art magazine in 1972. I got really turned on by magazine production—the layout and pasteup and so on, and later became the editor. Later, when I went to college, I began an under-ground black magazine. Eventually I convinced the university's paper to do an insert called "Black Print." The paper became the first college paper to use computers for production; I helped in the setup and training, and became fascinated with computers.

"Anyway, when I finally left college with a degree in physiology, I found it difficult to get a job. I took a proofreading position at a publishing house, which I hated. Finally, I decided I had to get out, and started looking for some other way to make money as a writer. I got a job as a technical editor for a hospital software company in March 1979, and then did some of its writing, too. I've been a technical writer ever since. I would really like to find some way to make a living with creative writing. But the problem with technical writing is that the money is so good. *Writer's Digest* rates it third, after film and TV script writing, in terms of income. How do you beat that?"

Mary

"I was working at a telecommunications company through a technical services agency, doing mainly secretarial stuff, but some desktop publishing. I was hoping to do some writing and editing, but my company didn't let me do much. Now, I had been in advertising for quite a while in the past, so I had done some writing, and I wanted to get into tech writing.

"Well, when they closed down our department, the agency moved me back to its offices to do some newsletters, brochures, and advertising. I kept asking my employers to place me as a tech writer, but they kept stalling. Then they sent me to work with a large company as a junior writer, which was good experience. I also took some tech-writing courses. I spent thousands of dollars on those courses, though looking back, it was a good investment.

"After the junior writer position ended, the agency really didn't want to help. They had me working in their offices again, and I kept asking for a raise; the agency was paying me for desktop publishing, but I was writing for the company. All the agency would offer was an extra 50 cents an hour, so I gave the company two weeks' notice. I was taking a chance, because I didn't have any work, but at the end of two weeks I offered to continue working for the agency—at a higher rate, of course—until I found a job. So I got my pay raise; it was just a matter of calling their bluff, really. Soon after that I got a direct contract at a local company; it was a short contract, but it was nice and I started to build my reputation. I had a little time off without a contract, though I did some work on a seminar for my son-in-law. I bought a computer and work at home now. Right now I have two contracts I'm working on, at pretty good rates.

"When I'm looking for work I call everyone I know. The STC has found me work a couple of times, I think. But I just call people I know, and I've developed a reputation for doing good work, so I can find work by word of mouth."

How Can You Start?

So how are you going to find a technical-writing job? If I were trying to get into the business today, the first thing I would do is join the STC (you can find its address in Appendix D). The STC has almost 20,000 members in scores of chapters, mainly in the United States and Canada. Most of the members are technical writers.

The STC can help you in several ways, the most important being the instant network it provides. You will meet people who hire technical writers, and people who know who is hiring technical writers and where the jobs are. Many chapters even have a "job bank," a listing of current positions and contracts. The STC also runs seminars and sells books on the subject of technical writing, and publishes a journal and a newsletter. You can also ask the members which local colleges run technical-writing courses; a local STC member quite likely teaches a course somewhere.

Go to the STC meetings, meet the members, and ask the right questions. How can someone with your entry-level skills find a job? Which companies like to hire journalism graduates (or technicians if you are a technician, or military writers if you are ex-military)? Which companies hire a lot of entry-level people? (Some hire mainly entry-level because they are cheap.) Which companies pay well, which pay poorly? Try to get to know the people who actually hire; even if they don't want to hire you now, if they get to know you and you develop your skills, you will find it easier to get hired later.

(By the way, I'm not on the STC payroll; in fact, at the moment I'm writing this I'm not even a member—I'm an intermittent member. I have been a member in the past, once when an agency paid my dues—remember to ask your employers if they will pay—and once when I paid myself. I let my membership lapse now and then when I get too busy. But the STC is a great way to get to know your colleagues and find work, especially if you are new to the business or new in town.)

Many people will be able to get hired almost instantly. If you are a journalist and you find a manager who likes journalists, you could get a job without any further training. If you are a technician and you find a manager who hates "those language types" and is interested only in people with solid technical backgrounds, you may be in luck. But you can improve your chances a few ways.

Get Training

Find a local college that runs a technical writing class, and take it (many cities have at least one technical writing class somewhere). Or find out whether your present employer runs technical writing classes (some "high-tech" companies have classes for their programmers and technicians). If you don't have any technical skills, take a few courses in computers, electronics, or telecommunications. Think about the local market first. Are there a lot of telecommunications companies? Computer companies? You don't necessarily have to take a degree course in technical writing, by the way. If you already have some writing or technical skills, you need to fill the gaps in your knowledge, not start over from the beginning.

Take a few classes in word processing and desktop publishing—a lot of companies think of technical writers as highly paid secretaries, and look mainly for "keyboard" skills. (You don't necessarily want to make a habit of working with such companies, but they can provide a good start.) Read a few books on technical writing. (See Chapter 3 for information on college courses and books.)

Update Your Résumé

Take a good look at your résumé. Does it stress the skills that would help you in a technical-writing position? If you are a secretary, stress the computer manual you wrote, the desktop publishing programs you have used, the technical writing and English grammar courses you took. A lot of companies would never consider you— you are not "technical" enough—but someone somewhere will, because they are more interested in page layout than technical information. Buy a good book on writing résumés—it's a skill few people have—and clean the garbage out of your current résumé. Remove the six months you were out of work, the month you worked delivering newspapers, your high school accomplishments (unless you are young or they really do relate to the job—maybe you edited the school paper, for example). Place the skills that will help you where the person reading your résumé can find them, and place the jobs that are not relevant out of the way—or off the résumé entirely.

Which skills should you stress? These are any technical skills you have; courses in computing; work in data processing; jobs installing or maintaining hardware or software; word processing and desktop publishing programs you have used (the more the merrier); programming skills; systems analyst jobs; user-interface design; books and magazine articles you have written; writing courses you have taken; teaching or company training courses you have run. Should you include typing speed? Well, maybe, but low down on the list. Some managers are interested in typing speed, but most aren't, and if you stress it too highly it looks as if you are a secretary (which, of course, you may be).

Get Online

You really should have a connection to the Internet, and enough knowledge to find your way around. There's a wealth of information for technical writers on the Internet, and thousands of job leads, too. So get an Internet connection, and then see Chapter 24 to find the places where technical writers hang out.

Read On

And read the rest of this book. You'll find lots of information about tracking down work. Most of it is intended for current technical writers looking for the next position, but you can use many of the same techniques even if you are new to the business. I know new writers who've managed to go directly to a technical-service agency and find a contract, for instance.

Most importantly, keep looking. Don't be discouraged. Every manager has a different idea of the perfect technical writer; you just have to find the one who's looking for you. And once you have found that first job you become, like magic, a technical writer! The next time you are looking for work you will be taken more seriously. Instead of saying, "I'm a journalist, but I'm trying to find a tech writing job," you can say, "I'm a tech writer." That's what defines a technical writer. Technical writing is not a profession in the sense that medicine or law is a profession. You don't need to pass exams or be certified, you just need to get your first tech writing job.

Teach Yourself

Technical Writing

It's impossible to make anything foolproof because fools are so ingenious.

Another of "Murphy's" laws.

How do you learn the technical writing skills you want to sell? There's no room in this book to teach you those skills, but I will give you an idea of what those skills are and where you can get them.

College Courses

You could, of course, take a degree course in technical writing (or technical communication, or business and technical writing, or whatever the school happens to call it). Go to your local library and ask to see the college directories. Not all of them are indexed by subject, but these are:

- ◆ *The Index of Majors and Graduate Degrees* lists over 90 colleges under "Technical and Business Writing."
- ◆ *Peterson's Four-Year Colleges* lists 69 colleges under "Technical Writing."
- ◆ *Peterson's Two-Year Colleges* lists 23 colleges under "Technical Writing."
- ◆ *The College Blue Book: Degrees Offered by College and Subject* lists 17 colleges under "Technical Communication" and 17 under "Technical Writing."

The Society for Technical Communication (STC) maintains a list of colleges with technical writing courses. If you have Internet access, you can find a list of around 160 colleges at the STC World Wide Web site. Try the STC's Academic Programs page at http://www.stc-va.org/Academics/school.html. (If you can't find it there, go to the STC's site at http://www.stc-va.org/ and search for the word *college*.) The STC also has a brochure called *Careers in Technical Communication* that lists some of the universities and colleges with technical communication courses.

There are other sites listing technical communication courses, too: try the STC site Schools with Technical Communication Programs page at http://luigi.calpoly.edu/techcomm/Other_TCPrograms/Other_TCPrograms.html. And you'll find many more training courses listed in Appendix E.

(You can find links to these sites, and the many other technical-writing related sites mentioned in this book, from the Web site associated with this book, at http://www.mcp.com/mgr/arco/techwr/.)

Note, however, that you don't need a full-blown degree to get started in technical writing. There are quicker and easier ways. Check your local community colleges. Lots of them now have technical writing or technical communication courses. These courses cover subjects such as basic technical writing, programming in BASIC, computer graphics, DOS, desktop publishing, publication principles, computer architecture, data communications, and telecommunications. Check around and you'll find technical-writing courses all over the place; they seem to be very popular right now.

You might even look into correspondence courses, from organizations as diverse as the University of California Extension, the United States Department of Agriculture, and the College of Technical Authorship in Great Britain. And there are even courses you can take on the Internet. (See Appendix E for information on correspondence courses and courses on the Internet.)

Seminars

There are a number of companies that present technical-writing seminars. For instance, there's the Seminars in Usable Design series, run by a company founded by JoAnn Hackos, the President of Comtech (a technical-documentation company) and the author of *Managing Your Documentation Projects* (John Wiley & Sons). You can also find a list of seminar companies in Appendix E.

Perhaps the best way to hear about these seminars is to join the STC; you'll end up on various seminar mailing lists. The main problem with these seminars, though, is that they are high-ticket events targeted at companies rather than individuals. If you can get an employer to send you to one, great. Otherwise, you'll find it more cost-effective to go to a community college.

On-the-Job Training

It's often possible to become a technical writer without any specific training. Perhaps you are a journalist and have found a manager who believes journalists make the best technical writers, or maybe your company transferred you into a technical writing position because you were in the right place at the right time. If you have become a technical writer without any training, it's a good idea to read a few books on the subject, if only to get an idea of what techniques are used in other companies. You might also consider going to a community college course, or see if your company will send you to a technical-writing seminar; some large companies even run their own technical writing courses so that their technical staff can learn how to write things that other people can actually understand.

Books

There are many good books on technical writing. *Books in Print* lists about 150 books about the subject. You might want to begin looking at your library. Whether you go to your library or your bookstore, look in these three book categories: Writing, Business Writing, and Computers (many book stores put the books on software documentation in this section).

You should definitely get a copy of John Brogan's *Clear Technical Writing* (see the Bibliography at the back of the book for more information on this and all other books I recommend here). Brogan's book is about words and sentence structure, removing redundancies, using the active form of verbs, replacing weak verbs, and so on. It has thousands of examples and exercises. Follow the lessons in this book and your writing will become clearer and easier to understand.

You might also read *Technical Writing: A Reader-Centered Approach* by Paul V. Anderson. This 800-page book is a great introduction, explaining how to write a variety of documents, from résumés to hardware manuals. The book covers sentence structure to page layout, visual aids to library research.

I like *The Technical Writer's Handbook* by Matt Young. This is a dictionary of terminology and misused phrases and words. You might want to read it from start to finish rather than use it as a reference book, though, to help you clear your writing of clutter. I particularly like Young's humorous writing style.

There are several good books on writing computer documentation. You could start with *The Complete Guide to Writing Software User Manuals* by Brad M. McGehee. For more detail, try *How to Write a Computer Manual* by Jonathan Price. This book began life as Apple Corporation's internal guide to writing manuals. It's an excellent book, covering not only writing computer books but also how to test and revise your work, how to review other people's books, and how to recommend changes to the computer program. It has an excellent glossary and pages of checklists.

Writing Effective Software Documentation, by Patricia Williams and Pamela Benson, provides dozens of examples of page layouts—how to lay out a table of contents, a glossary, reference pages, and so on. You could also take a look at *Technical Writing for Business and Industry*, by the same authors.

There are many excellent books on the subject, but spend a few moments reading before you buy. You can find many dry, boring tomes that seem to send the wrong message about technical writing: that technical books should be formal almost to the point of being unreadable. Take a look at this book's Bibliography for more recommended books, and for bibliographies available on the World Wide Web.

The Society for Technical Communication (STC)

Many of the STC's local chapters organize monthly speeches and lectures and occasional seminars. The STC is also a good source of books about technical writing, and publishes several periodicals. Ask STC members for information about college courses and commercial seminars.

Perhaps the most important thing a new technical writer can do is to join the STC. You'll see it mentioned throughout this book. This organization is a great way to get to know all the people you need to know in the technical writing business. Join, read everything it offers, go to all its events, talk with everyone you meet, use its job lines. You'll soon learn what you need to know to get started. (See Appendix D for more information about the STC.)

A Few Writing Tips

Finally, here are a few general pointers to help you produce useful, readable documents. You might think of this as "the bare minimum you need to know to write good technical documentation." It's a start, but for more information read some of the books I suggested in the "Books" section earlier in this chapter.

Before Beginning, Think About Your Readers

Who will read your manuals, and what sort of information are they looking for? Think about how the readers will refer to your book, about the sequence of information they will need. For example, many manuals explain computer program features one by one, in the sequence those features appear in the menus or in alphabetical order. That may be fine for a document intended only for reference, but it is very difficult for a new user to work with. Instead, consider putting the information in the book in the same sequence that the users will need it. For example, a book describing a simple spreadsheet program might begin with installation instructions, move on to a "quick start" section (how to open a spreadsheet and enter numbers and simple formulae) and then explain groups of features in the order of probable use—the simple features first, proceeding through the more complicated or infrequently used features to those that few users ever need.

Think of yourself as the reader's advocate. Think about what you'd want to know if you were in the reader's place, then provide that information.

Look for Connections

I believe that one of the main weaknesses of technical writers is that they don't look for connections. They write about each feature of a product as if it exists in isolation from the rest of the product. Rather, you should look for ways that working with that feature affects other features in the product. (This is particularly true for software documentation.) And consider how other features interact with the one you're writing about.

Avoid Tautology

If you've worked with computers much, you've run into tautological documentation. For instance, for some reason the Widget dialog box has opened, and it contains a variety of different options. You can't figure it all out, so you open the Help system and find something like this: "The Widget dialog box is where you configure the Widget feature. Select the Widget options and click OK." Useless. It explains the feature by telling what you already know: that it's the Widget feature. But how do you use it, what does the Widget feature actually do, what effect do all these options have? Avoid tautology like the plague!

Don't Use Two Words When One Will Do

Research into reading shows—and common sense suggests—that the more concise your writing (with the minimum of unnecessary words), the easier it is to understand. While it is important to ensure that you include all essential information, it is equally important to make sure that your writing is not cluttered with unnecessary words, words that do nothing to increase the reader's understanding. Look at the following two sentences, for example:

> Before reading this chapter, use the installation procedure to put the program on your hard disk.

> Before reading this chapter, install the program on your hard disk.

The first sentence is five words and ten syllables longer than the second. Not a lot really, but put five extra words in every sentence of your manual, and your readers will feel as if they are running in knee-deep water. And the first sentence doesn't tell us anything more than the second.

Here are a few examples of redundancies and simpler versions:

Redundant	Simpler Version
Most of the CODP packs	Most CODP packs
The alarm message indicates the alarm is	The message shows the alarm is
This chapter provides a description	This chapter describes
This manual is intended to explain	This manual explains
Reference should be made to	Refer to
Table 1 gives a listing of	Table 1 lists
The Print Option commands are to be used	Use the Print Option commands
Is capable of	Can
An alarm message is generated and printed	An alarm message is printed

Don't Use Two Syllables When One Will Do

Say *press* instead of *depress*, *use* instead of *utilize*, *move* instead of *transport*. If the shorter word doesn't say exactly what you mean, use the longer word. But if it does say what you mean, why add extra syllables for the reader to dig through? A syllable here and there doesn't make much difference, you might think, but the more unnecessary syllables, the longer it takes to read, and the less is understood.

Use Clear Language, Not Jargon or "Nonwords"

Because jargon and nonwords can often be found in dictionaries, many writers think it is acceptable to use such words. (Dictionaries are encyclopedias of use, not of correctness. Many incorrectly used words are found in dictionaries because they are in common use.) But words like *functionality* and *irregardless* slow reading and reduce comprehension, and are unnecessary because clearer alternatives are available. And the unnecessary use of jargon will often confuse your readers, especially those with little experience with a product. Why add jargon to computer documentation that may confuse new users? Why say *visual indicator*, for example, when *lamp* will do just as well, or *the octathorp* instead of the # *key*? (Or *user-friendly* instead of *easy to use*?)

Use the Active Voice—Speak to The Reader Personally

In "the old days," technical writers wrote as if they were describing the procedures from afar: "The operator depresses the Esc key" instead of "Press the Esc key," "The user should open the left panel" instead of "Open the left panel." They also wrote using the "passive voice," such as "the software should be installed" instead of "install the software." Apart from being unnecessary, the detached form of writing leads to more words cluttering the page. Active writing, on the other hand, is direct and easy to understand. Some of your clients may not like it; there are still a few dinosaurs out there. But in most cases, the active voice will make your writing clearer, and your clients will appreciate it.

Use an Eighth-Grade Reading Level

If you follow these rules, your writing will automatically have a low reading level. Researchers usually advise an eighth-grade reading level for technical documentation, not because few people have a higher reading level, but because the higher the reading level, the longer it takes to get the message across. Probably most of your readers have a much higher reading level, and may enjoy reading Shakespeare, Nietzsche, or the *Washington Post* in their spare time, but when they are trying to understand a new product, they want the information quickly. While they may not mind too much being challenged by the new product, they don't want the documentation to pose an extra challenge.

Many computer grammar-checkers analyze writing for reading level, but if you don't have such a program, try the Gunning's Fog Index on a few sentences to check your work. To apply the Fog Index, follow these steps:

1. Add the number of words in the paragraph.
2. Divide this number by the number of sentences in the paragraph.
3. Find the number of words in the paragraph that have three syllables or more, and divide this number by the total number of words to arrive at a percentage of long words.
4. Add the percentage number from step 3 to the number from step 2.
5. Multiply the total by 0.4.

The final number is the approximate grade level required to read the sentence. If you find your writing is way over eighth-grade level, go back and use shorter words, remove unnecessary words, and break the sentences down into shorter ones.

Break Up the Text into Lots of Bite-Sized Units

Information is more easily absorbed and understood when it is in small bites. Just as it is easier to digest a pound of steak if it has been cut into pieces, it's easier to understand information if it has been divided into manageable pieces! Technical writing "systems," such as Information Mapping or Edmond Weiss's two-page modules, are simply ways of breaking the information down into easy-to-understand blocks.

Use Lots of Headings and Subheadings

Punctuating a document with lots of headings serves two purposes: It helps to break the text into those bite-sized blocks I just mentioned, and it allows the document to be used as a reference document. The headers let the reader scan through the book, looking for the required information.

Use Lots of Tables and Figures

Tables make it easier for the reader to find information when scanning through the document, and diagrams help to make the text's explanations clearer. It's easier to show people something than tell them. When documenting computer programs, it's often useful to provide snapshots of the program. Don't use snapshots of *everything*, but use snapshots of screens with information that you are defining or explaining in the text, and of examples that the reader can follow. Reader surveys generally find that readers like snapshots, for a number of reasons. They help readers locate information (they can scan the document and quickly find the computer screen they are currently using), they help reassure readers that they are at the correct place in the text, and they show how the readers' screens should appear at that point.

Use Cross-References

Cross-references are often misused. Many writers think that instead of explaining something fully, they can just refer the reader to another area of the document. Such references are often frustrating for the reader. But there are many occasions when an explanation will touch on a subject explained elsewhere in the book. If that other subject is not essential to the understanding of the current topic, you don't need to explain it again, but you should use a cross-reference to help the reader find the related subject. Modern word processors contain excellent tools that make cross-referencing very easy; use them!

Include a Complete Table of Contents

Many publications omit subheadings from the table of contents. This is a mistake, because readers often use the table of contents as a form of index. Readers often refer to the table of contents before flipping to the index, because the table of contents allows them to pick an area of interest. The more subheadings included in the table of contents, the closer the reader can get to the required information, without referring to the index (an index is usually so detailed that it can actually mislead a reader). A table of contents can lead readers—they pick a general category (a section, for instance), then a subcategory (a chapter), then another subcategory (a heading within a chapter), and so on. Indexes don't lead readers in the same way, so readers tend to look at the table of contents first. You might even include *two* tables of contents: a general one, showing only the chapter headings, and a detailed one, showing subheadings too.

Include a Detailed Index

If the table of contents doesn't get the reader where he or she wants to go, the next step is the index. There is nothing more frustrating to the reader than an incomplete index. Again, word processors provide excellent tools for creating indexes; you can index a large book quite quickly.

Of course, professional indexers would disagree with that statement, and I'd agree with them that doing a really good index takes time. However, if the choice is between no index and doing an index yourself, without any training (and in technical writing, that usually is the choice), you can still create a pretty good index very quickly. If you really want to do the very best index possible, you can learn about indexing. The United States Department of Agriculture has a correspondence course on indexing (see Appendix E), and you can find more information about indexing resources online, at the American Society of Indexers Web page (http://www.well.com/user/asi/).

Consider Other Types of Reference Aids

There are other tools you can use to guide your users through your book. I like feature tables. Build a table that lists all the commands in your computer program, for example. You can do this in menu order. The table should include a one-sentence description of each command, and refer the reader to the page or chapter that contains a full explanation of the command. Such tables help readers because they fit in with the way many people learn programs; they start the program and then "investigate," opening menus and trying commands, just to see what will happen. The feature or command table explains each of the program's features in simple terms, giving the reader a quick overview of your program. And the user can refer to the table to find the area of the book that explains a particular command or group of commands.

You also might consider using tables that list all the program's features (and refer the user to the appropriate part of the book), list keyboard commands, display all the available fonts or special characters, or show all the special symbols used by your program. These can be put on the end-pages or inside covers of your book, or even on separate cards. You can even use a table to allow readers to use a reference book as a learning guide. Though the guide may be structured with the commands in alphabetical order, you could add a table that directs the reader through the book in a tutorial sequence, helping him or her learn the program feature by feature, in a logical order.

Proofread the Document!

This may seem obvious, but many technical writers omit this step, perhaps because it is the most boring part of the writing process. Nonetheless, nobody can produce an error-free document (Ernest Hemingway, for example, couldn't spell). You can make the process easier by using an electronic spell-checker (virtually all word processing programs have them now) and, perhaps, an electronic grammar-checker. Combined, these will catch most problems, but never all of them. So read the document after checking it electronically. (Electronic grammar-checkers can only make suggestions, and tend to find "problems" where none exist; only people who understand grammar can use grammar-checkers effectively! But if you know grammar well, you might not want to bother with a grammar-checker.)

Use a Professional Editor

Proofreading your own document is important, but so is having someone else read it, preferably a professional editor. Why? It is nearly impossible to catch all the mistakes in your own work. For some reason, writers tend to see what they thought they wrote, rather than what they actually wrote. If you don't have a professional editor available, at least let another writer go through your document for you. In some companies writers swap documents, proofreading each others' work.

4

What Is

Freelancing?

Man is a masterpiece of creation if for no other reason than that, all the weight
of evidence for determinism notwithstanding, he believes he has free will.

German physicist and philosopher G. C. Lichtenberg (1742–1799)

The word *freelance* comes from the Middle Ages, when it was used to describe a
mercenary soldier who would sell himself (and his lance) to whoever paid the most. Of
course, its meaning has changed—it no longer refers only to warriors—but the terms
of employment remain more or less the same.

The *Concise Oxford Dictionary, 7th Ed.*, says that a freelancer is a "person working
for no fixed employer." My *Merriam-Webster* dictionary says that a freelance or
freelancer is "one who pursues a profession under no long-term contractual commit-
ments to any one employer." These are good definitions, but you will often hear other
terms that tend to complicate the issue a bit.

You will hear the term *contractor*, generally applied to someone who sells his services
on short-term contract. You also may hear the term *job-shopper* applied to someone
who finds work using the technical-service agencies. *Temporary employees* are often
freelancers, going from one temporary position to another.

I'm going to use the terms *freelancer* and *contractor* interchangeably in this book to
cover all these types of employment, because they all have certain common characteristics. A freelancer moves from one temporary job to another. The advantages are
many, perhaps the most important being the ability to make significantly more money.
Specific terms of employment may vary, but the key characteristic is that both the
employer and employee intend employment to be of a limited duration. A permanent
job comes with an implied promise: "You have a job forever, or until you die, retire,
are laid off, or fired." The freelance relationship, on the other hand, is recognized to
be temporary by both parties: "You've got a job until the work is finished or the
contract expires."

Contractor or Consultant?

You also will hear the term *consultant*, a much misused term defined in one of my dictionaries as "one who gives professional advice or services." Although consulting is a form of freelancing—and many contractors call themselves consultants—it is important to understand that it is different from mere contracting.

A consultant has more responsibility than a contractor; the consultant may have control over the entire project, and may even provide other personnel to do the work. The consultant uses his own methods and techniques, and has control over how and when the work gets done. The contractor, however, is often a cog in a machine, doing the work how and when the client says. And an important difference is that contracting jobs are easier to come by than consulting jobs. There are tens of thousands of contract jobs available around the country every day, whereas consulting jobs may not appear until a consultant convinces a client to buy his services. Contractors are the "bread and butter" of the technical services industry, while consultants are the "caviar"; companies know they need bread and butter—so they shop for it every day—but may never buy caviar.

So consultants have to try much harder to find work. They spend much more time looking for work, so although their daily rates are much higher than those charged by contractors, consultants often make no more money. According to a 1988 survey published in Howard Shenson's *Complete Guide to Consulting Success*, the average data-processing consultant made $81,102 a year before taxes; but contract programmers can make that or more (one told me he made $125,000 in 11 months), and without the marketing problems that come with consulting. A successful consultant can make a lot of money—most of the technical writers making $100,000 or more are consultants—but there's no guarantee that consulting will automatically increase your income. And it's sometimes possible to make plenty of money ($80,000, $100,000, or more) as a *contractor*.

Once you have been contracting for a while, you may find that you automatically slip into consulting without any real effort, because the most important method for finding work as a consultant is also the most important method for finding work as a contractor: word of mouth. Most consultants also use other methods to find work, though, such as direct mail, advertising, or writing articles for journals and magazines.

Another term you should understand is *technical-service agency*. This is a firm that finds contractors for companies; such a firm charges the client a set amount per hour, pays the contractor an agreed-upon amount, and keeps the rest. For example, a client may pay $43 per hour for a technical writer. The agency pays the writer $28 (or $25, or $13, whatever is agreed upon), withholds taxes, pays any benefits it promised the contractor, and keeps the rest. The agency may keep anywhere from $5 to $25 of the $43 paid by the client. You also may hear the technical service agencies called *job shops, shops,* or just *agencies*. Some agencies call themselves *consulting firms*, though few of them truly are. A consulting firm is really a company that takes over a project and runs it for the client, both hiring and managing the people needed to do the work. Many so-called consulting firms merely provide warm bodies that the client then manages.

The term *agency* offends many agencies, though. They like to present themselves as "consulting companies." I was speaking to a recruiter at a job fair once, when I suddenly recognized her company's name and realized that I was talking to someone from a technical-service agency. "Oh, Acme Inc.," I said, "you're an agency, right?" She looked very offended and said, "Certainly not, we are a consulting firm." Oh, sure.

"An agency brings parties together for a potential transaction exclusive of the agency itself," wrote the vice president of one agency in reply to an article I wrote for *PD News*. He continued: "A technical-contract firm provides services to the marketplace by assigning its own employees to client projects. As long as the contract employee remains on assignment, the technical-contract firm is a vital component of the relationship." The vice president evidently felt that his company was a "technical-contract firm," a subtle distinction that most contractors ignore; as far as I'm concerned, if a company finds a contractor for a client and takes no real part in the project's planning or execution, the company is an agency, not a technical-contract firm.

Finally, many contractors use the terms *captive* or *slave* to refer to those people who don't freelance but remain permanently tied to one company. Some may find the terms *captive* and *slave* to be rather offensive. I'm not trying to offend anyone, I'm just telling you the terms that freelancers often use for people who work full time. One captive told me, "I *am* a captive; that's how I feel. I'd love to get out of working for other people, but I just don't know how." I think that many full-time employees feel like captives, and the whole point of this book is to describe ways to escape!

The Types of Freelancing

There are several ways to freelance, as this section describes.

Independent Contract, Hourly Rate

You have a contract with a client to provide your labor or skills for a specified number of dollars per hour. The client pays you directly, without withholding taxes. Such freelancers are often known as *independent contractors*.

Independent Contract, Fee Basis

You have a contract with a client to complete a specified project for a set number of dollars. Many people working on this basis call themselves *consultants* or *independent contractors*. They may agree to write a computer program's manual, a sales brochure, or a reference guide, but they are paid the specified fee regardless of how long the job takes.

Temporary Employee

You are an employee of the client, but only temporarily. Both parties understand the relationship to be temporary, and the client usually pays more than it pays its permanent staff. However, the client pays payroll taxes, and withholds your FICA and federal taxes, just as the company does with its permanent employees.

Contract with a Technical Service Agency

You are paid an hourly rate by a technical service agency, "on a 1099." That is, the agency does not withhold taxes from you, but pays you the entire earned sum, which the agency then reports to the Internal Revenue Service on Form 1099. The agency hires you out to a client company. You may be known as a *contractor* or *job-shopper*. This sort of arrangement is not always legal, though. The Internal Revenue Service can, in some cases, define you as an employee of the agency. We'll discuss that more in Chapter 19.

Pseudo-Salaried Employee of a Technical Service Agency

You usually should avoid this form of relationship. The agency pays what I call a *"pseudo-salary."* It tells you your salary, then divides the salary by 2080 (52 weeks times 40 hours per week) to come up with an hourly rate. The agency calculates your pay by multiplying the number of hours worked by the hourly rate. This relationship is often a way for an agency to make a very high profit from an inexperienced freelancer, because the agency charges the client a high contract rate, but pays the freelancer a low permanent-employment rate.

The relationship is especially unfair if the agency is too small to guarantee the freelancer's job when the present contract ends (although some of the larger agencies can do this), because then the freelancer gets a low income without even the security of continued employment. In fact this type of employment is not really freelance employment, though it's easy for beginners to fall into the trap. You should steer clear of this trap. There are also legal problems associated with pseudo-salaries and overtime pay (see Chapter 14).

True Salaried Employee of a Technical Service Agency

Some agencies probably treat their employees a little better—that is, they treat them as true salaried employees. Most agencies that have pseudo-salaries claim they pay real salaries. It's not a real salary unless they don't bother to link the salary to the number of hours you work.

There are probably other types of freelancing, and many freelancers jump from one type to another, depending on what is available. For example, for legal reasons discussed elsewhere in the book, a company may not want to hire an independent contractor. Instead, the company could take the freelancer on as a temporary employee. The freelancer's next job may be through a technical service agency, and the one after that may be as an independent contractor charging a set fee.

As you can see, these terms overlap a lot. There is one important distinction to make, though, because it affects how you pay taxes, deduct business expenses, and save for retirement: You are either someone's legal employee, or you are an independent business person, what the Internal Revenue Service calls a *sole proprietor*. (You could also be the president of your own corporation, though in most cases that's not necessary; see Chapter 23.) Where I have needed to make this distinction, I have used the term *independent contractor* or *independent freelancer* to refer to a *sole proprietor*, and *agency employee* to refer to someone legally employed by an agency (if your agency withholds taxes, you are an agency employee).

Which of the relationships is the most profitable? The independent contractor relationships are potentially the most profitable, because there is no middleman (no agency), and because you can deduct certain business expenses from your taxes. However, this is not always the case. For instance, you may find a company willing to pay you the same hourly rate if you become a temporary employee—and because the company also pays your taxes, you end up saving thousands of dollars in social security taxes. Or you may find an agency with a very rich client willing to pay enough money for both you and the agency to do well. (However, if you are an independent contractor with an employment-income pension plan, you may want to avoid becoming someone else's employee, because you won't be able to put that money into your pension. Pension plans are discussed in Chapter 13.)

Why Do Companies Use Contractors?

So why do companies use contractors? I sometimes wonder. An obvious reason is for short-term projects; if the company needs someone for only a few months, it has to hire a contractor. For example, many small software companies need a user manual written only once every couple of years—with, perhaps, minor updates once a year or so. Often the company's only option is to hire an outsider to do the book.

But I've heard of contractors working for the same company for 18 years. That is unusual, but it is common for contractors to stay with one company for a year or even three. A friend of mine has worked at his present company for about five years now (on an agency contract), and is making $80,000 a year, plus a few benefits. If he were an employee of the company he's writing for, he'd probably make $25,000 to $30,000 less. Why would a company do that? Many people claim it's cheaper to hire a contractor because the company doesn't have to pay benefits, but this is usually not true. Hiring a contractor is expensive, so why throw that money away?

A common reason is that "the left hand doesn't know what the right hand is doing." A company may have a policy that limits the number of employees in a particular department, but also requires that department to produce an amount or type of work that forces the department to hire someone; the manager may be able to get around this problem by hiring contractors, effectively bypassing the "no new hires" regulation.

Some companies also guarantee their employees permanent employment; they lay off personnel only as a very last resort, and then pay exceptional severance benefits. Such a company may hire long-term contractors if it is not sure that it will continue to require their services once the project is finished.

Weapons manufacturers often hire large numbers of contractors, and many critics claim it is the inefficiency of U.S. government procurement procedures that leads to extreme waste, from $1,000 hammers to contractors on 10-year contracts. If a company simply bills the government for the cost of a contractor, the length of the contract may not worry them, and it's also easier for them to get rid of contractors if the government suddenly stops funding a project.

Small startup companies are often good sources of contracts. Such a company may not want to commit itself to long-term employees, and may like the flexibility that hiring contractors gives the company—it allows the company to hire contractors while developing a product, and then release them when the company begins marketing the product and slows down the development phase.

A company also may hire contractors if it can't find permanent employees to do the job. "It seems that some professions go through phases," one personnel manager told me. "Sometimes everyone in a particular profession wants to work as a contractor, and you just can't find good permanents." That's a problem experienced by, for instance, companies, in some areas, trying to hire permanent technical writers; it's hard to find good writers, because so many of them have gotten hooked on high contract rates.

How Much Experience Do You Need?

You may be able to find a contract even if you have little experience; it's not unknown for companies to give contracts to entry-level people. Calling and talking with as many agencies as possible will help you find out. Talk with other contractors as well, but don't let anyone put you off contracting until you've checked every avenue. A reader of *PD News*, a publication for "job shoppers," once said that "a new shopper must have a minimum of 10 years' experience in his field." Yet I began contracting with only six years' (part-time) experience, and I know technical writers who began straight out of college. (*PD News* is now called *Technical Employment News*; see Appendix B for more information.)

Of course, it helps to be experienced and skilled—you will find work easier to come by and rates much higher—but if you are a new technical writer, you may still be able to find contracts. You can make good money and gain experience at the same time. You certainly don't need to be an expert to work contract. Howard Shenson (who writes about consulting issues), states that "very few [consultants] are the world's leading authorities in their fields. Instead, they are active, practical, energetic people who put the theory to work and make it pay. You have no reason to feel unqualified just because you do not rank as number one in your field." I know a successful consultant in the technical-writing field who stated quite clearly that he didn't know more about his specialty than many others did. "I earn much more money, though, because I've written books about the subject, so I'm taken seriously as a consultant," he said. (He knew that writing books is a great way to boost a freelance career, as we'll discuss in Chapter 25.)

A friend of mine once told me that he didn't want to become a contractor until he was the best he could be in his field; he felt he had to "grow" more in his profession. Six months later he was contracting at a very good rate, and his client was so happy with his performance that he tried to hire him full time. So don't feel you are not good enough to be a contractor. As one department manager told me, "Contractors are no different from their permanent-employee peers—they just want to make more money."

The Three-Step Method of Freelancing

In the introduction to this book, I told you about my Three-Step Method for becoming a freelancer. Here's a quick summary of how this system works. You'll learn the details in the rest of the book.

Step One

In Step One you contact the technical service agencies. If there is a demand for your skills you can find a contract through an agency, at a higher rate than you now make. You will start to learn a bit about the freelancing market—the kind of rates available, how much work there is in your area, and who is employing freelancers. This step allows you to start saving money—when I went through Step One I was able to save $1,000 a month, and still support a wife and baby. You will begin to strengthen your résumé, working on different projects and products, with different tools and techniques. And you will begin to build a network of contacts—other freelancers, employers, agencies, and colleagues in different disciplines who work on projects that need your skills.

Step One may last a few months, or several years (it took me 13 months). Or you may never leave Step One—but that's okay, too. Many freelancers spend the rest of their careers working through agencies. They find they can remain employed, earn excellent money, and leave all the sales and marketing to the agencies.

Step Two

In Step Two, if you decide to continue, you stop using the agencies to find work. You have built a network strong enough to track down the work, and a reputation good enough to get the contracts. You have also saved enough money to survive while you wait for your client to pay your first invoice. You also may need money for business stationery, mail, professional association fees, computer equipment, and so on, depending on how you intend to sell your services. Often the only office equipment you require, though, is a telephone.

Step Three

In Step Three you begin selling your services as a consultant, charging by the *project* rather than by the hour. If you are disciplined and work more quickly than most writers, you can boost your income dramatically, because you base your fees on how much the competition charges. Because your competition is slower than you are, you can make more money for every hour you work than you would if you billed by the hour. If you can build a strong reputation for doing good work, your fees can go even higher.

Step Four

Here's the "bonus step," Step Four. Once you've worked for yourself, once you're free of the shackles of permanent employment, you begin to see other possibilities. You might make a living by writing computer books for publication (see Chapter 25). You might start publishing your own books—a number of successful publishers began as technical writers. Or perhaps you'll drift into a related career (one writer I know now writes about intranets and also helps companies set up intranets) or even into a completely different career. Once you're your own boss, your horizons seem to widen.

"Money Isn't Everything; What About Job Satisfaction?"

You are going to hear this question a lot, mainly from permanent employees trying to rationalize their continued employment: "Sure," they say, "you make good money, but money isn't everything, you know." Of course, it's hard to argue with this statement. Job satisfaction is very important. But the statement is based on a couple of premises that may not be true: that freelancers don't have job satisfaction and that permanent employees do.

Some permanent employees do have job satisfaction, but so do many contractors. I believe the contractors who don't have job satisfaction are often working for companies whose captives don't have job satisfaction either, and for the same reasons— boring projects, patronizing or arrogant management, no gratitude for a job well done, and so on. But contractors can get out of these situations in a few months, while the captives remain stuck in a rut, until they quit, the company lets them go, or they retire. And which would you prefer: to work on a lousy job for a pittance, or to work on a lousy job for a lot of money? The choice is clear.

Freelancing can provide great satisfaction, not only from the job itself but because of the significant advantages that freelancing brings—as you will see in the next chapter.

Who Can Work Freelance?

This book was written for technical writers, but hundreds of technical professionals can use the same techniques to find work. Anyone whose skills are marketed by the thousands of technical service agencies throughout the country can follow the procedures described in this book to go freelance.

What Skills Do You Need?

Freelancing is very different from permanent employment, and requires a different temperament. This section specifies a few characteristics you should have if you want to do well as a contractor.

The Ability to Handle Money

People usually get into freelancing because they can make more money. The extra money allows them to have a higher standard of living—but don't think that if you make an extra $1,000 a month after taxes you can spend an extra $1,000. If you spend everything you earn, and perhaps even more, you might want to avoid freelancing. On the other hand, you are headed for trouble anyway, freelance or not; one day you will find yourself out of a job without any money. Freelancers have to be prepared for more "downtime" than captives (permanent employees). The freelancer needs a certain amount of money in the bank to finance time between jobs. While a captive may have one job for five years, the freelancer may have 10 contracts in that time. If you have skills that are in demand, you may be able to go directly from one contract to another, but it is wise to assume that you will have periods without work. Therefore, you need to save money.

Being without money can lead you to take a low-paying contract because that is all that is available at the time. Take the case of a colleague of mine. His second agency contract increased his income from $13 per hour to $25. The money went to his head. Instead of increasing his spending only slightly, and saving the rest, he started spending much more than he ever had before. In particular, he bought a new car and a living-room suite. He failed to prepare for time out of work.

But everything comes to an end. The department in which he worked closed down, and he went from $25 per hour to a $21 per hour agency contract, all he could find at the time. With money in the bank, he would have had time to find an agency contract that paid at least $28 an hour (or an independent contract that paid closer to $40 an hour).

You also need savings for the second phase of your freelancing: for when you get out on your own, independent of the agencies. Although the agencies pay every two weeks (some even every week), independent contractors may wait 60, 80, or even 90 days to get paid. You submit an invoice, which then goes through the company's accounting department, and comes out who knows when. I had to wait about 40 days after starting my first independent contract before I received a check. (This isn't the norm, but it does happen.)

You must remember that you are in business, and every business requires capital to help it through the lean times. No business can survive without capital, nor will you if you don't save. I know people working through agencies who would like to work on independent contracts (and earn more money), but are unable to do so because they have no savings. "Six weeks!" said one friend after I explained how long I'd just had to wait for the first check from a new client. "I couldn't wait six weeks for money. How would I eat?" This friend is on a good agency rate, high enough to save at least $1,000 a month.

Remember, your savings are an investment in your business. If you can't save, stay out of the business.

The Ability to Handle Uncertainty

I wasn't sure what to call this characteristic, because it is a bit of a paradox. I believe there is more certainty in freelancing than in permanent employment. In freelancing you know that your contract will come to an end, and you prepare for the next contract. Change is not a problem; it is simply one of the conditions of business. All businesses must find a succession of clients, and yours is no different.

In permanent employment, however, you assume your job will go on forever—but it won't. You don't know when it will come to an end, but eventually you will be laid off or fired, leave, or receive an offer you can't accept ("The company is moving to Gun Barrel, Texas. You've still got a job with us there!").

Sure, some people seem to stay with their company forever, but that is happening less and less these days. High-tech companies, especially, seem to start and crash within a few years, companies often relocate, and people's expectations have become higher—they are more likely to quit to find a better position than they would have a few years ago. ("Depression babies" traditionally hung on to a job as long as they could, but they are retiring now, and their children and grandchildren are more demanding.)

So why do I call this characteristic "the ability to handle uncertainty"? Well, many people need a permanent job, even though they are fooling themselves about the permanence. It makes them feel more comfortable and secure. I've had friends tell me, "I couldn't handle not knowing how long the job will last," as an excuse for not freelancing—and then some of those same friends got laid off from their "permanent" jobs.

Perhaps it is not so much the uncertainty that they object to as the job search—having to search for a client almost continuously. Job searches are a form of sales campaign, and many people do not have what it takes to sell a product, even if the product is their own services. And that leads us into the next characteristic.

The Ability to Sell Yourself

Everyone has to sell themselves at some point. Captives do it when they are looking for a new job, and freelancers do it when they are looking for a new contract. You don't need to be a high-powered salesperson, but it certainly helps.

For example, one technical writer I know moved from Atlanta to Dallas when her husband's company transferred him. Most freelancers would contact agencies in Dallas to find a contract, but she used her sales ability to find an independent contract instead. "I just spoke to everyone I knew in Atlanta, and asked them if they knew anyone in Dallas," she told me. "Eventually I got some names in Dallas and then just started networking." Before she arrived in her new home town, she had spoken to 400 people, and had a contract to go to.

You can avoid most of the selling by working through one or two agencies. But you can be more successful if you sell yourself through many different agencies, or if you sell yourself directly to the client. And if you sell yourself directly, you then get into "cold" telephone calls, sales letters, and even brochures. Successful freelancers are also successful salespeople.

An Inclination to Gossip

I could have used a euphemism to describe this characteristic, but "gossip" is more direct and honest. Freelancers who make good money "gossip"—not about people's private lives or scandals (well, not much anyway), but about the business they work in. If they hear about someone getting a new contract, they want to know where and with which company. They want to know how much money people make and how long a contract is likely to last. They ask if the company needs more people, even if they don't need a contract right now.

Eventually you get a feel for the market you are working in. You know where to look for work the next time you need it, and how much each company is likely to pay. You also get to know names of people to call when you need job leads, or the name of the hiring manager in a particular company. You should keep a card file, or better still, a computer database, noting the names of other contractors and managers, anyone who may be able to help you the next time you are looking.

Of course you need to be careful when you are talking about how much money people make. Some people may be offended if you ask them this—we are taught that it isn't nice to discuss money, and employers and agencies discourage employees from talking about pay, even threaten them with dismissal. But you need to know how much money people in your line of work earn. You are running a business, remember, and every business has to know how much the competition charges. If you don't know, you may overbid (and lose the contract) or underbid (and get the contract but lose money you could be earning).

I've met people who have been freelancers for years, usually working through agencies, who have no idea how much more money they could ask for. They don't gossip with people much, so they don't find out the range of rates. For example, when I wrote the first edition of this book, technical-service agencies in the Dallas area were paying technical writers from about $27 per hour to around $32 per hour. However, some writers were making $15 an hour, and one I knew made $38 an hour. The people making the higher rates are obviously in the minority, and if you don't know what is going on in the technical-writing market you might assume that $20 or $22 per hour—or much less—is a good rate. As one writer e-mailed me after reading the first edition, "[my current] assignment pays $18 an hour, which I thought was fantastic until I read your book!"

So talk to people. Don't make a nuisance of yourself, and don't spend too much of your client's time talking, but do get to know other freelancers, and do get to know the market you are working in.

A Reputation for Being Good at What You Do

If you work through the technical service agencies, you don't have to be very good—many agencies fill positions with "warm bodies"—but being good helps. As a freelancer, you are going to be interviewed more often, have your résumé read more often, and perhaps have your references checked more often.

While it may be possible for mediocre employees to "hide" in a large company (we all know downright incompetent people who somehow manage to hang on to their jobs for years), they will have trouble if they must search for a new contract every six months. If you are good at what you do, though, you can quickly build a reputation for yourself. And a good reputation is worth a lot of money in the freelance business.

Furthermore, if you really are interested in pushing your income near or over the $100,000 level, you'd better be good at what you do. You'd better work very quickly, yet still do a good job. To do that you'll have to be self-disciplined, and use all the tools of the trade efficiently.

Self-Motivation

The freelancer needs to be what my mother used to call a *go-getter*. You cannot just hang around waiting for a contract to arrive; if a contract just "drops in your lap," it probably won't be very good. You have to make things happen, to get up and start looking for work.

Let me give you an example. A few years ago I had a list of 140 technical service agencies in the Dallas area. I gave this list to several people who either wanted to work freelance, or who already worked with technical-service agencies. The ideal way to use the list is to contact all the agencies at once, as I explain in Chapter 8. But what did these people do? They called one or two agencies, or mailed résumés to 10 or 20, and then accepted the first thing that came along.

Self-motivation helps when working with the agencies, but if you want to work independently of the agencies, you need to be even *more* self-motivated. You must be prepared to make 20 to 30 phone calls a day (I'll tell you who you should be calling in Chapter 17), and keep going until you find something. Most people are not willing to make this sort of effort, so they are better off remaining captive.

The Ability to Handle Change

Freelancers must change gears constantly. One day they are working for a Fortune 100 company, the next they are telemarketing their services, and the next they are working for a small startup company. To me, this is one of the advantages of freelancing, but to many people it is irritating. They prefer to plod along at the same pace, year after year. If that describes you, stay out of freelancing.

The Ability to Learn Quickly

It helps if you can catch on quickly. If you can get rolling in a new project quickly and efficiently, you can be more productive, which can only enhance your reputation. A common complaint about freelancers is that they take too long to train—the company has to pay for some totally unproductive time while the freelancer settles in. The shorter this unproductive period, the better you will look.

The Ability to Get On Well with People

A freelancer's reputation is very important. You go from job to job and work with so many people that you start to get a name for yourself, in a way that doesn't happen to permanent employees. The name you make for yourself can be good or bad, and it comprises two basic components: job skills and human relations skills.

While getting on well with people will not, on its own, get you work, not getting on with people can, on its own, lose you work. However well qualified you are, if you have a reputation for being a jerk, you will find contract-hunting difficult. On the other hand, if people like you, they are willing to forgive a lot. I would rather be known as competent and likable than as a genius who's difficult to get on with.

You Don't Have to be Perfect

Clearly not all freelancers have all these characteristics. I know some financially irresponsible contractors, some who are not very good writers, and others who are no good at sales. If you work with the technical-service agencies, you can get away with a lot. But the more of these characteristics you have, the more successful you can be, and independent freelancers—those not using the agencies—will need to have just about all of them.

5

The Advantages

of Freelancing

> No man has received from nature the right to give orders to others. Freedom is
> a gift from heaven, and every individual of the same species has the right to
> enjoy it as soon as he is in enjoyment of his reason.
>
> Denis Diderot

Why would anyone want to work freelance? Why give up a secure, permanent position for the uncertainties of freelancing? I hear both sides of the story. One afternoon I was chatting with an employee of a company for which I was contracting. "My wife tried contracting," he told me, "but it really wasn't worth the hassle. By the time we figured it all out, she wasn't making any more than she would as a full-timer, so she gave up." That evening I was talking with a programmer who had been contracting for about 15 years. He traveled around the country, from contract to contract, but now wanted to stay in the Dallas area. "I've made $125,000 this year," he told me. "Figure I'll make $140,000 next year." I continually run into these two opposites: people who tell me they just couldn't make freelancing pay, and people who tell me they've built $100,000+ incomes from freelancing.

Freelancing is what you make it. If you know the ropes, it can totally change your life. If you don't, it will just be a temporary phase between permanent jobs. If you last as a freelancer, these are the advantages you will enjoy.

Variety

For some people, of course, it is the very sameness of permanent employment that makes it so unattractive. I just can't imagine having the same job day in and day out, year after year after dreadful year. The monotony of it frightens me. The same people, the same buildings, the same ideas, the same product.

No, I need more variety than one job could give me. Changing jobs every six months, or even every year or two, keeps work interesting. New people, new tasks, and new experiences help you maintain interest in your work. And if one gets a bit boring, you'll be in a new one soon anyway!

Money

Skilled freelancers who know how to sell their services can make a lot more money than their permanent-employee colleagues. You may make 50 or 100 percent more on the first job you take, even allowing for lost benefits. By finding a specialty and building a reputation for yourself, you may be able to make several times your last salary. As you saw in Chapter 1, annual incomes of $80,000 are not unusual, and many freelancers make over $100,000.

Get Paid for the Hours You Work

People earning salaries are often expected to work much more than a 40-hour week. If you calculate your hourly rate, you may be surprised how low it is. Working freelance, you get paid by the hour, even if you charge a fixed fee for the project, because you base that fee on your estimate of the time it will take.

Get Paid Now, Not Later

As a permanent employee many of your benefits are in the form of promises: "Stay with us and you'll get a week of vacation this year (if we don't lay you off before the end of the year). Eventually we will give you five weeks' vacation each year (if you manage to last 15 years). You'll get promotions later (as long as you don't fight with your boss). And we have a wonderful pension plan (if the company stays in business long enough for you to collect)."

Working freelance earns you money up front, not implied promises that are broken as often as they are kept. You get a check every week or two, and that's it. No I.O.U. If you decide to leave the job, you are not throwing away all the "pending" payments.

Time Off

Freelancing lets you plan time off and take as much as you want. If you want to spend a month skiing each year, do it. One friend sells his services as a technical illustrator for most of the year, and then takes off during the summer so he can play baseball with his sons. Unlike salaried employees, who are limited to one or two weeks' vacation in the first year of a job, you can take as many as you want. And as a freelancer, you not only can have more time off, but usually can say when you want to take it. Sure, you need to be aware of your client's deadlines, but if you are on a six-month contract, it doesn't usually matter if you take off week 5 or week 15, whereas an employee often has more restrictions.

Work for a couple of years and take a year or two off if you want. A British contract writer I met recently did just that. He sailed his boat from Greece to the Caribbean so he could winter in the islands, and then sailed back to England. It is much easier for a freelancer to take a sabbatical than for an employee. When you need your boss's permission, it helps to be your own boss!

A More Balanced View of Life

If you've worked with one company for 5, 10, or 20 years, you've got a lot invested (all those implied promises the company hasn't yet fulfilled). Problems at work start to take on a new dimension. An argument with your boss is not just irritating, it may cost you thousands, even tens of thousands, of dollars in lost vacation, savings plans, and pension. The job has become so important that a serious problem becomes insurmountable.

I can hear my friends complaining now: "There's nothing wrong with work," they are saying. "Why shouldn't someone love their profession?" I'd better make a distinction between a job and a profession. A profession may be very important to you; it defines who you are and what you do. There's nothing wrong with feeling good about being a doctor or a writer or a programmer. The danger comes when your self-esteem depends on a job rather than a profession. A job is simply the use to which you put your profession. Placing too much importance on a job is placing all your eggs in one basket—someone else's basket!

It seems strange that in the United States of America, a country that prides itself on its citizens' individualism and independence, so few people are truly independent; they allow themselves to be directed and controlled by others in exchange for an illusion called "job security."

Easier to Leave a Bad Job

Because you are not waiting for payments you have been promised, leaving a freelance job is a lot easier than leaving a full-time position. But there is another reason it is easy to leave: You have a different mind-set. You expect to leave eventually anyway, so all you are doing is advancing the date a little. (But be careful not to do this too often. You don't want to get a reputation for running out on contracts.) I have found that permanent employees are much more wary of losing or leaving a job, not only because of all that they will lose, but also because they don't feel "comfortable" without a permanent job. "I've always had a job," one laid-off employee told me. "I just don't feel safe without one." Freelancers, even those who have been employed for many years prior to going freelance, learn to accept the ups and downs. They know that being between work is just part of the game.

Easier to Find New Work

Finding a contract is often easier than finding full-time work. While it may take several months to find full-time work, it may take only a couple of weeks to find contract work. Why? Probably because companies are more careful about hiring a full-timer—someone whom they want to stay years or even decades—than they are about hiring a contractor who may stay only a few months. They put a lot more effort into hiring full time, and spend much more time making their decisions—and keeping you waiting.

A Wide Range of Experience

Working a variety of contracts over a few years can help widen your experience and make it easier to find a job. You will work on a range of products, with different tools and technologies. You will learn more about your profession than you could by staying with the same company for years. Freelancing helps you stack your résumé with skills, making job- or contract-hunting easier.

Travel

In Chapter 8 you'll hear how freelancing can help you travel. Using some of the periodicals that carry advertisements from technical service agencies, and by looking for work online, you can find work anywhere in the United States, and possibly even overseas. Many freelancers move from job to job, throughout the country, leading a gypsylike existence.

The Opportunity to Move

Maybe you don't want to travel, but you do want to move. I'd lived in Dallas too long; I was raised in England, and the Texan summers were just too much for me! (Where I came from, a hot summer's day is in the 80s. In Texas, that's a warm winter's day.) I wanted to move to Denver, to be close to skiing. Because I was freelance, I was able to do that. I saved up some money, then put everything in a truck and left. My free-lancing skills helped me find work when I got to Denver. (I got a contract within a few weeks of arriving, after talking with someone at the very first Society for Technical Communication meeting I attended in Denver.)

It's even possible to move to your dream home and work elsewhere. How? By using the Internet to find work. We'll look at that in Chapter 24.

(**Disclaimer!**: If you follow the preceding advice, leaving your city and stable business environment and moving to the other side of the continent, then find that you have trouble securing contracts and end up bankrupt and destitute, living on the streets, don't come crying to me. Try this only if you are sure you have the skills to find the work when you get where you are going!)

A Stepping-Stone

The money, free time, and flexibility that freelancing gives you can be used in many ways. You can use it to make your life easier and more comfortable right now, or you can use it to fulfill an ambition you have. A programmer friend of mine works freelance to save the money that will allow him to start his own software business. I used freelancing to get my writing career going. I've now written around 30 books, including two computer-book best-sellers, and have begun my move into a different genre, too. The time and money provided by freelance technical writing were essential to my career.

You might have found your life sidetracked. After 15 years as a technical writer, you suddenly discover you would rather be an archaeologist. What do you do? You've got a spouse and three kids, so you can't just drop out and go back to college. But a high hourly rate could help you save money to take the time to study, and to make those long trips through Central America or North Africa.

More Job Security

Contractors have more job security than permanent employees.

Does that statement confuse you? It is my opinion, and that of many other contractors I know, but most permanent employees and perhaps even many contractors think it is nonsense. Contractors, after all, are out of work every year or so, or even every few months. How can you call that job security?

Here's what I think of as job security: *The security of knowing I can find work when I need it, with minimal time out of work.*

Let me give you an example. I joined a telecommunications company, on a contract with a technical services agency, at the same time another writer joined the company as a permanent employee. He needed to build a pension, he told me, and wanted more job security than contracting could provide. Twenty-one months later he was laid off, spent a few weeks out of work, and had to take a lousy job. I, on the other hand, worked contract for two other clients and lost not one day of work. My colleague was laid off again, several times over the following two years. (Finally he saw the light; he's been freelancing for about eight years now.)

A freelancer who knows the contract market and knows how to sell his services has more job security than a captive who finds himself thrust into the real world totally unprepared. You may be employed today, but if you are laid off tomorrow, what are you going to do? Contractors know the answer to that question; most captives don't.

No Office Politics

Don't office politics make you sick? A real advantage to freelancing is that you don't have to worry about them. As long as the client is paying an acceptable rate, I don't care too much about what is going on around me: who is likely to get the next promotion; who is being fired next; what the new boss is like. I don't even care too much about talk of layoffs and bankruptcy, because I know I'll be leaving soon anyway.

I don't have to play stupid office games to get ahead (compliment the right people, wear the right clothes, say the right things). Companies usually judge freelancers on their work; because they are not seen as company people, it doesn't matter if free-lancers don't "fit in." And if it all gets too bad, you can always get another contract.

I know that office politics damaged my earlier career. While working in the oil business in Mexico I advanced rapidly, and soon found myself in a management position—just as the oil business started to fall apart. The company transferred me back to Dallas, out of an environment in which performance counted and into one in which image was more important. I had an instant black mark against me: When I had joined the company a few years earlier, I had worn an earring.

Earrings on men, as you might imagine, were not common in the oil field in the early 1980s. But working on the oil rigs I experienced nothing more than rough, but generally good-humored, mocking. In the world of office politics things were worse. On the rigs, people tell you things to your face; in the office, they smile while they stab you in the back. It was only through the office grapevine that I heard what managers had said, and discovered why I had lost an important promotion.

No, give me contracting. I don't like playing these silly office games. I don't like having to mold my personality into an image approved by some old man in a little gray suit. I know I'm not alone in this. Most people don't enjoy these silly games. They don't have to get involved, if they freelance.

No Background Checks

You are less likely to run into background checks as a freelancer than when applying for full-time work. The United States is turning into a nation of control freaks, it seems. Apply for a job, and the employer wants to know about your recreational drug use, your medical history, your credit record . . . what has all this got to do with your employer? Freelancers rarely run into clients who want to test them or check on them.

You Can Say What You Mean!

Have you ever worked with a manager who made your life difficult? Someone who was simply rude, who got in the way of you doing your job? If you are a freelancer, you can tell people like this to take the job and shove it.

Here's an example. A few years ago I was doing a job for a small telecommunications company. I was talking with a programmer, gathering information. She was friendly, quite willing to provide the information I needed. But when her boss walked in and saw me talking to her, he went crazy. He decided I should have scheduled the meeting in some way, talked to him before I talked to any of his programmers. Nobody had told me this, but he decided, retroactively, that that was the way it had to be. He didn't explain this politely; he was quite rude about it.

Now, if I had been an employee, I'd think twice before going up against a manager, even if he wasn't *my* boss. But I wasn't an employee, I was a freelancer. I began by explaining that one reason I was a freelancer was that I didn't have to put up with the rudeness of petty bureaucrats like him. I don't want to be subjected to the rudeness of arrogant managers. And I'm willing to lose a contract now and again as a matter of self respect.

I *didn't* lose the contract, though. While I was shocking this manager by talking back to him, the person who had hired me to do the job walked in. He broke up the "discussion," dragged me off to his office, and apologized for the behavior of the other manager.

Extra Money on Referrals

Some contractors make extra money by establishing a relationship with a technical service agency and feeding the agency "leads." For example, if the agency needs someone to fill a position, and if you can find someone to take and keep the position for at least a month or two, you can earn a referral fee. Or if you know of a company that needs a contract employee, you tell the agency, and the agency fills the position; then you could get a fee. Not all agencies will do this, but the ones that will typically pay from $500 to $1,500 for each contractor hired or position filled. One technical writer I know made $5,000 in one year from fees.

Freelancers Like Being Freelance!

The best advertisement for freelancing are freelancers who are happy with their careers. The Society for Technical Communication asked freelancers about their work. When asked about their expectations, 55 percent of the contractors and consultants said they felt freelancing was better than they had expected; only 7 percent said it was worse. Ninety percent of those surveyed said they prefer freelancing to salaried work, and only 8 percent were actively looking for a salaried position. A 90 percent approval rating is a pretty good endorsement for the freelancing lifestyle!

The Disadvantages

of Freelancing

> Nothing is as easy as it looks.
>
> One of "Murphy's" many laws

There are several disadvantages to freelancing, so you must decide if they outweigh the advantages. I can imagine some situations in which you would be better off not freelancing—if you have serious medical problems, for example, or if you simply don't have the temperament suited to the lifestyle. It's easy for those of us who love freelancing—who can't imagine working for anyone else—to believe that there is only one way to work, and that's for oneself. Unfortunately, freelancing is not suited to all. So, in the interest of balance and to help you make the best decision, here are a few reasons why you might not want to freelance.

You Don't Get Any Benefits

Perhaps one of the most significant problems is that you may not receive the sort of benefits you would normally get from a permanent job. You may have to buy your own medical insurance, for example. (Of course this is a problem mainly in the United States, not in most of the rest of the industrialized world, where health insurance is not linked to employment.)

However, many agencies do have benefits, often very good packages that include medical, dental, long-term disability, and even vision insurance, at very reasonable prices. If you go totally independent, working without the assistance of an agency, you have to find your own benefits, but as you will see in Chapter 13, you can usually replace these benefits by buying your own policies and setting up your own pension plans.

Sometimes, though, you may find that the cost of replacing your benefits is so great that you cannot afford to go freelance. If, for example, you have been with a company long enough to be close to becoming "vested" in a pension plan, you should calculate how much you will lose if you leave; it may be worth waiting a while to get the pension money before you go freelance. If you or a dependent have serious health problems, you may want to consider staying with your present company, or at least only working with agencies that have good health insurance.

Remember, however, that most insurance plans have preexisting condition clauses, so they may not cover medical problems you already have. (U.S. law has changed recently, in theory to make moving between jobs easier, but there are still restrictions. See Chapter 13.) It's a shame that the United States, in theory a Mecca for free enterprise, has chosen a medical system that actually puts a damper on free enterprise.

By the way, I don't regard vacation as a benefit; companies do not pay their employees to take vacations, they simply withhold some of the employee's pay until he or she takes a vacation, to give the employee a constant income throughout the year. As a freelancer you must simply ensure that your income is sufficient to allow you to take vacation and still earn more than a salaried employee.

You Must Have More Savings—Business Capital

In some ways a freelancer needs to be more financially responsible. Your savings are your business capital, and a certain portion should be treated as such. However, freelancers usually have more money to play with anyway, so you can be "irresponsible" with a lot of money and still have some left over to save for your business. And when you become established, you may find that work is so easy to get that you don't have to worry too much about money.

When I started freelancing I didn't dramatically improve my lifestyle. I did spend a bit more, and take longer vacations, but I didn't rush out and buy a hot tub and a Porsche. Instead, I saved most of the extra income, and used that money as business capital.

You Don't Have Long-Term Work Relationships

Some people want the same work, day in, day out. They don't like change, and prefer to know that they will be working with the same people and doing the same thing two years from now. If this describes you, then don't go into freelancing. Your long-term relationships must occur outside of the workplace if you are a freelancer. That's not to say that you won't make lasting friendships with people you meet on a contract, but usually you will simply move on to the next company and the next set of employees with hardly a thought for the last.

You Have No One to Point You in the Right Direction

Some people like to be given a direction to go in, a set of steps to take that will lead them up a company's career ladder. As a freelancer, you are on your own. Either you make your own career ladder, or you forget about professional progress and just work for the money. No one is going to act as your mentor or guide.

You Can't Get Involved in Office Politics

One of the advantages to freelancing is that you don't have to bother yourself with office politics. Yet to some people, this is a disadvantage. I know people who have done well in their careers thanks to office politics. They play games, such as forging strong friendships with "mentors" in management and ensuring that they're seen to be the first at the office each day.

Such games don't work for freelancers, because freelancers aren't around long enough for anyone to care, and the company's "rules of the game" don't apply to them anyway.

You Must Be a Salesperson

Another major disadvantage of freelancing is that you have to sell yourself. How often you have to do so will vary, but one way or another you must persuade someone to buy your services. People who don't mind sales work, or even enjoy it, do well as freelancers. If you can handle calling 40 strangers a day looking for a contract, and enjoy going on interviews, then the sales aspect of freelancing shouldn't worry you. But if you have an inordinate fear of rejection, or suffer from what salespeople know as "call reluctance," you may have problems freelancing. Even if you have no great fears, but simply find constant marketing to be too much of a grind, you may find freelancing to be more hassle than it's worth.

However, this is more of a problem for people in Step Two and Step Three (see "The Three-Step Method of Freelancing" in Chapter 4). People in Step One, working through agencies, don't have to worry too much about selling themselves; they let the agencies find the work.

Incidentally, you don't have to be some sort of caricature of a used-car salesman to do well in sales. Contrary to popular opinion, the most important characteristic of a good salesperson is not the ability to lie, or the ability to smooth talk. Most sales trainers will tell you that what really counts is hard work and persistence. You have to contact a lot of clients. The more clients you contact, the more sales you'll make. So don't worry about compromising your principles; you don't have to do so to succeed in selling your services. And you should also know that as your business becomes more established, and as you become more skilled and build a reputation for yourself, you'll have to do less and less marketing. I know writers who do very little marketing, because the work seems to come to them. And although I haven't looked for work in almost two years, companies still call me with projects.

No Established Pension Plan

If you work freelance, you have to find your own pension plan. If you work for a company, you probably will have some kind of plan set up for you. However, as I'll discuss in Chapter 13, the freelancer has several advantages over the captive worker here. For a start, if you are making more money you can afford to save more. Many agencies have pension plans, too. The very best pension plans, however, are limited to the true independent contractor.

Feelings of Uncertainty and Insecurity

I believe the major factor stopping many people going freelance is a general feeling of insecurity. People spend most of their lives inside social organizations that provide them with guidelines and rules: first the family, then school, college, and a company. These organizations promise certain things. "As long as you behave yourself," the organizations say, "we'll look after you. We will feed you, clothe you, and provide you with social status and a position in the pecking order. You may not like us much," they sometimes say, "but at least you'll know what to expect."

But going freelance is different. You're on your own, with no one to point the way. Sure, you may have an agency telling you it will find work for you, but you can't bank promises. I know perfectly healthy, skilled, experienced people who have unequivocally stated they feel nervous without a job. If that sounds like you, you have two options: Try freelancing anyway (and hope you will get over the nerves), or continue working as a captive.

More Time Spent Job Hunting

Freelancers usually spend more time looking for work. Whereas the average employee may look for work every three or four years, freelancers may look every six months or year. If you don't like the feeling of being out of work, or of being unsure what you will do when your current job comes to an end, then freelancing may not be for you. But if you know how to find work and have the confidence that comes with knowing that your skills are in demand, then you have no reason to be nervous about freelancing.

You won't necessarily spend more time out of work, though. You will start job-hunting before your contract ends, so you may go straight from one contract to another. One contractor in Dallas told me he has been freelancing for seven years and has had only one week out of work. Others find contracts that last for years; I've met contractors who haven't had to look for a job for five years or more.

You Don't Get Vacations

This *isn't* a disadvantage, but I wanted to discuss it because so many people think it is. "If you work on contract, you don't get any vacation," I often hear. What do people think, that I never take time off? "But you don't get paid for your vacation, that's what I mean," people say. Well, I've got a surprise for those people: Neither do they.

No company pays people to take vacations—after all, why would they pay you not to work? Companies pay employees to work for them, but they don't pay all the money they owe in each paycheck. They hold some of the money back, and then continue paying the employee while the employee is on vacation. Sometimes they hold the money back and *never* pay it, because the employee is fired or laid off before using the vacation time.

On the other hand, the freelancer receives all money owed in each paycheck; the client doesn't hold any back for later. I make more money each week than I would if I were a permanent employee, so does it matter if no one is paying me while I'm on vacation? Of course not.

Of course some agencies do give vacation pay, but don't automatically assume that you are onto a "good deal" just because an agency offers you vacation pay; the money still comes out of your hourly rate. I would rather receive the money up front, for a couple of reasons. First, I would like to have the money earning interest for me rather than the agency. And second, I would get the money even if the contract ended early; most contracts that pay vacation stipulate that you must work a certain amount of time before you can get the vacation money.

No One Will Train You

Companies usually want to hire people who are already trained. This isn't always true—sometimes they will hire entry-level contractors—but more often than not, the company wants someone who can come in and produce as quickly as possible. This may be a disadvantage, especially if you don't have a lot of experience in your line of work. You may decide to remain as a permanent employee for a few years while you learn your trade, and then go freelance. A programmer friend of mine is working for a company that is training him in UNIX. Although he could get more money as a contractor, he has decided not to leave until he is proficient in UNIX.

An alternative is to educate yourself in your free time. My friend could learn UNIX at a local college, for example, although it is difficult to beat the experience that comes from the hands-on use of a technique in the real world.

As I've mentioned earlier, though, freelancing is often a great way to learn things. In many cases freelancers pick up many diverse (and valuable) skills by hopping from place to place. In the technical-writing field, the fact that nobody will train you is usually not too important, because you can quickly learn the required skills in your free time or simply pick them up while you work. (It's easier to learn how to create Web pages than to write C++ programs, for instance.) Training is more of an issue in other fields, such as programming, where the required skills may take thousands of hours to learn.

You Want to Transfer to Management

Many people transfer out of the "nitty-gritty" of their professions into management positions. A technical writer, for example, may become a department manager. These avenues for advancement are not normally available to the contractor. A writer remains a writer.

However, many technical writers build their own advancement. Some start their own agencies, selling technical writing services, for instance.

You Won't Get Unemployment Pay

If you are out of work, you cannot claim unemployment pay. But unemployment usually pays only a limited sum for only a limited time. Successful freelancing will allow you to save enough money to tide you over times of unemployment.

You May Not Be Covered by Workers' Compensation

You probably won't be covered by Workers' Compensation insurance, although if you are injured at a client's office, you may be covered by your client's liability insurance. Still, it's important to make sure you have adequate medical and long-term disability insurance. See Chapter 13 for information.

You'll Make Too Much Money

Too much money? Well, okay, this is one of those "disadvantages" that are real, but which people can't take too seriously. I know someone who would like to work with a big company, in a nice, stable position. He's a company man at heart. But he's been working freelance for a few years, and every time he applies for a full-time position and discovers how much money he'll *lose* by giving up freelancing, he can't bring himself to do it. He's spoiled, he's become a captive of the high-paid freelance life. Poor guy.

You May Not Get Paid

I left this until last because it is not very common. It does happen, though, and you should protect yourself as much as you can. If you work for an agency, make sure it pays at least every two weeks; many agencies pay each week. If you work on an independent contract that pays you by the hour, invoice the client at least every two weeks. If the client is a small company, you should try to arrange favorable payment terms—10 days from the invoice date, for example. You can usually be more confident that large companies will pay, and you may find that most will want to pay within 30 days of the invoice.

If you are working for a fixed fee, you should arrange to get some of the fee up front, and the rest at set intervals throughout the project. If the checks are late, find out why immediately, and get the problem sorted out right away; don't let your losses accumulate (if necessary, don't do any more work for the client until the checks arrive, so you don't have too much unpaid time). Incidentally, small agencies are probably more likely not to pay than the larger agencies or client companies.

Using these methods, you can make sure that if a client does default, your loss is limited. Another advantage is that the lower the loss, the easier it is to go to small claims court. Small claims courts are cheap and easy to use, tend to favor the "underdog" (individuals up against companies), and may be the only way you will ever see your money. If you ever need to go to small claims court, get the *Small Claims Court Citizens Legal Manual*. This explains exactly how to use this court and what your alternatives are. Or contact the Nolo Press Self Help Law Center, which should have useful information. (You can find information about both these items in Appendix F.)

I've never had a client default. I'm sure I've met people who've run into these problems, but they happen so infrequently that I just can't remember any such cases. By the way, remember that if the client doesn't pay, then the client doesn't own the work. Copyright law protects writing. So if the client doesn't pay and uses your writing, the client has broken copyright law—that's criminal law, not civil law. We'll discuss this in more detail in Chapter 20.

Can *You* Succeed?

Will you succeed? Or will the disadvantages overwhelm you? I hope you can make a success of freelancing, as so many others have, but there are no guarantees. While the great majority of people who have contacted me after reading my book have thanked me for helping them start or improve their freelance business, now and again I hear from someone who hasn't managed to get things rolling.

For instance, one woman wrote to me saying that I'd written "a great book," but that she'd had so many setbacks that she'd decided to go back to full-time employment. And in one review, the reviewer had written that "the work is not as easy to get as he claims." I must admit I'm a fairly optimistic person. I'm not interested in what the "average" or "median" writer makes, I'm interested in how much writers can earn if they make all the right moves—if they are good at marketing themselves, if they are persistent, if they do a good job for their clients.

Is the work not as easy to come by as I claim? Well, I'll admit that I know writers who complain that there's not enough work around. But I also know writers who have so much work they have trouble finding free time, who *turn down* work because they just can't take more. The work *is* as easy to come by as I claim *if* you make all the right moves, but it's very hard to come by if you don't know what you are doing.

Still, there will always be people who won't make it, perhaps because they are not suited for the work. I don't mean that in any derogatory way at all—we all have different strengths and weaknesses which make us more suitable for some things and less so for others. Many people hate marketing and sales, but those activities are an integral part of freelancing. If you are uncomfortable selling yourself to someone, you won't be as successful as you might otherwise be.

Sometimes people are in situations that make it difficult to get a freelance career going, too. For instance, the woman who said she was going back to a full-time position later told me that she *had* been doing okay, making $30 to $35 an hour. But then she moved to a small rural town (30,000 people), and since that time had trouble finding contracts. A small market means fewer opportunities.

Still, with hard work and imagination, it's possible to overcome difficulties and make it as a freelancer. I suggested to that woman that she market her services in the nearest metropolitan area—it's possible to do so without clients realizing you are actually living in the middle of nowhere. You can get a local phone line in the nearest major city that automatically calls long distance to your home, and a post office box that forwards mail. And, of course, e-mail addresses are impossible to pin down to a geographic location. She would have a long drive once or twice a week for a while, during the time that she was building her business, but it might be worth it. Another thing she could try is finding work on the Internet, using some of the techniques discussed in Chapter 24 (if it's possible to live in Malaysia yet find work in North America and Europe, as one writer does, I'm sure it can be done on a more local scale).

Ultimately it all comes down to you. Are you suited to freelancing, and are you willing to do what it takes to succeed? The benefits are fantastic; they're well worth making the effort. I've provided enough information for you to get started. Read the book carefully, try a few of the techniques, be creative, and get your freelance career rolling.

How Much Do You

Currently Earn?

Having money is rather like being a blond. It is more fun but not vital.

Fashion designer Mary Quant

Before you begin freelancing you should calculate how much your permanent job pays you for each hour you work. That may sound simple; after all, you already know your salary or hourly rate. But your employer pays a lot more than you receive in cash—you have to calculate the value of the benefits you receive. Also, if you receive a fixed salary and work long hours, your hourly rate may be much less than you imagine.

When I speak of the value of benefits, I don't mean how much the benefits cost your employer. I mean how much it will cost you to replace the benefits. The important thing to remember here is that however much a benefit costs your employer, if you don't use it, it isn't worth anything. For example, you may have a free membership in a health club, a membership that you have never used. This may cost your boss a couple of hundred dollars a year, and may cost you even more to replace it, but since you don't use it, you should not include it in your calculations. Companies and personnel managers often claim that their employee benefits add 25 to 30 percent to a salary. Often this is exaggerated, but even if your company does spend this amount, so what? When you deduct the cost of the benefits you never use, you usually find that you can replace the benefits for far less.

You want to know how much it costs to replace your benefits, but the actual value of the benefits—and thus your hourly pay—varies depending on the situation to which you are comparing your permanent employment. For example, it will cost you less to replace your medical insurance if you are working with a technical service agency that has a company-subsidized policy than if you are working with an agency that doesn't. So the amount you earn is a relative number used to compare work situations.

You must calculate how much you get per hour, because that is how you are going to be paid when you are freelancing. If you are working for an agency, you will be paid an hourly rate; if you are working as an independent, you will either bill for the number of hours worked or charge a set fee that you determine according to an estimate of how long the job will take.

I've seen a few ways to calculate a job's total value. One formula suggests that people take their base salary, add the value of their benefits, and add a value derived by multiplying the number of days not worked (vacation, sick leave, and so on) times their "daily" salary. This method is nonsense. Assigning a value to vacations and adding that value to the salary (which already includes payment for vacations) is ridiculous. After all, if my salary is $30,000 and I take 33 days' of vacation, how much do I receive? I get $30,000, of course, but this formula would have me believe that I'm really paid $33,807, because that is the "value" of the time off.

But vacation and sick time have no monetary value. Rather, the more vacation or sick leave you take, the less you work, which means the higher your hourly rate. For example, a job that pays $30,000 a year and provides three weeks' paid time off pays $15.31 per hour. If the same job provided four weeks' paid leave, the hourly rate would be $15.63 per hour. (These examples assume a 40-hour work week.) When you assign a value to vacations, you are assigning a value to time not worked. So why not assign a value to weekends, or evenings, or lunch hours . . .

Assigning a value to vacations muddles what should be a simple calculation. The most sensible way to calculate the value of a job (and the only way to compare a salary to an hourly rate) is to calculate how much you earn each hour. (At the end of this chapter we'll look at other ways that freelancers muddle the calculation.)

When Should You Make These Calculations?

Your hourly income is not an absolute number. Because it includes not only wages or salary but also benefits, and because they vary in value depending on your work situation, your hourly income is in some senses a comparative value.

For example, suppose that you earn $15 per hour in wages and benefits excluding medical insurance, and work for 1,880 hours a year. What is your total hourly rate? Well, it depends on how much it costs to replace your medical insurance, and that depends on several things. If you are going to add yourself to your spouse's policy for $10 a month, you are earning about $15.06 per hour. If you plan to use an agency policy that will cost you $50 per month, you are paid about $15.32 an hour. But if you are comparing your job to working through an agency that doesn't have a policy, and you estimate that it will cost $500 per month to replace your medical policy, then you are making $18.20 an hour (that is, you need to make $18.20 an hour to match your present salary and benefits).

So when do you calculate your hourly rate, and what is the point of doing so? I recommend that you first calculate your hourly rate when you decide to work freelance. Some of your figures will have to be estimates. You won't know exactly how much it will cost to replace your medical insurance, but you can guess. Then, when you get your first contract-job offer, calculate again, using the actual figures. And what will the hourly rate tell you? It tells you how much you must earn, in a particular job, to equal your present income.

Let's take an example. An agency has offered you a job. It has medical insurance for $600 per year, but that doesn't include long-term disability, which will cost you $900 per year. You estimate that you can replace other benefits (which we'll look at in detail in a moment) for $1,000 per year. Your present salary is $30,000, and you work 2,000 hours in a year. So your hourly rate at your present job is $16.25. The following indicates how you arrive at this figure:

Salary	$30,000
Insurance	$600
Long-Term Disability	$900
Other Benefits	$1,000
Total	$32,500
Total Hours	2,000
Hourly Rate	$16.25

So what does the figure of $16.25 tell you? It means that working through that particular agency, you must make $16.25 an hour (and be able to work 2,000 hours a year) to match your present income. (Remember, however, that many agencies pay time-and-a-half for overtime, which further complicates the issue.)

Now suppose the agency doesn't have medical insurance, and you estimate it will cost you $400 per month to insure your family:

Salary	$30,000
Insurance ($400 x 12)	$4,800
Long-Term Disability	$900
Other Benefits	$1,000
Total	$36,700
Total Hours	2,000
Hourly Rate	$18.35

You need to make $18.35 to replace your income.

Calculating Your Income

I have included a worksheet near the end of this chapter. Follow the instructions in the following text and use the worksheet to find out how much you earn.

How Much Are You Paid?

Write down all your income: salary, hourly wages, overtime pay, and bonuses. Include *all* the money, even money paid during vacations and sick leave.

Medical, Dental, and Vision Insurance

This one is a bit complicated. If you are married and can get onto the policy provided by your spouse's company, write down that cost. That is probably the cheapest insurance you can get. (If you live with someone in a "common law" relationship, you may still be able to get onto their medical insurance, depending on your state's laws.)

Many technical service agencies now have medical insurance (almost all the large ones do). Some charge the full cost to the contractor, but others charge only a portion. One agency charges $50 a month for a company policy, another charges only $10 a month, and yet another charges the full amount ($327 a month). If you have to get your own policy, the cost is going to depend on several things. You can get family coverage through a Health Maintenance Organization (HMO) for about $400 a month. However, if you want to include maternity insurance, you may need to add $150 a month or more. Also, if you have a history of medical problems you may find insurance very expensive, possibly prohibitively so—you may need to stay in your permanent position just to maintain your insurance. See Chapter 13 for more information about health insurance.

Another option is to continue your present insurance for 18 months using a COBRA (Consolidated Omnibus Budget Reconciliation Act) continuance; see Chapter 13 for more information. I suggest you examine all your options before filling in this cost. Check a few policies for prices.

If your present employer provides dental and vision insurance and it appears you won't be able to replace it, estimate how much you will lose in a year without it.

Finally, remember that if you are an independent contractor you can deduct part of your medical insurance from your taxes. Currently (in the 1997 tax year), you can deduct 40 percent of the premiums. So, for instance, if you are paying $4,500 a year, and are in a 28 percent tax bracket, you'll save $504 in taxes—so your real cost of medical insurance is $3,996. (The deduction is scheduled to increase in steps, up to 80 percent by the year 2006. It'll be 45 percent for 1998 to 2002.)

Long-Term Disability

You need a long-term disability policy, although many freelancers don't have one. Just imagine the consequences of a sickness that stopped you working for a year or two, or even just a few months. Many agencies include a long-term disability policy with their medical insurance policies, but if they don't, you can replace it (if you are in good health) starting for around $95 a month, depending on your age, occupation, and the amount of coverage you want. See Chapter 13 for more information.

Term Life Insurance

Company life insurance rarely has any significant value. Although some companies give their employees life insurance with a value of one or two times their annual salary, more commonly companies provide a $10,000 or $20,000 policy. How much is that worth? That depends on your age, sex, and health—it may be worth as little as $10 or $20 a year. Even if your company gives you a large policy, it may be worth only a couple of dollars a week.

For example, if I were a permanent employee, I would probably have a salary of $45,000 to $55,000, so my employer might provide a free life insurance policy with a benefit of $90,000; replacing that policy would cost me $90 a year. Also, the tax law changed recently. If your employer provides you with a life insurance policy with a benefit over $50,000, you now have to pay tax on the cost of the amount over $50,000. For example, if you have a $100,000 policy, you have to pay income tax and FICA on half of what your company pays for the policy.

If you don't think your employer's policy is worth replacing (you already have your own or don't need one), don't write down a value.

Tax-Free Savings Plan

Wherever you work, you will have a tax-free savings plan. Even if your company or agency doesn't have one, you can still use an IRA (Independent Retirement Account). However, many agencies also have 401(k) plans; and if you are self-employed, you can have an SEP (Simplified Employee Pension) or Keogh plan. These plans let you save even more than an IRA allows.

So how much is your current employer's plan worth? Remember that the value of your present employer's savings plan is limited by how much you manage to save. If your income is too low to allow any savings, the plan has no value to you. If you put less than $2,000 a year into the plan, having your employer provide the plan has no value, because you can put that amount into an IRA. If you save more, write down the reduction in your tax bill that is due to the portion of the contribution above $2,000. Therefore, if you put $3,000 into your pension plan, write down the savings in tax produced by $1,000. Take a look at Chapter 13, and spend some time investigating pension plans. You may find that your employer's plan has absolutely no value, because you can put just as much into a plan you set up yourself or get through the agency. (Some agency plans have a waiting period before you can join them, though, so remember to ask.)

Employer Contributions to Pensions and Tax-Free Savings Plans

Employers often contribute to a pension plan for you. It may be difficult to estimate the value of these benefits because that value depends on how long you are going to stay with your employer. For many people, especially young people just starting a career, these benefits often have *no* value because such workers don't intend to stay with one company long enough to get their hands on the money.

Your employer's contribution to a pension plan doesn't immediately become your property. You may have to wait over three years to "own" 25 percent, four years to own 50 percent, and five years to own 100 percent. So it's up to you. Decide if you are likely to stay long enough to become "vested"; if so, find out how much your employer contributes (often 3 to 5 percent of base pay for a pension, and a similar sum in matching contributions to a tax-free savings plan). Remember also that if you don't contribute much to your savings plan, your employer isn't going to have much to match.

If you have been with the company a long time, these calculations are easier. In such instances, you are already vested, so all your employer's contributions are immediately your property.

Health Club

Does your company provide a membership to a health club? Do you use it? If not, ignore it.

Cafeteria

Does your company provide a cafeteria? Do you use it? How much does it save you each year?

Education

Many companies pay for certain educational courses taken by their employees. If your company is doing this for you, estimate how much you would spend each year if you had to pay your own way.

Employee Discounts

Does your company produce or sell a product that you use and can buy at a discount cost? If so, do you ever buy any of this product, and would you do so if you didn't have a discount? For example, if a manufacturer of high-cost computers lets its employees buy PCs at a 40 percent discount, the cost may still be more than the cost of a comparable mail-order clone. Would you buy the product if you didn't get such a discount, or would you be just as happy with the clone? Include only the savings over and above what you would pay if you had no discount. And remember, if you buy one computer every three years, divide the savings by three.

Day Care

Does your company provide day care while you are at work? If so, how much will it cost you to replace the day care? Don't add that cost to your benefits, though. Using 1996 tax-year figures, you can get a tax credit of between 20 and 30 percent (depending on your income) of the first $2,400 you spend on day care for one child under 13, or $4,800 for two or more children. For example, if your adjusted gross income is over $28,000 and you spend more than $2,400 a year for one child's day care, you can deduct $480 from your taxes. Spend more than $4,800 for two or more children and you can deduct $960 from your taxes. So the value of the benefit is the cost of replacing the benefit minus the tax credit. (Not that these are credits; you deduct the value of the credit from the tax you would otherwise be paying. They are not deductions from the estimated income that you are using to calculate your taxes.)

FICA

You don't need to worry about FICA (Social Security tax) if you are going to work for an agency, because usually the agency will pay FICA for you (and is normally legally obliged to do so)—it's just the same as having a job with any other company. So if you are going to be an agency employee, skip this step. However, if you work as an independent contractor—that is, if you are paid without anyone withholding taxes from you—you must pay Self Employment tax instead of FICA.

There are actually two different taxes involved in this calculation. If you are someone's employee, your company or agency pays part of the tax; you pay 7.65 percent of the first $62,700 and 1.45 percent of everything above that (1996 figures). But independents pay the full amount, both the "employer's" and "employee's" share—a 12.4 percent social security tax and a 2.9 percent Medicare tax (1996 figures). You will pay both taxes—a combined 15.3 percent on the first $62,700 of your income, and only the Medicare tax (2.9 percent) on everything above that.

However, you can deduct half of the Self Employment tax from your federal income tax, so you get some of it back! (Aren't taxes wonderful? Who thinks up these systems?) If your total Self Employment tax is $7,600, for instance (twice the $3,800 paid by an employee earning the same amount), you can deduct $3,800 from your income tax. Deducting $3,800 could save you $1,254 (depending on your tax rate), so the extra Self Employment tax paid would really only be $2,546.

To complicate things further, you don't pay Self Employment tax on your entire income, only on 92.35 percent of your income. So if you earn $60,000, you pay Self Employment tax on $55,410. (Hey, I never said this all made sense.)

For example, an employee earning $60,000 will pay $4,590 (7.65 percent of $60,000), while an independent will pay $8,478, half of which is deductible. So the independent will really end up paying about $7,291, around $2,700 more than the employee. (Okay, here's how it works: 92.35 percent of $60,000 equals $55,410, which multiplied by the 15.3 percent tax equals $8,477.73. But you can deduct half of this amount from your taxes. So half of $8,477.73 times a tax rate of 28 percent equals $1,186.88. $8,477.73 minus $8,477.73 equals $7,290.85. Round it up to $7,291. The calculation will vary, of course, if you are in a different tax bracket.)

Here's a table to help you calculate your additional Self Employment tax, the tax you'd pay on your income if you were a freelancer and not a salaried employee. Base this estimate on your current salary.

Line	Step	Example
1	Enter your income.	$50,000
2	Multiply line 1 by .9235.	$46,175
3	If line 2 is less than $62,700, multiply line 2 by .153 (15.3%). If line 2 is over $62,700, enter $9,593.	$7,065
4	If line 2 is less than $62,700, leave this line blank and skip to line 6. If line 2 is more than $62,700, subtract $62,700 and enter the remainder here.	
5	Multiply line 4 by .029 (2.9%).	
6	Add lines 3 and 5: **This is your total Self Employment tax.**	$7,065
7	Divide line 6 by 2.	$3,533
8	Enter your top income-tax rate.	.28 (28%)
9	Multiply line 7 by line 8: **This is the amount the deduction saves you.**	$989
10	Deduct line 9 from line 6: **This is the true Self Employment tax you will pay**, allowing for the income-tax deduction.	**$6,076**

Now you need to calculate how much FICA you'd pay if you were an employee.

11	If line 1 is less than $62,700, multiply line 1 by .0765 (7.65%). If line 2 is over $62,700, enter $9,593.	$3,825
12	If line 1 is less than $62,700, leave this line blank and skip to line 13. If line 1 is more than $62,700, subtract $62,700 and enter the remainder here.	

continues

continued

Line	Step	Example
13	Multiply line 12 by .0145 (1.45%).	
14	Add lines 11 and 13. This is the amount of FICA paid by an employee.	**$3,825**
15	Subtract line 14 from line 10. This is the value of the **additional tax** you pay as an independent freelancer.	**$2,251**

This simply gives you an idea of how much additional money you'll lose to Self Employment tax. If you've been listening to other freelancers, you may be surprised at how small this sum really is. I've heard freelancers claim that they're paying an extra $5,000 or more in Self Employment tax, because they haven't taken into account FICA, the 7.65 percent deduction off the top, and the 50 percent deduction of income taxes.

Miscellaneous

There are various benefits that your company may be providing that are very difficult to estimate. For example, you may get funeral leave and moving allowances. If these miscellaneous benefits are likely to be of value to you, add them to the list. However, since you will rarely need these benefits and they are often of very limited value, you probably should just forget them.

Hours Worked per Year

Write down the number of hours you work each year—hours actually worked, not vacation and sick time you were paid for. If you receive a salary, don't just write down 2,080 (52 weeks times 40 hours) unless you actually work 2,080 hours. Subtract the hours you spent out of the office playing golf, taking long lunches, taking personal days, on vacation, on military or funeral leave, out sick, or off for holidays—time you didn't work but for which the company paid you. And *add* all the extra time you may have worked, weekends and evenings.

Worksheet

Use this worksheet to figure out how much you make each year. Refer to the preceding instructions for specific information about each line.

Line	Income—Payment Per Year	Total
1	Salary/Wages	$
2	Overtime Pay	$
3	Bonuses	$
4	Other	$
5	Total Payments—add the values on lines 1, 2, 3, and 4	$

Line	Benefits—Costs per Year	Total
6	Medical/Dental/Vision Insurance	$
7	Long-Term Disability	$
8	Term Life Insurance, Personal	$
9	Term Life Insurance, Family	$
10	Tax-Free Savings Plan	$
11	Employer's Contribution	$
12	Health Club	$
13	Cafeteria	$
14	Education	$
15	Employee Discounts	$
16	Day Care	$
17	FICA	$
18	Miscellaneous Benefits	$
19	Total Benefits—add the values on lines 6 through 18)	$
20	Total Income (Payments + Benefits) —add lines 5 and 19	$
21	Total Number of Hours Worked per Year	
22	Your Hourly Rate—divide line 20 by line 21	$

Now you know what you earn. Employees paid hourly are often surprised how high the rate is, and salaried people working long hours are often amazed at how low.

Anyway, now you have a benchmark. You know you must make that much to "break even." You may find you can easily make $10 or $15 an hour above your break-even point, which is $20,000 to $30,000 a year more than you now make. You may be able to increase your income by much more than this. But even if you are not able to make a large increase in your income, I suggest you make sure your first contract is at least several dollars an hour higher than your break-even point. As a freelancer you will be looking for work more often than a permanent employee; you must make more money to see yourself through the times you are selling yourself instead of working. You may be lucky and rarely have any "downtime," but you should prepare for such an eventuality nonetheless.

Many newcomers to freelancing are surprised by hourly rates that sound high. They make $14 an hour in salary, so when an agency offers $21 an hour they jump at it. What they don't realize is that when they add benefits to their salary, they are really making $18 or $19, so the contract is increasing their incomes only a dollar or two an hour. Make sure you know what you earn and you will know how much a contract must pay to make it worth your while.

More Expenses

We've just looked at direct job-related expenses: the cost of replacing a salary and benefits. But there may be other expenses. In Step One of my Three-Step plan, there are few other expenses. But if you enter Step Two, you may have other expenses—and if you reach Step Three, you certainly will.

In Step One you are working through the agencies, at a client's office. You have no more expenses than if you were a full-time employee. You may be working side-by-side with full-time employees, doing exactly the same thing as they.

But if you are selling yourself directly to clients, you will have more expenses. You'll spend more time running around visiting clients, and perhaps mailing a brochure of some kind. But the real expenses don't start until you enter Step Three, the "consulting" phase. At this point you are probably working at home. Then you have to consider the cost of computer equipment and software, two major expenses.

Exaggerated Expenses

For some strange reason, it's common in freelance publications to exaggerate the expense of doing business as a freelancer. I've seen articles claiming that if you want to match a salary of $40,000, you'd better be making $80,000 of freelance income. I've even seen a claim that a $100,000 freelance income is the true equivalent of a $40,000 salary. Both figures are total nonsense, based on exaggerated expenses.

Why do freelancers exaggerate their expenses? I'm not quite sure. It may be the same thing *everyone* goes through: Money never seems to go as far as it should, so you wonder "where your money is going." The freelancer has an easy target to blame: the cost of doing business. I think some freelancers also exaggerate their costs because they want to justify their high rates. In effect they are saying, "Hey, so I charge $80 an hour, but you don't know how much I have to spend to stay in business!" And often freelancers simply don't understand the calculations they must make, or don't keep good track of their finances.

So here are a few misunderstandings you'll run into. Understand these and you'll be able to ignore other freelancers when they try to frighten or impress you with their vast business expenses.

Miscalculating Taxes

One good way to increase the estimated "expense" of being a freelancer is to miscalculate the additional taxes you'll have to pay. For instance, one writer started her breakdown of expenses by calculating Self Employment tax on her entire income. But this should be the last calculation; you don't pay Self Employment tax on your entire income, you pay it on your income *after* you've subtracted expenses. (In steps Two and Three, you'll have business expenses that are deductible; see Chapter 18.) She also ignored the 7.65 percent reduction in income, forgot that she was paying 15.3 percent on only the first $62,700—she applied it to her entire income—didn't calculate the savings from deducting half from her income tax, and then ignored the fact that she'd have to pay FICA if she were an employee.

Assigning a Value to Vacations

The most common mistake freelancers make is to assign a value to their vacation, then deduct that vacation as if it were a business expense. This is really quite bizarre, but I've seen it done several times. It makes absolutely no sense, so it's difficult to argue against!

If you made $100,000 last year, and you took three weeks of vacation, you still made $100,000. It doesn't matter whether you took three, six, or nine weeks; if you made $100,000 during the year, you made $100,000 during the year! And yet some writers will tell you that you should calculate the value of the vacation, and subtract that value. For instance, one writer says that you should allow $400 per day of vacation. So if you take three weeks' vacation (15 days), the value of your vacation is $6,000. Thus, you didn't make $100,000 a year, you actually made $94,000. Of course, this formula makes no sense. Similar calculations made for sick leave and days off make no sense, either.

Exaggerating the Cost of a Pension Plan

Here's another common mistake. Let's say you make $60,000 after business expenses. You can pay up to $12,000 into a pension fund. Some freelancers would take that $12,000 off their income when trying to compare their freelance income with a salary. But that makes no sense, because the $12,000 is not something you must spend to make sure that you have the same benefits you would have if you were salaried. Rather, being able to afford to put such a large amount into a pension fund is one of the *advantages* of working as a freelancer; it's nonsensical to turn it around and use it as proof of how expensive it is to work as a freelancer.

Deducting Expenses That You Can't Deduct If You Are Salaried

Another way to make freelancing look really expensive is to include the cost of things that you'd pay for even if you were salaried. The most common one is to deduct the cost of driving. If you are salaried, you are driving to work, right? Driving to work is not deductible, though, even for most freelancers (see Chapter 18). However, when it *is* deductible (as it is to many writers who visit clients once or twice a week, for instance), that's an *advantage*, not a loss; in other words, you can now deduct something that you *wouldn't* be able to deduct if you weren't freelancing. Your income is not reduced, it's *increased*!

As a freelancer you'll find that you end up deducting certain expenses that you'd have even if you were an employee. While this at first glance seems to indicate that your expenses are higher than an employee's—after all, those expenses will reduce your income as far as tax calculations are concerned—these expenses create a reduction in taxes—in effect an increase in after-tax income—that you wouldn't have if you were an employee.

Deducting Expenses That Are Not Business-Related

How about deducting expenses that are not directly business-related? For instance, in one assessment of the cost of freelancing a writer deducted $600 for life insurance. Fine, it's a good idea to have a good life insurance policy. But it's not directly related to the cost of doing business. Few companies provide $600 worth of life insurance to their employees, so it's unreasonable to include $600 as a cost of doing business. (The Internal Revenue Service wouldn't regard it as a cost of doing business, anyway.)

Estimating Excessive Business Expenses

My business expenses are typically $12,000 to $15,000 a year. One year they were only about $8,000. I've heard writers claim that you'll need $20,000 or more a year. I've no idea what they are spending this money on. Personally I believe my expenses are higher than would be necessary for most writers. I have a very high phone bill, because I work on book and magazine projects around the country. I have a very high online-services bill, because I write books about the Internet. And because my freelance business is more profitable than most, I have more to spend on expenses . . . so I'm not quite as careful as I could be. I'm sure that if I worked locally (no books and magazine articles for companies spread around the country) and if I were more careful about spending only money I really need to spend, I could keep my expenses below $10,000 a year. So why do some writers estimate expenses of $20,000 a year? Well, there must be special cases in which there are good reasons for spending $20,000, but this is far more than most writers need to spend. (And if you're in Step One, this is not an issue; business expenses increase to these sorts of levels only in Steps Two and Three.)

Deducting Profit

I've heard a couple of writers say that you must also deduct profit. Here's how the theory goes. You are running a business. Businesses have to make profits—$10,000, $20,000, or whatever. This whole concept makes no sense, anyway, so the sum you choose as profit is fairly arbitrary. Anyway, you deduct all your business expenses, then you deduct this arbitrary profit, and what's left over is your income. But wait, what's the profit? Well, yes, that belongs to you too; you just removed it from the calculations, to make your final income look smaller than it really is. Ridiculous.

No, a $100,000 freelance income is *not* the equivalent of a $40,000 salary. Believe me, it's worth a lot more. After paying everything you need to match what you'd get from an employer, you'll have *much, much* more than a $40,000 salary! Don't let other freelancers frighten you with inflated claims of business expenses.

Part II

Step One: Using the Agencies

8

Finding the

Technical Service

Agencies

Everyone lives by selling something, whatever be his right to it.

Robert Louis Stevenson (1850–1894)

Now that you are ready to find contract work, you have to find the agencies. I don't recommend that you work with only one agency. Sure, the first agency you contact may find you something in a few days, but on the other hand, it may not. "I tried to work on contract," a captive employee once told me, "but the agency never came through. They kept saying they had something coming up and they would call me, but they never did." He implied the mistake he had made by using the words "the agency." Had this would-be freelancer contacted a group of agencies, his chance of success would have been far greater.

A few years ago I gave 140 mailing labels to a friend, each one carrying the address of a local technical-service agency. My friend, a technical writer, mailed résumés to 80 agencies, and received around eight responses over a two-week period, eight agencies that had "possible" contracts. That's not such a great response, though. The last time I had used a similar list (I mailed résumés to about 90 agencies) I received about 20 responses, and began working on a new contract two weeks from the day I mailed the résumés.

But my friend had such a bad response that I began to feel a little guilty. I had assured him that this was the way to go, that he had to get his name out to as many agencies as possible. He was obviously disappointed. Then I began to consider what would have happened if he hadn't mailed to 80 agencies. What if he had contacted only, say, 10 agencies? He may have got only one or two responses, or perhaps none.

My friend was looking for work at the end of October, when several local companies had laid off technical writers. The last quarter of the year is supposed to be a bad time to find a contract—companies haven't completed their budgets, people are thinking about Thanksgiving vacations and Christmas shopping and so on. I don't know how much of this is true, but many people who have been in the business long enough to get a feel for the ups and the downs say it is so.

So, here is my friend looking for work in a tough market. All the more reason to contact as many agencies as possible! Yes, his response was low, but he needed as many leads as he could get, and his response would be lower still had he limited his search to a few agencies. Of course he *should* have mailed to all 140, which would have increased the response. And it didn't cost him much anyway. Sending a two-page résumé and a cover letter to 140 agencies should cost about $75, a minimal expense compared to the return on your investment.

Why You Must Contact *All* the Agencies

You *must* contact all the agencies you can find. This section explains why.

Most Agencies Don't Place Many Technical Writers

Most agencies rarely place technical writers, if ever (though some of the larger ones always seem to have a few writers working). However, that doesn't mean it is difficult for technical writers to find contract work, it just means that they have to work with a lot of agencies. If only one agency in 10 has a technical-writing position each month, there is no point contacting only five. If your skills are not needed as often as others, you must try harder to find the contracts. Incidentally, there are some agencies that place only, or predominantly, technical writers. (It often seems that such agencies don't pay writers very well. That's simply my observation of a few such agencies, though, and it may not be true of most. You can find a list of some of these agencies in Appendix C.)

Some Agencies Have Specialties

Some agencies have specialties, even if they don't recognize it. Some have intention- ally built up business in a particular industry, and others have, just by chance, found most of their clients in one or two types of business. The problem is, though, you can't tell which agency places the most technical writers and which works mainly with airframe engineers. Only if you get your résumé to all the agencies in town are you sure of getting the right ones.

If Business is Bad, You Must Try Harder

If the market is down, you have to find as many leads as possible. You can't do that by calling five agencies and then sitting by the phone.

The More Offers You Have, the More Choice You Have

Some people seem to believe that a contract is a contract is a contract, that one is the same as another. Clearly that's not true, though freelancers often act as if the best contract is the first one they are offered. But contracts vary widely. One writer I know went from $13 per hour to $25 per hour literally overnight. And contracts don't just vary in monetary rewards either; you may be offered a boring contract, a contract 90 minutes' commute from home, or a contract in an industry other than the one in which you want to specialize. When you limit your choices by working with just a few agencies, you limit your ability to choose how and where you will work, and for how much.

More Offers Means More Confidence

Imagine you are in urgent need of a job, but you don't feel close to getting a contract. An agency calls and offers you a contract, but at a rate 25 to 50 percent lower than what you believe to be the "going rate." What do you do? Do you say, "No, thanks, you're not paying enough," and hang up the phone? Do you tell the agency that you can get more money elsewhere and hope the agency increases the offer? Or do you jump at the chance to start making money again?

Now imagine having a couple of contract offers, plus a few more "in the works." How are you going to feel? A bit more confident, right? You know that if you turn an offer down, you've still got other options. The people at the agency will feel your confidence. And it is natural to think that confident people have something to be confident about, that confident people are not worried about being out of work, because they are well qualified and good at what they do. Believe me, you get better offers when you are not in a hurry to find work than when you are desperate to be earning money.

This may sound a little hokey, a little like psychobabble, but any good salesperson will tell you it's true: Sales is a mental game, and other people can feel your confidence (or lack of confidence). You are selling your services, so don't ignore the psychological aspects of selling.

Make the Agencies Compete

Not only will the agencies "feel" your confidence, but you can even tell them that you have other options open. Of course, you have to be tactful about this. Don't act arrogantly or imply that they need you more than you need them. Simply mention that you have been discussing contracts with a few other agencies and hope to hear soon about some contracts. In effect you are saying, "If you want me, you'd better move, because other people want me, too." Just make sure you don't beat anyone over the head with your ego.

If you are tactful you can play the agencies off against each other. If an agency knows you are close to making a deal with another, the hourly rate that it offers you is likely to be higher.

Continuing Job Offers Help You Learn the Market

Another great advantage to getting your résumé to as many agencies as possible is that agencies keep résumés on file. I found that if I mailed to, say, 90 agencies, I would get one or two calls from agencies each week, for several months afterward. This helps you plan for the next contract, make useful contacts in the agencies, and get a feel for what is going on in the contract market. When you are working and an agency calls you to see whether you need a job, the agency may try to steal you away from your present contract. When the agency asks you how much money you are making, exaggerate a dollar or two, and see what sort of counteroffer they make. Listen carefully to gauge the agency's responses. They may say, "Oh, we can beat that" (you are asking for too little or just about the right amount); "Well, that's a bit high" (you've got about the right rate and they're just bargaining with you, or you really are asking too much); "That's a pretty good rate" (the same); "That's not bad" (you probably can get a little bit more).

Each time you think you have found the top rate, try ratcheting it up a little, a dollar or two. You may find you are a long way below the limit, but no one's going to come out and tell you that. After talking money with several agencies, from a position of strength, you will begin to discover how much money contractors in your profession can make. Naturally you should also be talking to fellow contractors, asking what they make and how much various agencies and companies pay. (But don't be discouraged if a contractor tells you an hourly rate that sounds too low; he may not know the real rates, so just keep asking other people. You're interested in the high rates, not the ones that writers who don't know any better have settled for.)

I'm not suggesting that you drop one contract to take another. That is something you should think about very carefully before you do it—you don't want to ruin your good reputation. But by talking with the agencies, even when you don't need work, you will learn how much money you can ask for the next time you need a contract. And if an agency has offered you a high rate in the past, the next time they call you, you can remind them of that fact!

Avoid the Bad-Contract Cycle

All these advantages combine to help you avoid a vicious cycle that goes something like this: You are short of money so you take the first contract that comes along; the job may not last long or pay much, so the contract comes to an end before you have built up any savings, by which time it's Christmas and nobody's hiring; however, you can't afford to wait until January, so you take the first contract that comes along, which may not last long or pay much; on and on, ad nauseam.

Work with One Agency?

A few contractors will disagree with me on this; some believe that you should work with only one or two agencies. One contractor told me she had ruined her reputation by working with "several" agencies. Clients got her résumé from so many agencies that they began to be suspicious of her for "not being selective enough" in her job search. I find it hard to imagine how this could happen. While most agencies will check with you before sending your résumé to a client, it's true that some will submit your résumé without talking to you, and occasionally a client will see the résumé from more than one agency. I've had it happen to me, but I don't think it did me any harm, and I doubt that it would happen often enough to ruin someone's reputation. In fact most companies that use agencies understand how the system works, and are not particularly surprised to see two agencies submit the same résumé. (If you're particularly concerned about this issue, state in a cover letter that you send with your résumé that the agency must not submit you to a client without checking with you first.)

A 14-year job-shopper described something that had happened early in his career: "I had handled four continuous contracts with one excellent technical shop. I became complacent. The local economy changed and the shop moved to another city. I was unemployed for four weeks." He went on to say that he now has a computer database of 264 agencies around the country, and has been out of work for a total of three weeks in the last 10 or 12 years.

Working with one agency is a bad idea, unless that agency is prepared to guarantee you work. And agencies won't do that unless you are an agency employee—and you'll earn less money. (Even then, they may not honor their guarantee.) No, contact all the agencies you can find. The next section describes how to do that.

Finding the Agencies

Your first task is to find all the technical service agencies in your area. Any large metropolitan area has scores, maybe hundreds, of agencies. If you have a computer you should make a list of these agencies. Get a database program or a cheap mailing-label program (you can buy one for less than $10). If you don't have a computer, just put the addresses into a notebook for now. Leave space to make notes next to each address.

Here is how you find the agencies.

Check Appendix C

Start by contacting the agencies in Appendix C. These are large, national agencies, or agencies that specialize in technical writing. Many have branch offices throughout North America. (Some of the entries are for agencies overseas.) Send your résumé to all of the agencies on this list, or call them and ask for the address of the nearest office. Appendix C also lists several World Wide Web pages that contain links to technical-service agencies.

Ask Colleagues

Speak to any freelancers you know. Talk to friends and coworkers who work contract or have worked contract in the past, or just know someone who works contract. Ask them if they know of any agencies. They may be able to name several, and if you are lucky you may run into someone who has already compiled a list. You also can get good information about the agencies from other freelancers—the agencies that pay well, the ones to avoid, the ones with specialties, and so on.

If a contractor advises you not to work with an agency, try to find out why. You may find that the agency doesn't pay regularly, for instance, or is so unethical that either you or the client will get burned. However, many contractors are too quick to exclude agencies.

My list of agencies once fell into the hands of another technical writer, who typed it into her computer and passed it on to other writers. I had no problem with that, but she removed many good agencies from the list. Many, she said, were personnel agencies (but many personnel agencies also sell contract personnel), and others were disreputable. When I tried to find out what "disreputable" meant, I discovered that contractors had told her they had got a "bad deal" from these agencies, or that they "don't pay very well." That is a strange reason for excluding an agency. How can you possibly know why another contractor got a bad deal? Perhaps the client simply refused to pay any more, forcing the agency to pay a low rate for that job; perhaps the contractor felt he was worth more than the market paid for his services at that time; maybe an aggressive recruiter at the agency managed to convince the contractor to take less than he could have received elsewhere.

One contractor told me that he would "never work for agency X, because of what they had done at client Y." It turned out the agency had told the client it was paying the contractor $28 per hour, but was paying only $20 per hour. That is unethical, certainly, but I had worked for the same agency, at a different client, and with a good hourly rate. Just because they paid this other contractor badly doesn't mean they pay everyone a low rate. The secret is knowing how to negotiate your own deal; you shouldn't worry about the deals other writers make with the agency. (I'll discuss agency negotiations in Chapter 9.)

Whenever someone tells me that an agency gives bad deals, I usually know of someone else who has worked through the same agency with no complaints. And I often wonder, if the deal was so bad, why did the contractor take it? Because it was better than any other offer the contractor had at the time, of course! You shouldn't worry about whether the agency gave someone else a bad deal, you are interested only in the deal they will give you. If the deal is no good, you don't have to take the job. Avoid particularly unethical agencies or those with serious financial problems, but don't avoid an agency just because another contractor was not happy with the money they paid; otherwise you will have no agencies to work with at all.

Build a List With Other Writers

Why not get together with a few other writers and create an agency list together? While working with the Freelancer's Special Interest Group at the STC's Rocky Mountain chapter, I organized a few writers to create a local-agency list. We found a few small lists from people, then systematically searched a variety of sources (such as the Yellow Pages and newspapers) for more. We then shared the list with anyone who wanted it.

"Ah," you say, "I want my own list! If everyone has it, I'll never be able to find work!" Well, it doesn't work that way. First, even if the list finds its way to 100 different people, they won't all be looking for work at the same time. Most will never use the list anyway, and, sadly, many of the people who do use it won't use it properly—they'll send a résumé to a couple of agencies one week, a couple more the next. So don't worry about hurting yourself. The benefits of a cooperative project of this kind far outweigh any disadvantages.

Check the Yellow Pages

You can find many agencies listed in the Yellow Pages. Check the following (and similar) categories:

> Employment Contractors—Temporary Help
>
> Computers—Software and Services
>
> Computers—Systems Designers and Consultants
>
> Data Systems—Consultants and Designers

These categories include a lot of the agencies you are looking for. Unfortunately they also include a lot that are of no use to you. The first category, for example, includes agencies that sell unskilled labor or secretarial help. Some of these "temp" agencies, however, now sell technical services. Volt, for example, is a large temporary agency that also places technical professionals, and Kelly (of "Kelly Girl" fame) now has a technical division.

Some of the agency names will tell you that they are no good to you, or that they are probably just what you want. For example, don't bother with Accountants On Call or American Driver Leasing, Inc., but add DocuCorp. Other agencies have display ads listing the professions they work with. For example, the Dallas Yellow Pages has an ad from an agency called B&M Associates—"Experts in contract technical services," the ad says. It lists the types of contractors: "Engineers, Designers, Drafters, Technicians, Computer Science, Programmers, Technical Writers, Artist/Illustrators."

Some of these ads may list, for example, programmers, but not technical writers. Include these agencies in your list. You are interested in any agency that works with the sort of people you are likely to work with. An agency that places programmers will, now and again, be asked for writers too.

If an agency is clearly of use to you, add it to your list. If it clearly isn't, leave it off. If you are not sure, call and find out. (By the way, the Yellow Pages doesn't list zip codes, so you need to get those when you call. If you are trying to build a list of agencies in another town, you can save phone bills by finding zip codes in a zip-code directory. You can get a directory from the post office, bookstore, or library; you can also find a zip-code directory on the Internet, at http://www.usps.gov/ncsc/.)

The Computer categories mentioned include many agencies, but they also include many one-person consulting companies—other freelancers, that is. You will find that out when you call them, although it will be apparent if the business is listed under an individual's name. You may want to include these on your list, though. If they are also writers, include them on your list; they often run into jobs that they can't handle by themselves, or can't handle at all, so it's well worth letting them know that you are looking. If they aren't writers, but work in the same sort of business, add them too. For instance, freelance programmers sometimes run into projects that also require documentation. If they have your résumé on file, they may call you.

Don't scrimp. If you are not sure about an agency or consulting company, add it to your list. It costs very little to send out a few extra résumés, and the payoff may be tens of thousands of dollars.

Research Contractors' Publications

Contact the companies in Appendix B to get sample copies of their publications. They may send a free sample or they may sell you a copy. Or, if you know any contractors, see whether they have a copy you can borrow, or check a library. These companies also publish directories, listing hundreds of agencies. For instance, *Contract Employment Weekly* publishes the *Directory of Contract Service Firms*, which lists 1,000 companies. Of course these agencies are all over the country, so only a few will be in the city in which you want to work (unless, of course, you want to travel). The publisher of *The Computer Consultants' and Contractors' Newsletter* also publishes *The Consultant's Ye**ow Pages*. This lists over 6,000 agencies throughout North America; it's available in a paper edition and on a floppy disk.

Go through these publications looking for agencies in your area. Check all the ads and the lists of agencies, which may be divided into individual states (some agencies may have display ads but may not be listed in the contracts list, so make sure you check all the ads).

Check the Newspapers

The job ads in your local papers often include ads from agencies. Check categories such as "Engineering and Technical" and "Data Processing." Some newspapers list jobs by job title rather than the general category, so check a few different, related titles for agencies. For example, you might look under "Writer" or "Technical Writer" as well as under "Computer Programmer" because agencies using programmers sometimes need writers.

Some companies openly proclaim themselves to be agencies (they usually call themselves "consultants"), but others may have names that imply that they are agencies (Butler Service Group or Consultants and Designers, for example, or names with "Associates" at the end). And some agencies are recognizable by the long list of different skills they are searching for. Check the papers every week, because some agencies don't advertise all the time.

Use the Internet

You can also find agencies online, through the Internet. For instance, you should subscribe to mailing lists and newsgroups that contain job leads; many of these leads will come from agencies. I'll discuss that in more detail in Chapter 24.

From these sources you should be able to build a good list. Continue adding to the list whenever you hear of another agency. Once you are working freelance, your colleagues should be able to provide you with yet more names. By the way, when you collect information about an agency, include not only the address and voice-phone number, but the fax number and, if available, an e-mail number.

If you don't live in the area in which you want to work, you can still put together a list. You can use the contractors' magazines, of course, and many libraries stock Yellow Pages from around the country. Libraries also stock newspapers from other cities, but if your local library doesn't, you can write to the newspaper you want (your librarian can help you find the address) and ask about purchasing a copy (many papers have special services for people moving to their cities). You might even take a trip to the other area—after all, if you plan to work there you may as well see what it's like first.

Mailing Labels

Now, what do you do with these addresses? If you have a computer you can use the list to print mailing labels. Buy a database program that allows you to print mailing labels (such programs can cost as little as $10).

If you don't have a computer, buy photocopier labels from a business supply store. Copier labels are mailing labels on sheets that you can run through a photocopier. You type the address list once, onto blank sheets of paper, and then each time you need to use the list, you photocopy the addresses onto the copier labels. The labels are self-stick, so all you need to do is lift them off and stick them to the envelopes. You can get boxes of 2,000 labels for about $10 if you look around. Buy a generic brand; they are much cheaper than the well-known brands, and work just as well.

Preparing the Mailing

A few weeks before you come to the end of a contract or plan to leave your present employer, contact the agencies. Allow three or four weeks, or even do two mailings, one about two months before, and one about three weeks before. You need to leave enough time to find the job, but not so much time that you can't take any jobs that come along.

What are you going to mail to the agencies? Not much: a two-page résumé and a one-page cover letter. The cover letter should explain when you are available for work, or how much notice you need to give your present employer, and state that you are looking for contract work (many agencies also place full-time personnel). Don't say how much money you want to make. There is never an advantage to stating up front how much you will accept, before you know the details of the job.

I know some people will disagree with me here, but I usually put the résumé and letter on simple white paper, nothing fancy. I don't even personalize the cover letter; I just type "Dear Sir/Madam" at the top. I suppose it doesn't do any harm to use attractive paper (except for the extra cost, of course), but I'm not so sure it makes any difference to the agencies.

What you put on the paper is more important than the paper itself. Limit the résumé to one or two pages (many recruiters say no more than one page, though I always use two). Put your name, address, and phone numbers at the top of the résumé. Some experts suggest that you leave three lines between your address and the main text; this allows the job shop to cover your address with its own label when it faxes your résumé to a client. Below your address, summarize your skills. Remember that you want a recruiter to be able to glance at your résumé and know who you are and what you do. Résumés with extraneous text often get laid aside.

Your next step is to mail a résumé and cover letter to every agency on your list; there's no need for a complicated cover letter, just a simple letter explaining that you're a writer looking for work will do. For some reason, many freelancers mail the résumés bit by bit—10 today, 15 on Friday, 10 next week. I don't know why they do this, and I can't think of any advantage to doing so. You lose the benefits listed at the beginning of this chapter, because you end up spreading the résumés too thinly; there will be too much time between the contract offers you receive.

Once you've mailed your résumés, you can start calling the agencies. This may not be necessary for many people (the agencies will call you), but if times are hard or you don't have a lot of experience, you may need to call and talk to the agencies. This will remind the agencies that you are looking and will give you an idea of what is going on in the market.

Incidentally, if you don't have a lot of experience, you may want to build a relationship with some of the larger agencies. Once you have mailed your résumé, call these agencies and talk to the recruiters; try to get an interview and get to know the people at the agency.

You may find that one of these larger agencies can help you by including you in a package; clients sometimes hire an agency to provide all the staff for a project, and trust the agency to find the right people. Some agencies will put inexperienced people in, and may even lie to the client about that person's experience. Not too good for a client, but a good way for you to get the experience! Of course, this often backfires— I know of one case where an agency lied and the client found out and fired the contractor. But sometimes it works—the same agency placed the same contractor with another client, where he kept the client perfectly happy. (I'm not justifying this practice; I'm just stating that it does happen, and that some freelancers have taken advantage of it in their careers.)

Faxes and E-mail

When I first wrote this book, the most efficient way to contact the agencies was by mail. But these days you have two more ways to contact them: fax and e-mail. When you create your agency list, don't forget to collect fax and e-mail addresses. Then, if you have a computer, you can make your own fax and e-mail mailing lists; these let you contact dozens, even hundreds, of agencies in about the time it would take you to contact just one through traditional methods. (Good fax programs will let you automatically fax a single document to a list of numbers. E-mail programs also allow you to create mailing lists, so you can send one message that is distributed to everyone on the list. We'll look at online access in Chapter 24).

Life on the Road

Many contractors live a gypsylike life, traveling from one contract to another—a year in California, six months in Alabama, 18 months in New England. If you would enjoy working like this (and I must admit, it sounds attractive to me), I strongly recommend that you subscribe to *Technical Employment Weekly* and *Contract Employment Weekly*. These magazines list contracts all over the country, but they also have special services that can be especially useful, such as résumé mailing services (they'll mail résumés to agencies that advertise in the magazine). You just provide one résumé, and they do all the copying and mailing.

Both publications also have a "hot sheet," a list of contractors seeking work that includes your name, address, phone number, and job description. They sell mailing labels so you can mail out your own résumés to their advertisers, fax services, electronic bulletin board services, Internet job postings, and so on. (See Appendix B for more information about these services.)

And don't forget the Internet; you can often find jobs online. The Internet is a good place to look for work all over North America, and even overseas, too. For instance, techwr-l, a technical-writer's discussion group, frequently receives messages containing contract offers from companies throughout Europe and North America. See Chapter 24 for more information.

Working with the Agencies

So what happens now that your résumés are in the mail? First, a few of your résumés won't reach the agencies. The Post Office will return as many as 10 percent, maybe more, as undeliverable. Just remove these agencies from your list.

The next step, you hope, is that you begin to receive calls from agencies. Exactly how many calls depends on your experience, the industry you work in, the economy, and the time of year. If you don't get many responses, don't worry; start calling the agencies on your list and talk to them.

Now that you have contacted the agencies, what next? You need to know what to ask them and what to tell them, so move on to the next chapter.

Negotiating with

the Agencies

It is well-known what a middleman is: he is a man who bamboozles one party
and plunders the other.

Benjamin Disraeli (1804–1881)

Whether an agency contacts you, or you call an agency, there are several questions you should ask before you make any decisions. The agency often won't have the answers the first time you speak with them, but they should be able to answer at some point.

Before I list the questions, let me just explain how the agencies operate. A company's personnel department has one major purpose: to find suitable people to work for the company. The technical-service agencies have two main jobs: In addition to finding suitable people, they also have to sell their services to client companies. Small agencies usually have the same people doing both things, selling and searching. Large agencies, however, divide these tasks. An agency may have one or two recruiters, searching for potential contractors, and one or two salespeople, looking for potential clients and selling the contractors to them.

When a salesperson discovers a company that needs a contractor, the recruiter has to start looking for candidates. (The salesperson and recruiter may be the same person in some small agencies.) The recruiter checks the résumé file (where your résumé is sitting, waiting for just this moment). He or she also may run a classified advertisement in the local paper, and call the job banks run by local professional associations. The recruiter then starts calling all the potential candidates, and anyone who may know of a potential candidate. That is where you come in, of course.

When the recruiter calls you, he may tell you that a position is available. This is close to the truth—the recruiter knows a company that has a position open. But it is important to remember that the agency usually doesn't have a job to offer, however confident the recruiter may sound. The agency is usually competing against several other agencies, and the client also may be looking for independent contractors. And sometimes the client may not yet have approval to hire anyone. So when you start talking to an agency about a position, don't expect too much, and don't be disappointed if you never hear from the agency again. If the agency doesn't get any further with the position, the recruiter probably won't bother to call you back to tell you.

You Need These Answers

Although you need answers to all the following questions at some point, the first six are the most important; you should ask them immediately. If the answers are not to your liking, there is no point in letting the agency submit your résumé.

Is the Job a Permanent Position or Contract?

Some agencies provide both full-time and contract personnel. When you send out your résumé you will be mailing to agencies that work both ways. You also will find, as your network grows, that people are hearing about you from other sources. Perhaps a coworker mentioned you to a headhunter, or a recruiter passed on a lead to a friend in another agency. However it happens, you will start receiving calls from people you've never heard of before. Some of these may be employment rather than contract agencies. So if you don't know for sure that the agency you are talking to is a contract agency, ask if the job is contract or permanent.

Is the Agency Looking for Contractors or Employees?

This is not quite the same as the preceding question. As I mentioned in Chapter 4, some contract agencies only hire people full time. Even though the job is a contract (that is, the client is paying the agency an hourly rate to provide people for a limited time), the agency hires people full time and pays them a salary. Other agencies employ both full-time people and contractors. It is important to understand that the Internal Revenue Service regards both types of workers as employees.

The agency withholds taxes from both types of employees, but regards one type (the contractors) as temporary employees and the other type as permanent employees. The permanent employees get the usual employee benefits (paid vacation, medical insurance, and so on) and receive a salary, whereas the contractors are paid by the hour and sometimes don't get any benefits. Of course, the line blurs sometimes—some contractors get vacation pay and medical insurance—but the most important distinguishing characteristic is that the permanent employee receives a salary (or a pseudosalary) while the contractor gets paid by the hour. (See Chapter 14 for a discussion of pseudosalaries.)

For reasons already explained, the best deal is contract, so you don't want to work for a contract agency as a full-time employee. You should bear in mind, though, that even agencies that say they never hire contractors may do so if they really need you. And agencies that encourage you to become an employee will still let you work contract if you insist. (The reason they want you to be an employee is that they make more money, money that should be going into your bank account!) Anyway, don't let anyone talk you into becoming an employee of an agency, unless it is your only option.

What Industry Is the Job in, and What Type of Work?

You may have preferences about the type of work you are looking for, or may have specialized in a certain type of work. For example, many writers prefer to specialize in the telecommunications industry. On the other hand, it may be a good idea to try something different now and again, so you don't become "typecast." You must decide what you would prefer to do, and what will look good on your résumé the next time you are looking for a contract.

How Long Is the Contract?

The agency may tell you a position is "long term," but who knows what that means? Ask how many months the contract will last. This affects how much your hourly rate should be. If the contract is only a few weeks, the rate will usually be—and certainly should be—higher than if the job is expected to last eight months. Incidentally, it seems that clients are more likely to extend contracts than to end them early. Sometimes, of course, contracts do end unexpectedly early, but that is just one of the occupational hazards. It is comforting to know, however, that the opposite is usually the case.

How Much Is the Agency Paying?

Now we get to the nitty-gritty, the most difficult part of the negotiations. When you ask how much the agency is paying, the agent probably will say "Well, how much are you looking for?" Or the agent may mention a wide range, with the top figure high enough to interest you (later the agent can say the client wouldn't pay the top rate). Of course, the agency doesn't want to offer an amount higher than you are willing to work for. I've had agencies tell me $18 an hour, go to $24 an hour when I didn't sound interested, and end up at $40 an hour when I told them I was already on $38 an hour. (Does it sound like I enjoy playing games with the agencies?)

You must find out what the current rates are for someone with your experience. You have to do your homework, and talk to a lot of agencies. Eventually you will get a feel for how much money you can ask for. The first contract you accept may be at a lower rate than you could have gotten, but if you have done the calculations in Chapter 7, you know how much to ask for to ensure that you work with a smile on your face. And as you talk to other freelancers and contract agencies, you will get an idea of what rate to ask for the next time you need a contract.

Try not to give too much away when you talk rates with an agency. If the rate sounds like a lot, don't get excited. As much as it sounds, it may still be lower than you can get. Don't sound as if you need a job soon; the more urgently you need a job, the lower your rate will be. Try to sound confident, in control. Let the agency know you have other "irons in the fire," that they are not the only agency you are talking to. Even if the contract they offer you sounds great, don't let the agency hear the excitement in your voice. Let the agent think you will carefully consider the contract, not that you'll jump at it. (Don't overdo it, of course, and sound totally disinterested, or the agency won't call back.)

If you are in a salaried position, don't discuss your present income. If anyone asks, say what I used to say: You are not willing to discuss your present salary, because you know it is less than someone with your skills and experience can earn—which is why you want to work contract. I believe it is unreasonable for agencies to base your rate (or companies to base your salary) on what you used to earn. You should be paid the market rate for someone with your skills and experience. If necessary, come up with an excuse not to tell the agent, or even make up a salary. When I was first looking for contract work I simply told the truth: that my salary was lower than many people with the same experience because for two years my employer had a pay freeze (I worked in the oil business, when times were bad). Therefore, I went on, I didn't want to discuss my salary because I didn't feel it had any bearing on what my hourly rate should be.

Don't be scared to ask for a high rate. Many contractors feel that if they don't take the first position that comes along, it may be a long wait for the next one, so they don't want to jeopardize the contract by asking too much. This may be true for some people (entry-level writers, for example), and for some areas of the country; whether these factors apply to you is something you will have to determine for yourself. Many writers, however, will find mailing résumés to every agency in town results in dozens of job offers, so they don't need to grab the first offer that comes along. Don't be panicked into taking the first job that comes around from fear of losing it. (Of course, if you are out of work and need a job in a hurry, the picture changes a little.) The more you need a job, the less money you are likely to get—so don't let an agency know how badly you need the work!

Finally, remember this:

The lower the rate you ask for, the lower the rate you will get.

What Company Is Offering the Contract?

Most agencies won't tell you this until they have an interview set up, but some will, so why not ask anyway? It is important information that has a direct bearing on your decision, so why not find out as early as possible who is hiring?

Where Is the Contract?

Even if the agency won't tell you who the job is with, the agent should be able to tell you where it is—which city or area of the city. Remember, a long trip to work each day costs more in commuting expenses and time that could be better spent (working overtime, or playing with your children). For example, you are comparing two potential contracts: one is close to home and pays $25 per hour, the other pays $27 per hour but means an extra hour of travel each day. You would usually pick the lower-paying job. If the first job allows you to work overtime, you can work the extra hour and make another $27 a day, compared to the extra $16 a day you would get from the second job's hourly rate. And you have lower commuting expenses.

What About Overtime?

How much overtime is available? How much overtime does the client expect? Is the overtime paid at the same rate? You may not want to work overtime, so you need to know if the client expects you to do so. Some clients may want a job done in a hurry and expect long hours. One client offered me a job that required 80 hours a week. It's a great way to make a quick buck, though it can be depressing after a while.

Although most contracts pay the same rate for every hour worked, some contracts may pay time-and-a-half for overtime. This can make overtime very attractive. A high hourly rate, multiplied by 1.5 after the first 40 hours, makes it hard to turn down overtime! Such overtime rates used to be rare when I was working with agencies—most agencies didn't pay overtime rates—but it's worth checking. As you will see in Chapter 14, agencies that don't pay time-and-a-half for overtime may be breaking the Fair Labor Standards Act, but few agencies seem aware of this fact.

Does the Agency Have a Medical Policy?

How much is the agency's medical policy, and what does it cover? Most agencies can provide a medical insurance policy. If you need insurance, you should ask how much it will cost (remember to mention if you want to include dependents). You will usually pay the full cost of the policy, although some agencies will share the cost with you. For example, I was paying an agency $260 a month for a comprehensive insurance package. It included an excellent medical policy, vision and dental insurance, a small life insurance policy for myself and my wife, and a long-term disability policy. At the same time, however, a friend was paying her agency only $50 a month for a similar policy. However, remember that any benefits the agency pays for come out of what the agency budgets as your cost. While one agency may pay some of the medical policy, another may give a higher hourly rate. In fact, although my friend paid $210 a month less than I did for insurance, she also earned $3 an hour less.

Ask what the insurance covers. There is no need to go into detail until you get close to a contract offer. But eventually you need to know if it covers visits to a doctor, and vision and dental, and find out what the deductible and out-of-pocket expenses are. Even if you don't need a medical policy, you might want to ask about the agency's coverage anyway. If the agency doesn't have an insurance policy, or if it has a particularly bad policy, you can use that as a bargaining chip to get a higher hourly rate.

Incidentally, you may want to find your own medical insurance elsewhere. It's not really good to keep switching insurance companies each time you switch contracts; eventually you may get caught between contracts and in a position in which your insurance doesn't "work." And if the agency is small, the policy is not too strong, because insurance companies can dump the policy if it gets too expensive for them. One insurance company dumped me when they discovered that my wife was pregnant, for instance. This was totally illegal, but the medical-insurance laws are set up so that there is essentially no punishment for doing this, and getting restitution is next to impossible. (I called the Department of Labor and was told that it would investigate; I was also told that the department would never inform me of the results of this investigation!) See Chapter 13 for more information on medical policies.

Does the Agency Have a Long-Term Disability Policy?

The agency's medical policy often includes a disability policy. You must make sure, though, as it is very important. Many people forget about long-term disability coverage, but being out of work for an extended period can have serious consequences. If the agency doesn't have coverage, you can buy a policy from an insurance agent, but you should use the lack of coverage as a bargaining chip to get a higher hourly rate. (See Chapter 13 for more information on long-term disability policies.)

Does the Agency Pay for Vacations or Sick Leave?

Ask this question and a lot of agencies will sound offended and tell you that this is a contract job, not a full-time job, and that any vacation pay would come out of your hourly rate anyway. They are quite right, but some agencies *do* pay for these benefits. And yes, it does come out of money that could be on your hourly rate. If I were working for such an agency, I would calculate the value of the benefits and ask for the agency to increase my hourly rate correspondingly: "A bird in the hand is worth two in the bush." I would rather have the money now than wait for it, for several reasons. First, I would prefer to have the money earning interest for *me*, rather than the agency. And if for some reason the contract ends early, I would rather walk away having already received my vacation money than have to argue with the agency about whether I'm owed vacation or not. Anyway, it's always good to see an extra dollar or two on your hourly rate; at the very least, it means you can tell the next agency that calls that you are on a high hourly rate.

Vacation and sick leave are linked to the number of hours you work, so ask what the ratio is. For example, the agency may pay for 40 hours' vacation for every 490 hours you work. In other words, for every 490 hours you work, the agency pays you for 530. Multiply your hourly rate times 530 hours (the time worked plus the vacation time). Now divide the total by 490, the hours worked. For example:

$30 per hour × 530 hours = $15,900

$15,900 ÷ 490 hours = $32.45

Then $32.45 is the true hourly rate (assuming that you work enough to get the vacation pay). Also, ask when vacation pay becomes "vested." For example, an agency tells you that you must work six months to get six days' vacation pay. Once you have worked your first six months and received the first six days' pay, do you have to work a full six months again to get more vacation pay? If the contract ends five months later, will you get five days' pay or will you get nothing?

In the preceding example I would ask the agency to pay me $32.45 an hour instead of giving me vacation pay. However, this negotiation is like buying a car and trading in your old one. Make the best deal you can on your hourly rate *before* you say you want a higher hourly rate instead of vacation time. The increase in your hourly rate should come from the vacation money, not from the dollar or two "negotiating room" the agency may have left for itself.

Does the Agency Pay a Mileage Allowance?

Some agencies will pay you driving expenses between your home and the contract. It may not be much per mile, but it all helps. Most contractors and agencies think this mileage allowance is tax free, but it usually *isn't* (see Chapter 18 for an explanation of why commuting is not tax deductible).

Does the Agency Have a 401(k) Plan?

If the agency has a 401(k) pension plan, you can save a larger portion of your income than an IRA allows. However, many 401(k) plans are set up to restrict participation to people who have worked with the company for a year or two.

What Other Personal Considerations Do You Have?

You may have other considerations. For example, does the client have a dress code? Do you want to work at a company that will let you wear jeans? Do you want to work in an office that has banned smoking—or would you prefer to work in a company that still allows smoking? Would you prefer to work in a company with a cafeteria? You should ask these questions later in the process, and you should remember that the more job offers you have, the choosier you can be—which is yet another reason to work with as many agencies as possible.

Road-Shopping: A Few Questions to Ask When Working Out of Town

In addition to all these questions, if you are taking an out-of-town contract you should ask a few more.

Is the Job Paying a Per Diem?

Per diem is Latin for *"per day,"* and most dictionaries say that the term means "a payment or allowance for each day." In the contract business in the U.S., however, *per diem* means an extra payment for expenses, usually expressed in dollars per week. If the job the agency is offering is out of town, you should ask whether the agency will pay a per diem. If it does, and tells you how much, make sure you know what the agency means. If the agency says it pays a $70 per diem, ask whether that figure is per week or per day (it is probably per week).

The agency usually pays the per diem without withholding any tax. Don't think it is not taxable, however. You must keep records of your expenses while you are away from home. If the per diem ends up more than your expenses, Uncle Sam will want a share of the excess. And the per diem may be taxable—and probably *will* be taxable—even if you can prove your expenses. (See Chapter 18 for more information.)

What Are the Tax Rates in the Area You Are Going to?

If you are going to work in an area that has a state income tax (as most states do), you need to know how much that tax will be. It may be lower than you pay in your home state, of course, but it may be considerably more. For example, a contractor from Texas (which has no income tax) who goes to work in a state with an income tax will find a sizable chunk of income disappearing—perhaps 7 percent or more. Forty dollars an hour in Texas is worth much more than $40 an hour in New York.

How Much Are the State and Local Sales Taxes and Living Costs?

State and local sales taxes are an indication of how much higher prices will be. The higher the sales tax, the more you will pay for living expenses while you are away. Ask about general living costs in that area. You also may want to go to a library or bookstore and look at *Rand McNally's Places Rated Almanac*. It will give you a good idea of relative costs throughout the United States; it also lists state income-tax rates. These questions about living costs and taxes are essential if you are road-shopping. Don't leave home until you know the answers! If you live in Gulfport, Mississippi, and think that an agency's offer of $28 an hour is excellent, just wait till you get to San Jose, California, and see what the money buys!

By the way, here's a nice little toy you can use if you have World Wide Web access (see Chapter 24): the Center for Mobility Resource's Relocation Salary Calculator. Point your Web browser to http://www.homefair.com/homefair/cmr/salcalc.html. You'll find a form into which you can enter your current income, a special code indicating your current location, and a code representing the area to which you are moving. Click the Calculate button and the form calculates how much you must earn to match your current income.

How Much Is Accommodation?

Ask how much accommodation costs in the area you'll be moving to. A contractor from Dallas, for example, would be shocked by California's accommodations costs. You may want to add a dollar or two to your hourly rate to pay the higher rent. Some people who "road-shop" buy recreational vehicles, and live in them while they're "on the road." RVs can be a great way to maximize the income from your road trips.

Will the Agency Pay Moving Expenses?

Some agencies will pay part of the expense of traveling to the place of employment, so ask how much the agency will pay.

Get the Answers Straight

Now that you've asked these questions, you should have a good idea of the contract the agency is offering. If you get past this stage and interview with the client, you should remember to ask some of these questions again. Sometimes the client will not interview you; you may be offered the contract before you ever see or speak to anyone from the company. But before you sign the contract, you should try to talk to the person you will be working for. Ask the agency for the person's name and phone number, then call. You should ask the client how long it expects the contract to last, exactly what sort of work you will be doing, and whether the client expects or allows any overtime. And if you have any special personal considerations, ask about those too. (You generally shouldn't talk about money, though; hourly rates, per diems, and other compensation is between you and the agency.)

You must ask these questions for several reasons. First, the agent you are working with may not understand your business. The client probably gave the agency a list of requirements, but the agent may have misinterpreted the type of work you will be doing, and accidentally given you the wrong impression. Second, the agent may make a mistake. An agent works with dozens of clients simultaneously, and may simply get two mixed up and tell you a contract is for a year when it is actually for three months. Finally, some agents are simply unethical. They may lie, or just exaggerate. For example, if a client said a contract probably will be three months but may last six, the unethical agent might tell you the contract will last for at least six months.

When you discuss a job with an agency, don't expect to get the contract; you have a job lead, not a job. When an agency tells you that you probably have the job, or even that you have the job, don't believe it until you have signed the contract! You should continue talking to other agencies. You can tell the other agencies that you probably have another job lined up, but you are still willing to consider other positions until you have signed the contract. This will put you in a strong bargaining position with those agencies.

If you have done any type of sales work, you will understand this. Until the client has signed the contract (and, in some types of sales, until the commission check arrives), most experienced salespeople do not assume they have a sale, regardless of what the client says. Too much can go wrong between the client saying yes and the signing of the contract. The client's boss may say no, or the purchase order may get bogged down in red tape. Or, the client could even resign, get laid off, or die (I've had it happen!). Worse, when the agency tells you that you have the job, the agent may be lying.

Most agencies want you to think they have the contract, and that all they need to do is find the right person. More commonly, though, an agency is competing against several other agencies, or even against the client. In other words, if the agency can find a good person at the right price, the client may buy; but if the client finds someone he prefers from another agency, or even working as an independent contractor, he'll go with that person. Whatever the situation, a company rarely "buys" contractors from just one agency, so when an agency tells you that the local IBM office or Boeing plant deals exclusively with it, you can usually discount the claim as nonsense. If you do run into this type of misrepresentation, I don't recommend that you refuse to do business with the agency. Just keep quiet and humor the agent. Unfortunately, so many of the agencies exaggerate their abilities that if you refuse to do business with the ones you catch in a lie, you'll be left with a small number of agencies—agencies that you haven't yet caught lying! No, your best defense is simple: Know your market, know how to deal with the agencies, and don't believe anything until you see it on paper (or better still, until your new client shows you where your desk is).

This chapter concludes with a reprint from one of my articles originally published in *PD News* (now *Technical Employment Weekly*), titled *What Is a Fair Rate?* You will hear contractors complaining about the agencies, claiming they got "ripped off," or that the agency doesn't pay enough. Certainly many agencies will try to get you as cheap as possible and sell you for as much as they can, but it's up to you to market yourself properly.

What Is a "Fair" Rate?

Is there any such thing, in a free market economy, as a "fair" rate? After all, isn't "what the market will bear" the closest we can get to a definition of "fair"?

Of course, I'm talking about job-shop hourly rates here, and there appear to be two basic positions on the subject. On one side, many people believe there is such a thing, that job shops should not offer less than the "fair" rate for a job, although no one seems to be able to tell me what that rate is. Most job-shoppers seem to fall into this category. They don't know how to describe a fair rate, but they know it when they see it, and they are quick to complain if they are not getting it.

Many on the other side of the fence, the people running the agencies, have a different view: If a job-shopper is willing to take a job at the stated rate, it must be fair. They've got a point, too. After all, no one is forcing you to take the job.

There's another party in this relationship, though: the client. I would bet that most clients assume the bulk of the money they pay an agency goes to the contractor. Perhaps that is a good rule of thumb: "The agency gets a cut of what the contractor makes, not the other way around."

Of course, that doesn't always happen. Let me tell you about a situation I observed in Dallas recently. This took place in the offices of a well-known telecommunications company. I can't tell you who, but you would recognize the name if you heard it. One agency had managed to place three or four technical writers in a documentation department on long contracts.

The rates were good for writers in Dallas—one contractor was earning the agency $43 per hour. But all the "contractors" were pseudosalaried. The agency had found writers inexperienced in the world of contracting and persuaded them to take the kind of hybrid salary/hourly rate I described in an earlier article (see Chapter 4). The result was that the agency was getting quite a deal. The writer they billed for $43 an hour actually cost them about $18, including benefits—quite a nice spread.

Now, as we all know, contractors like to gossip, and this particular department had several writers making a lot more than $18 an hour. It also had trouble keeping information confidential, so it wasn't long before the lowest-paid contractors knew not only what they could make on a good contract, but how much the agency was billing for them. Not a healthy situation.

To make a long story short, people started looking elsewhere for work, for higher rates. Before long the client learned what was going on and, not surprisingly, was angry to learn that the bulk of what the agency was charging was paying for the agency's overhead and the salesman's Corvette.

Most clients are not unreasonable people. They know everyone has to make a profit, that agencies are not charities, but they also assume that most of the contract money is going to pay for experienced, skilled people; after all, if they can get people at less than half the price, why the hell pay $43 an hour?

Perhaps it would be poetic justice if the agency had been hurt by what it did, but I'm not sure it was. The client forced the agency to pay the contractors more, but it had been making over $20 an hour per contractor for almost a year already.

Sometimes agencies do get hurt, though. A few weeks ago a friend of mine came to the end of her contract. "No problem," said her agency, "we've got a contract for you," and promptly set her up with a job scheduled to begin the day after the old one ended. Just one problem: a rate so low that she would be better off taking permanent employment. Now, the agency may have miscalculated and bid too low, very low. However, I learned from other sources that the client company was willing to pay quite a high hourly rate, enough for the agency to pay my friend $7 or $8 an hour more, and still make $7 an hour themselves (yes, after payroll taxes).

The client offered my friend the job and she accepted it. But she found a better contract, and jumped ship the day before the new one started. The agency scrambled around for a substitute, but before they could find one the job went to another agency (paying considerably more money, by the way). The second agency may be making a small cut, but a small cut of a lot is a lot more than a large cut of nothing.

I don't much like the agencies making such large markups, but sometimes I think the "free market" theorists are right. I've seen contractors accept bad rates not because they had to, not because there was no food on the table and they had a sick child at home, but because they were not prepared to make the effort to find a good rate. Many contractors don't know what rate their skills and experience can bring—a situation they can easily remedy by talking to other contractors in their field. Often contractors know how much a good rate is, though, but still settle for less. Why?

The problem is they don't market themselves well enough. Too few job-shoppers realize they have to sell themselves to not one but two groups of people: the client and the agency. Too many job-shoppers believe that marketing is what the agencies are for, so they can just sit back and wait while the agencies deliver contracts to them. Yes, you can work like that, but if you work with just one agency, you had better have an excellent relationship with a very good one, or just resign yourself to paying a lot of money for their services.

If you want to do well as a contractor, you have to be a salesman. You might believe that only independent contractors need sales skills, but if you are getting an "unfair" rate, maybe you had better examine your own ability to sell yourself before you complain about the ethics of your agency.

Unethical Agencies

Let every eye negotiate for itself,

And trust no agent.

William Shakespeare (1564–1616)

So far I've explained how the agencies can help you. Sure, you need to know how to negotiate and how to make the best deal, but that's business. I am now going to tell you something that will upset many people, perhaps even my friends in the technical service business. I'm going to explain why using technical service agencies is often not in the best interests of the client companies.

There are two types of problems with technical service agencies. One type is the unethical behavior of many agencies, and the other is the inherent weakness in the whole system of hiring people from an agency.

Now, I should point out that the problems I discuss in this chapter hurt the client company, and only occasionally hurt the contractor. But it is always a good idea to understand how the business in which you are working operates, and there are specific reasons that you should know about these problems.

For example, if you work through an agency, that agency's unethical behavior can tarnish your own reputation, however good you may be. If you are an independent contractor, you will find many companies unwilling to hire you unless you go through an agency. The information in this chapter may provide enough ammunition to persuade your potential client that the agencies are not such a good deal. And if you are ever in the position to employ contractors, you will know why you should hire independents. (I discuss how you can do so legally in Chapter 19.)

Before I start, I want to apologize to any friends or associates who I may offend. Some agencies work in the most ethical manner possible, but many don't. If what I say offends you, please assume I'm talking about someone else's agency!

The first thing a client should remember is that the agency is selling something. When an employee of a corporation has to hire another person, he or she usually wants to hire the best person for the job. But if that employee decides to allow technical service agencies to compete for the business, another factor has entered the picture: the profit motive. Although the company employee does not profit from hiring someone, the agencies do. They don't want the client to hire the best person available, they want the client to hire one of their people. (If that person happens to be the best available, that is fine, but if not, so what?)

Think of buying a car as an analogy. You wouldn't go to a car dealer and say, "I want to buy a car, find me the best one." You would find that the Ford dealer wants you to buy a Ford, and the Isuzu dealer claims that the best car is an Isuzu! That's why you educate yourself before buying a car. You may read car magazines, look at several models, sit in them, even test-drive them. You may research the dealer price of the car, and ask other owners how they like the vehicle.

If you want to hire a contractor, you also should gather much of the information yourself, and not rely on the biased opinions of an agency that stands to make tens or even hundreds of thousands of dollars.

Why Companies Should Avoid Agencies

Here are 10 reasons companies should avoid the agencies. I will explain each one in turn.

◆ Most agencies don't check references.
◆ Some agencies do check references, then give the contractor the benefit of the doubt.
◆ Competition among agencies hurts the clients.
◆ Many good contractors do not work with agencies.
◆ The agency may keep 60 to 70 percent of the pay.
◆ The agency may encourage the client to take a less qualified person.
◆ The agency may stop the client from rehiring the contractor.
◆ The agency may stop the client from offering the contractor a permanent position.
◆ Some clients don't want independents, so they hire through agencies—and unknowingly get independents.
◆ Clients can hire independent contractors and save 20 to 50 percent.

Most Agencies Don't Check References

All agencies will deny this, but it's a fact. Some agencies do check the references of potential contractors, but most do not. I know this to be true from my own experience, and from talking with other contractors and agents. I have been sent on interviews (and been accepted for jobs) when the agency has not checked my references. My references are important to me; I get good ones, so I always offer my references when I go for an interview. "That's okay," one client told me, "I let the agency handle all that." Of course, the agency didn't.

Here's how the agencies operate. They discover that a company needs a writer. They check their résumé files, and call all the people who appear to have the necessary qualifications and experience, and ask each contractor whether they can submit the résumé to the client. (Some agencies will submit a résumé without even asking the contractor first.) They also may ask for the names of other people who could do the job, and then call those people. The agency then submits as many résumés as possible, and arranges interviews. The agency does all this in a very short time, possibly a few hours even, because it knows that the competition is hard on its heels.

Imagine that the client wants to hire one of the writers. Remember, the agency has not had time to check references—they've barely had time to get the résumés to the client. The agency is now being offered a profit of $1,000 a month, maybe even $2,000 or $3,000. The agency doesn't have to work for this money—it has done most of the work already! So, what does the agency do? Check references and discover that the writer isn't worth minimum wage? Risk throwing away thousands, even tens of thousands of dollars? Absolutely not! They accept the contract and hope that the writer meets at least minimum requirements.

Some Agencies Do Check References, Then Give the Contractor the Benefit of the Doubt

Some agencies do check references. You must remember, however, that agencies are usually competing against each other. As I've already mentioned, the agency doesn't want you to hire the best contractor; they want you to hire *their* contractor! So long as the contractor isn't a mass murderer, and turns up for work at least some of the time, the agency may still submit his or her résumé. (I know of an agency that—quite aware of the writer's work record—submitted a writer who only turned up at work 50 percent of the time. The agency got the contract, too, at least for a few weeks.)

Because references carry so little weight in the contractor search process, undue importance is given to the résumé and the interview. Anyone can have a good résumé. If few companies check references, the contractor knows there isn't much chance of being caught in a lie. And many people do lie—or merely exaggerate—because they know they can get away with it. Clients looking for contractors generally use short interviews, perhaps believing that the agency is screening the people anyway. And don't we all know incompetent people who do well in interviews?'

So if an agency checks a résumé and discovers what it regards as minor problems with the résumé, it may ignore the problems and hope they'll go away.

Competition Among Agencies Hurts the Clients

In a free-market economy, a statement like that is almost heresy. But competition means the agencies have to cut corners. If a company is looking for a contractor without the assistance of an agency, the company will continue looking until it finds the best person. The agencies, however, don't have enough time. They have to find someone they can sell to the company before a rival agency does. They have to submit as many people as possible as quickly as possible. The agencies provide the company with information about the contractors. They give the client a résumé, which they may have modified to fit the client's requirements. They tell the client that the contractor is good, perhaps even say that he or she has good references, and tell the contractor what the client is looking for, so the contractor knows how to respond in the interview.

But when several agencies are submitting people, they can't *all* have the best person for the job. If the client company gets all its information from the agencies, it must decide based on interviews and the sales abilities of the different agencies. The agency that has both a skilled salesperson and a contractor who does well in interviews has a distinct advantage.

The idea of competition and the free market has become an ideology that people believe in blindly. There are clearly some things that competition and free markets cannot do. (Why don't we have a free-market military? Free-market police forces?) It makes no sense for a company to make agencies compete among each other for contractors, because they end up cutting corners and lying. I personally believe it makes more sense for a company to work with one good agency, and encourage the agency to spend the time and effort it takes to find good people. Or, better still, forget the agencies and have the human resources department do the hiring.

Many Good Contractors Do Not Work with Agencies

Many contractors can find work, at higher rates, without the help of the agencies. I work on a per-project basis (see Chapter 21), and make $100 an hour or more. If I worked through an agency, I'd make in the mid $30s if I was very lucky.

So experienced writers who have built a strong network avoid the agencies. They use them only if they have to, and even then will probably keep looking for a better deal. Not all of these people are good at their jobs, of course—many will have excellent sales and networking skills instead—but usually these people are more experienced and skilled than the average contractor. So a company that uses only agencies (and will not accept independent contractors) loses a pool of talented people.

Of course the fact that an agency doesn't pay much doesn't necessarily mean that the client pays a low rate; it usually means that the agency has a very high overhead or makes a large profit. An agency I once worked for had one person in overhead (salespeople, secretaries, administrators, and so on) for every four or five contractors. After paying for those people, and for their office space, desks, computers, and so on, there wasn't much left for the contractors. Such agencies pay lower rates than agencies with low overhead. But some agencies with low overhead also pay low rates—because they want to make a higher profit. An agency that bills $43 an hour for a contractor may keep $6 or $25.

Now, the client doesn't know how much profit the agency is making, or how much overhead it has, and usually doesn't know how much money the contractor receives. So the client doesn't know if the agency pays well or not. Of course, many clients don't care. They should, though, because the lower-paying agencies have fewer qualified people to choose from.

The Agency May Keep 60 to 70 Percent of the Pay

Although clients often assume that contractors make good money, that is not always the case. One company I worked for, for example, paid my agency $37 per hour for my services, of which I received $28 per hour. At the same time, the company paid another agency $43 an hour for a less experienced writer, of which the writer received about $16. How, you may ask, does this hurt the client? Well, when the contractors learn how much money the agency is making and how much other contractors earn, they get disgruntled. The quality of their work declines, and they may look for a contract elsewhere, leaving the client in the middle of a project.

The Agency May Encourage the Client to Take a Less Qualified Person

If an agency has, for example, two contractors in whom the client is equally interested, and one of the contractors is demanding significantly more money, what does the agency do? If the client picks the one who costs the agency less, the agency makes a greater profit. So even if the more expensive contractor is also significantly more experienced or more skilled, the agency may encourage the client to take the cheaper one; the client will pay the same, but the agency will make more profit.

The Agency May Stop the Client from Rehiring the Contractor

Companies may want a contractor to return to do more work later, but the agency may not allow this. First, if the contractor is on another job through the agency, the agency probably will not want to risk losing a contract by asking the other client to release the contractor. Second, if the contractor is no longer working through the agency, the agency will usually allow the contractor to return to the client only if the agency gets the contract. Most agencies have a clause in their contracts stating that the contractor cannot return to work for the client within a stated time without the permission of the agency; the contractor may have to wait a year or 18 months before returning. If the company has to rehire the contractor through the agency, the contractor may turn down the contract if the agency doesn't offer enough money. This is especially likely to happen if the contractor has since begun working as an independent.

The Agency May Stop the Client from Offering the Contractor a Permanent Position

The contractual clause I've mentioned often stops contractors from taking permanent positions with a client. The contract usually has a clause that allows the client to "buy" the contractor, so long as the agency agrees.

If the company wants to convert a temporary contract into a full-time position, and the contractor accepts, the agency may not allow it. Or if the agency does allow it, the client may have to pay a fee—30 to 40 percent of the first year's salary. That may translate into $10,000 to $20,000, often enough to kill an offer. Some agencies simply will not allow clients to buy their contractors, believing it sets a bad precedent. Such contractual clauses may be unenforceable in some states, and they're often ignored; even so, they may still be enough to frighten off clients who are unsure of their legal position. (Of course, from my point of view, this really doesn't matter; freelancers shouldn't be taking full-time positions anyway!)

Some Clients Don't Want Independents, So They Hire Through Agencies—and Unknowingly Get Independents

Some clients avoid hiring independents to avoid problems with the Internal Revenue Service. Instead, they hire through agencies. While most agencies hire contractors and pay them as employees, some do not, especially small "Mom and Pop" agencies. The agency takes the money from the client and pays the contractor on a 1099. This means the agency does not have to pay payroll tax or get involved in complicated paperwork. But this setup is usually illegal, and leaves the client company—thinking it is safe—at risk. Contrary to popular opinion, the fact that the agency hires and fires the contractors doesn't mean the problems are the agency's alone. The Internal

Revenue Service and the Labor Department recognize something called *joint employment*.

For example, Labor Department publication WH1297, "Employment Relationship Under the Fair Labor Standards Act," says this:

> Employees of a temporary help company working on assignments in various establishments are considered jointly employed by the temporary help company and the establishment in which they are employed. In such a situation each individual company where the employee is assigned is jointly responsible with the temporary help company for compliance with the minimum wage requirements of the Act during the time the employee is in a particular establishment. The temporary help company would be considered responsible for the payment of proper overtime compensation to the employee . . . Of course, if the employee worked in excess of 40 hours in any work-week for any one establishment, that employer would be jointly responsible for the proper payment of overtime as well as the proper minimum wage.

As you will see in Chapter 14, any agency paying a contractor on a 1099 may be breaking the Fair Labor Standards Act, because the agency is not paying time-and-a-half overtime rates. That means the client company, acting in good faith and assuming it has no responsibility, may be liable for the unpaid overtime and a penalty of an equal amount.

The client may actually be at greater risk using an agency than hiring an independent contractor. With an independent contractor, the client may be able to use the Section 530 "Safe Harbor" described in Chapter 19, but after the client has hired an agency, the safe harbor disappears.

Clients Can Hire Independent Contractors and Save 20 to 50 Percent

The best reason for a company to avoid agencies is that it just doesn't need them. By spending some time looking for contractors and checking references, a company can get better people for less money. How does the client do this? The same way the agencies do. A few classified ads in the local paper, a call to the local professional association job banks, and a call to potential contractors already known to the client will soon get the word onto the grapevine. And because there is no agency taking a cut, many of these people are cheaper than less qualified people hired from an agency. A writer who charges $40 or $45 an hour in an independent contract could cost the client $55 or more if an agency is taking a cut.

The cost of looking for a writer without an agency is minimal, the savings enormous, and the time spent quite short compared to the problems that arise when a company staffs a critical project with unsuitable contractors.

There are ways for companies to work with agencies and avoid most of these problems. They can tell the agency how much the contractor should get paid, and negotiate how much the agency will get on top of the contractor's hourly rate. They can demand to see written records of reference checks, and even check one or two of the references themselves. They can interview thoroughly, perhaps having several employees talk to the interviewee. And they can demand nonrestrictive contracts—contracts that allow them to hire the contractor again later or offer the contractor permanent employment, possibly after several months of working through the agency. They can ensure that the agency is not using independent contractors. And, perhaps most important, the client should simply remember that the agency is trying to sell something.

These are ways to improve the agencies' performance, but I believe the client is usually in a better position if it hires the contractor directly, without a middleman. The agencies will tell you that they take the drudgery of searching for contractors away from the client; that they handle the payroll, and keep the Internal Revenue Service off their client's back; and that it is difficult to find good people. All this is true, but the client must decide whether it is worth the additional cost—$5, $10, or $15 for every hour that the contractor works—and the potential problems.

chapter **11**

The Interview

Questions are never indiscreet. Answers sometimes are.

Oscar Wilde (1854–1900)

Once an agency has a client interested in you, the agent will arrange for an interview. This doesn't always happen; sometimes an overly trusting client will allow the agency to staff a particular project, and take the agency's word that all the people are qualified.

Normally, though, the client will want to talk to you first. There isn't a great difference between an interview for a contract job and an interview for a permanent position. The client wants to speak to you and get a general impression of what you are like and whether you will be able to do the job. The things that would encourage clients to hire you full-time are the things that will encourage them to hire you for a contract.

Prepare for the Interview

Before going on the interview, talk to the agency and get as much detail as possible. When the agency first talks with a client they ask for information about the type of person that the client is looking for: the profession, of course, but also such things as the type of projects the contractor has worked on and the type of equipment he or she has used. For example, a client looking for a technical writer may specify that the writer must have written hardware documentation and know how to use desktop publishing programs. The specifications may be even more precise than that: perhaps the contractor must have worked on central office telecommunication switches, and know how to use Ventura Publisher and Microsoft Word. The client also may specify the amount of experience required (entry-level, three to four years, and so on).

You can use all this information to your advantage. Find out everything the client told the agency, and remember to stress the experiences you have had that most closely fit the ideal that the client is looking for. For example, you may not have worked on exactly the type of equipment the client produces, but you may have worked on a similar product, or a product that shares certain features with the client's. You may not have worked with the same tools or computer software that the client has, but you may have worked with similar ones. Even if you don't fit the bill exactly, you may still

99

be able to get the contract; if you have enough experiences that are similar to those on the client's checklist, and if you appear to the client to be the sort of person who picks up information quickly, you may get the contract anyway.

It is important to appear confident in these interviews. As one contractor said, "The shopper must be totally confident in his ability to handle a project professionally and with little or no guidance." You must use the interview to convince the client that you are able and confident of your abilities, and don't need "hand-holding." Even if you are entry-level—as I've pointed out elsewhere in this book, even newcomers to a profession may be able to work on contract—you should still project an image of competence and ability. The client wants someone who can be trained quickly— someone who needs to be told something only once, not three or four times.

Take Control of the Interview

You can create a good impression by asking a lot of questions. Don't overdo it, of course, but most clients are happy to tell you about the project. Ask questions such as these: What is the project? How long do you expect it to last? What skills are you looking for? What sorts of tools and techniques are you using? How big will the team be? Has the company done similar work before, or is this a new venture? The more questions you ask, the more will occur to you, and the interview will quickly turn into a conversation.

You will find that many clients don't know how to conduct an interview. They usually leave that up to their human resources department. But although that department hires permanent employees, many companies hire contractors directly, bypassing human resources. That leaves the manager not knowing what to ask, apart from a few obvious questions. If you "lead" the interview you will give an impression of being enthusiastic and intelligent (well, you probably *are* enthusiastic and intelligent, after all!). When the client mentions aspects of the project that are similar to other things you have done, tell him about those things, as if in passing, and then ask another question about the job, perhaps a question that will play on the similarities between the client's project and the other work you have done.

Another advantage of this approach is that you quickly get on friendly terms with the interviewer. Rather than continuing an interrogation that makes both you and the interrogator uncomfortable, asking plenty of questions and commenting on the answers turns the interview into a conversation, even a chat. And, as any salesperson knows, many purchasing decisions are made for personal reasons—whether you are selling computers, encyclopedias, or your time. Clients don't think "I like this person, I think I will buy from him," but clients who feel comfortable and relaxed are more likely to purchase from you. After all, clients have to buy from someone, why not someone they like?

This principle is even more important in contracting. If you are selling encyclopedias, clients may purchase even if they don't like you (after all, they'll probably never see you again), but if clients are thinking of buying your time, they are not going to hire you if they dislike you . . . because they will have to spend every workday with you for months, perhaps even for years. Personal relations are critical in sales, so getting on friendly terms with your client as quickly as possible is essential.

Here's another important reason to be on good terms with the client. Even if you don't get this job (as much as you charm the client, you simply may not have the experience required), the client can become an (unknowing) member of your network. Keep the client's business card, add the information to your database when you get home, and call back when you are looking for work. Even if the client doesn't need your skills now, he or she may in the future.

It would be unethical to bypass the agency and go to work for the client a week or two later, but there is no reason you can't keep in touch and go to work for the client in six months, cutting out the agency to get a larger slice of the pie. Even if you never work for this client, he or she may still be a source of job leads. And if you *do* work for the client, you can get a testimonial or reference—and it doesn't matter how good you are, the testimonial or reference won't be quite as nice as it might be if your client doesn't much like you!

Asking questions sometimes puts you in the role of adviser, even consultant. I have had clients ask me how I would handle a particular project, not as a way of testing me but because they really were not sure how to get the job done. As a writer, for example, I may be interviewed by a small company that needs software manuals but has no writers of its own—that is why the company is looking for contractors, of course. It doesn't know how to put these books together, which makes it very difficult for the company to interview contractors; how does the company know whether you can do the job if it doesn't even know what the job is? Acting confidently puts the client at ease; like a small child that is lost, the client wants someone to take over, to tell it what to do. If you can come in and act "quietly confident," showing that you know how you would do the job and are sure you can get it done, the client will relax and feel good about hiring you. Of course, you must take care not to be overconfident or arrogant; otherwise, the client may wonder if you are all talk and no action. I'm certain, though, that a contractor who meekly sits back and waits for the client to take a commanding role will find it much harder to sell his or her services; clients are usually looking for someone to take the job off their hands, not someone who needs constant attention.

However, some companies are *not* looking for someone to take over: They want a cog for their machine, not a power source. The client may simply want to see that you have all the qualifications on the checklist, and not worry too much about qualities such as initiative, confidence, and independence. This sort of interview might just be a way to look you over, to ensure you have no obvious personality disorders that would disturb the atmosphere, and to make sure that what is on your résumé is correct. The interview could just be a formality; don't swear or spit on the floor, and you're in. This sort of interview is most likely for large projects, such as those undertaken by weapons manufacturers, when a company is hiring dozens, even hundreds, of contractors at once.

Check Up on the Agency

Remember to ask the client some of the questions you have already asked the agency (the ones listed in Chapter 9). Make sure you are getting the full story from the agent; the agent may not know exactly what is going on at the client's office, or may intentionally paint a rosier picture than the facts warrant. For example, the agent may say it's going to be a certain six-month contract, whereas the client may say it's three months with a possibility of an extension of two or three. An agency may imply that you can work as much overtime as you like, when the client will allow only three or four hours a week. Make sure that the impression you have of the contract is the correct one.

Contracts

I can't do no literary work the rest of this year because I'm meditating another lawsuit and I'm looking around for another defendant.

Mark Twain

If you are working through an agency, you don't need to draw up your own contract, because the agency will have its own. Read it carefully, and make sure you know what it contains, in particular how much you will be paid and how often. (You should be paid at least every two weeks.) Also check to see what the contract says about overtime, whether you will receive time-and-a-half for all hours over 40. Ensure that everything you've been told appears correctly in the contract. Take your time going over the contract. In most cases you'll find it's in order, but mistakes may be made, so it's worth your time being careful. If you want to be really careful, talk to an attorney.

Restrictive Covenants

Most agency contracts contain a restrictive covenant, which seems to create more discussions among contractors than any other part of the contract. For example, one agency I worked for made me sign a contract containing the following:

The Employee covenants and agrees that the Employee may not:

i) during the period of employment and for one year following the termination for any reason of the Employee's employment, solicit or sell, for his own account or for others, data processing professional services that are competitive with the services of the Employer, to any company for which the Employee or employees under his managerial control (where applicable) has solicited or performed any data processing services on behalf of the Employer during any part of the year immediately preceding the termination of his employment;

ii) during the period of employment and one year following the termination of the Employee's employment for any reason, work or render data processing professional services, for his own account or for others, for any customer or the Employer for which the Employee has performed any services (or for which other employees under Employee's managerial control performed services), during any part of the year immediately preceding the termination of his employment with Employer; provided, however, that this restriction on employment shall, in the case of multi-location customers, be limited to the location or locations of the customer in question in which the Employee performed services and offices within a fifty-mile radius of such location or locations where the Employee performed services; and

iii) during the period of employment and for eighteen months following the termination of the Employee's employment, either directly or indirectly, hire any employee of the Employer in any capacity whatsoever, for his own account or on behalf of any person or corporation other than the Employer, nor attempt to induce any employee of the Employer to leave the employ of the Employer to work for the Employee or any other person, firm, or corporation within the geographic area where the Employer now or hereafter does business.

The agency is trying to ensure that you don't use your position with the agency to sell the same services to a client of the agency that you worked with while employed by the agency; that you don't go to work for a client of the agency that you worked for while employed by the agency; and that you don't try to steal the agency's other contractors. The second part of the clause is the most significant, because it limits you from going back to a client for up to *two* years after you leave it.

Can an agency really enforce such a contract? Maybe, maybe not. Texas, for example, is a "right to work" state, which does not allow limitations on a person's right to work. That means, according to some contractors and attorneys, that such a clause cannot be upheld. One friend of mine decided he wanted to continue with the client he was working for, but without the agency that originally got him the contract. He stood to gain financially, but what spurred him to action were what he believed were unethical dealings by the agency. His attorney told him to leave the employer for a couple of days and then sign a new contract. Of course he needed the cooperation of the client, but it agreed. The agency didn't challenge the deal. . . perhaps because the agency had a lot of business with the client and didn't want to risk losing it.

Such deals are common. I know several writers who have broken these clauses and returned to a client. If you want to do so, you can do it only if the client agrees, and the client may not do so. The client may believe it is unethical, and also may have signed an agreement not to "steal" you. Even if the agreement isn't legally valid, it may be enough to scare off a client. On occasion, though, there are very good reasons for breaking a contract with an agency, and you may be able to persuade the client to work with you. For example, if an agency is not paying you regularly, or has defaulted on some of its other obligations to you, you may be able to convince the client to dump the agency.

More Complicated Contracts

Most agency contracts are straightforward. Read them carefully and check to see that they make sense. It's not until you get to step 2 or 3 that you need to be concerned about them. Once you have to negotiate your own contracts, you must think a little more about what they say. We'll come back to contracts in Chapter 20.

Buying Your Benefits

Insurance. An ingenious modern game of chance in which the player is permitted to enjoy the comfortable conviction that he is beating the man who keeps the table.

U.S. author Ambrose Bierce (1842–1914)

Working freelance means you lose benefits that an employer usually provides. Don't forget to replace these benefits. Working without medical insurance, long-term disability insurance, or a pension plan may give you a lot of money to play with, but can be disastrous if you get sick or live long enough to retire.

Most people can replace these benefits, although a writer in the U.S. with a stable job and serious medical problems should think hard before working freelance. Unless you find an agency with a good medical policy, you may be uninsurable.

Medical Policies

Medical insurance is probably the biggest problem for freelancers in the U.S. It is getting more and more difficult to find a good medical policy, and once you have one, you don't know for certain whether you are really insured—until you get sick. You may have a health insurance policy, but your insurance company may not honor it. Why? Well, it may go out of business before you get sick—or worse, soon after you get sick (then you can't get another policy). The insurance company may close down the "plan" your policy is on, which means the insurer doesn't have to pay claims to you or any of the other sick people it had insured.

If you get seriously ill, your insurance company may look for a way to dump you. The easiest way is to dig into your medical history to find something that you didn't put on your original policy application, and then accuse you of fraud. That's easier than you might imagine; there are often mistakes in medical records—illnesses that you have never had, for example. You can't possibly remember your entire medical history, and so much is open to interpretation anyway. Some insurance companies take advantage of that, using your inability to provide all of the information as a reason to cancel your policy if you get seriously ill.

105

This is not just a problem for individuals, though; it's very difficult for small companies to get reasonable insurance these days. In fact, in some ways you are better off on your own policy than a small company's policy. Insurance companies are allowed to dump people only if they close down an entire plan. Usually, each organization is a plan, whether a business, professional organization, club, or union. The bigger the plan, the safer you are, because the risk is being spread further.

For example, if a business has 10 employees and one of the employees (or a dependent) gets cancer, the insurance company may cancel the plan, because the cost of treating the cancer will outweigh the profits that the business could make from such a small group. Every employee loses insurance coverage, and the business probably won't be able to get more insurance, unless the person with cancer agrees not to join the new policy. (There is talk of banning insurance companies from dropping plans in such cases, but at the moment they can do so, and often do.) In some cases insurance companies simply drop people from plans quite illegally, and there's usually not much that can be done about it.

Finding Your Own Insurance

How do you replace your medical insurance, then? First, I recommend you buy *Winning the Insurance Game* (by Ralph Nader and Wesley Smith), which gives a number of ways to protect yourself when you are shopping for insurance (for example, check the company's rating in *Best's Insurance Reports*). Read this book, and then look for medical insurance. (This book, and all others mentioned here, are listed in the Bibliography.)

Of course, you should see whether the agency you are going to work with has a medical plan. Many, if not most, agencies now have plans. If your agency doesn't, or you are working as an independent, you have to find insurance elsewhere. Even if your agency does have a policy, though, you may want to consider getting your own, especially if it's a very small agency. In addition to the problems already discussed, moving from agency to agency could cause problems if you get sick. When you move to a new agency the new policy will probably have "preexisting condition" restrictions: The policy either will not cover, or will cover only to a very limited degree, conditions that you had before you signed on to the policy. Of course this is a problem that can occur to captive employees also, when they are fired or laid off, but the problem may be worse for contractors because they move between policies more often. Note that the way that preexisting conditions are dealt with has improved somewhat thanks to the Kennedy-Kassebaum bill, though they can still pose a problem in some cases.

Veterans Plans and COBRA

If you are a military veteran, of course, you may not want to bother with health insurance at all, if the military's medical services in your area are good. If you do need insurance when you go freelance, the Consolidated Omnibus Budget Reconciliation Act (COBRA) may help. COBRA forces insurance companies to continue medical coverage for employees who leave a company for any reason other than "gross misconduct." I don't know exactly what gross misconduct means, but if you are laid off or (in most cases) fired, you can continue your medical insurance for up to 18 months. It will cost more than a company policy usually costs, because you will have to pay the full cost of the policy, paying both your share and your ex-employer's share (plus an extra 2 percent if the company wants to charge a service fee). You remain covered under COBRA until you are eligible to join another employer's plan, unless you have preexisting conditions, in which case you are still eligible for the full 18 months.

This is an excellent way to keep medical coverage. Remember that if you work for an agency that has a medical policy, you can extend that policy when you leave—as long as you joined the medical plan before you left, even if you were on it only for one day. As long as you are a legal employee of the agency (if the agency withholds taxes and reports your pay to the IRS on a Form W-2) and the agency has more than 20 employees on a typical day, you have the right to a COBRA extension. I extended one agency's policy for $260 per month, which included not only an excellent medical and dental policy for my family but disability insurance as well. (There is no federal law that states employers have to continue disability insurance, but they may do so if it's all part of the same package.)

If you do decide to use your COBRA rights, you have 60 days from quitting to inform your ex-employer, and then another 45 days to pay the first premium. The law requires all employers to provide information about COBRA to all employees leaving the company, so if you don't get this information, call the company.

If you are an independent contractor and you have problems getting medical insurance, you might consider getting a short-term contract every couple of years with an agency that has a good medical policy, just so that you can extend with COBRA. (You might even get a full-time job for a few weeks!)

There are some problems with COBRA. Your ex-employer may stop providing insurance to its current employees, in which case it can drop you, too. And your ex-employer may refuse to extend your insurance. This is illegal, but I'm told by insurance-law attorneys that it is quite common. If this happens, contact the Department of Labor immediately and try to get help. If the department won't help you, keep trying, because getting help depends on speaking to the right person at the right time.

Kennedy-Kassebaum

U.S. law changed a little at the beginning of 1997, with the introduction of the regulations from the Kennedy-Kassebaum bill. The bill doesn't' make a whole lot of difference to health coverage in general; in fact this bill has been called by some a "minimalist" bill. However, it does make a few changes that are of particular interest—and benefit—to freelancers.

The title of the bill is the Health Insurance Portability and Accountability Act of 1996. The term *"portability"* means that employees should be able to take their health-insurance policies with them when they leave jobs. However, the Kennedy-Kassebaum bill *does not* provide portability, despite the title of the bill. Instead, employers (and that includes an agency you work through) cannot deny coverage for preexisting conditions to new members of an insurance plan for more than 12 months. That's a lifetime limit; once you've been excluded from coverage for a particular condition for a year, your insurance company—and any other company covering you under a company policy later—must cover that condition. (Note, by the way, that the

12-month limit is extended to 18 months if you don't join the insurance plan as soon as you are eligible.) So if you have a medical condition that has not yet been covered for 12 months under your employer's insurance plan, you may want to wait until it's been 12 months since the condition was diagnosed; that way you'll be covered when you move to another plan. Also, insurance companies cannot define minimal health levels as a condition for joining a group plan. The plan's open to all employees or open to none.

There's another important change, too. If you leave a company and then take COBRA coverage for 18 months, at the end of the 18 months insurance companies offering individual policies in your area must take you. They can't deny coverage for preexisting conditions. However, note that the law appears to allow the insurer to charge what it wants, so it may still be able to force people out of the policy by pricing it too high.

The changes brought about by this bill are certainly better than nothing, but the bill still leaves certain perils. If you or a dependent has a medical condition that requires long-term care, going freelance may not be a good idea. You can make sure you get coverage at the first agency you go to, but what happens when that contract comes to an end? You can take COBRA coverage for a while, but you may still find yourself with job offers from agencies that don't have medical plans, or from clients or agencies that want to pay you as a true independent, without providing you any benefits. The Kennedy-Kassebaum bill may not help you much at that point; although you'll be able to get individual coverage, it may be way too expensive to be practical. (At the time of writing it was too early to say what the practical effect of Kennedy Kassebaum will be; we'll have to wait and see how the final regulations are written. I suggest you contact your local state insurance board to find out the regulations concerning how high insurance companies can price their individual policies.)

If you have Internet access, you might want to view the Kassebaum-Kennedy Health Insurance Bill Clears Congress page, at http://epn.org/families/fakeka.html, for a discussion of what the bill does and doesn't do. Or see the entire bill, all 200 pages of the Health Insurance Portability and Accountability Act of 1996, at http://epn.org/library/h3103.txt.

Your Spouse's Policy

How about your spouse's policy? If your spouse has a good company policy, check into being added to that policy; this is usually the cheapest way to get good medical insurance. Incidentally, if you live with your mate but are not married, you may still be able to get on your mate's policy. If your state legally defines your relationship as a common-law marriage, your insurance company may be forced to accept you on the same conditions as a spouse. Many states have very simple requirements. Just living together for a few weeks may be enough. If this applies to you, check the definition of *"spouse"* with your insurance company and your state board of insurance.

Health Maintenance Organizations

You might want to look for a Health Maintenance Organization (HMO). With an HMO you pay a premium each month and get low-cost medical care when you need it—a visit to the doctor might cost $10, for instance. The HMO owns the hospitals or has an arrangement with the hospitals to pay directly. However, the most common complaints about such organizations are that you must use one of the HMO's doctors, and you don't always get the care you need because the people treating you have a vested interest in not spending too much time or money on special tests or treatments.

On the other hand, one major benefit is that HMOs may be less likely to kick you out. An HMO can't suddenly close your plan and boot you out, for instance, a trick played by many companies providing individual policies.

Individual Policies

Eventually you may find you have to search for an individual policy. Perhaps your COBRA policy runs out before you get a job with an agency that has a medical policy, or maybe you manage to find enough independent contracts and don't need to work through agencies anymore. So what next?

Finding an affordable medical policy is not easy, so give yourself plenty of time. Don't start looking a week before you need it. I suggest you start comparing policies at least two months before, preferably more. Insurance is a complicated business, and I don't have the space to explain all the options and possible problems, so read *Winning the Insurance Game*. Investing the time to read this book could save you much money and trouble in the future.

I'm wary of most individual policies, though. Many insurance companies churn these plans as a way to avoid paying for covered illnesses. Here's how this nasty little trick works. Periodically the insurance company closes down the plan. The company can do that quite legally. Because the entire plan is being closed down, everyone on the plan loses their insurance, so the company is not picking out just the sick and throwing them off the plan (though insurance companies will do that in some circumstances). Then the company sends a letter to all the people covered under the plan it's closing. The company announces a new plan, and says that everyone is eligible to apply to join the new one. Because the plan is new, the company can define eligibility and demand medical examinations. If you're healthy, you get onto the new plan; if you're not, you don't.

Group Insurance

Probably the most affordable way to get a medical policy, if you can't get a policy from an employer, is to join some kind of "group." You might want to look at Workers Trust, an "association of democratically managed businesses and self-employed people." A similar organization, Co-op America, also has a good policy. (See Appendix F for information on both these policies.) Both the Workers Trust and Co-op America policies are remarkably comprehensive, even covering "alternative" medical services.

You can join all sorts of organizations that have health insurance: The National Association for the Self-Employed (see Appendix D), the Society for Technical Communication, the American Association of Retired Persons (AARP), and professional associations are examples. These group policies are often no better than individual policies, so if an organization of which you are a member offers a group policy, don't assume it's the best deal. It may be a good policy, but check it out thoroughly (*Winning the Insurance Game* tells you how). In fact, when the insurance agent arrives at your house, make sure he's selling the right policy; you may be offered a completely different policy.

Also, don't let the word *group* fool you, or the advertising which often implies that you can buy a policy that rivals that of a big company—you can't. If you go to work for virtually any big company, you can join its medical policy without any medical examination or proof of insurability. To buy a "group" policy, on the other hand, you usually have to provide information about your medical history and may even need a medical examination. You can also have your policy canceled if the insurance company finds mistakes or omissions in the information you supply. And many group policies have enormous gaps in coverage; they are so specific about what they do cover that an awful lot gets left out. If a plan has a long list of what it does pay, and itemizes what it does pay while you are in the hospital, there are probably many things it won't pay, items that may not even appear in the "exceptions" section. Plans often have ridiculous limits (a maximum of $3,000 for surgery, for example, or $50 a day for the hospital room).

And be careful of plans that pay for hospital care but not for prescriptions outside the hospital; you can spend a lot of money without ever seeing the inside of a hospital. On the other hand, buying a plan with "holes" is one way to reduce your premium, so if you can save $3,500 a year by buying a plan that pays only $80,000 of a $100,000 medical claim, it may be a logical move—so long as you understand exactly what the plan does and does not cover.

However, there are some groups that have excellent health policies. There's a general rule of thumb, though: If *anyone* can join the group, the policy will not be too different from one you could buy outside the group—it may be discounted a little, perhaps. But if the group's membership is restricted, the policy is likely to be better. To join some professional associations, for instance, you have to prove you are employed in a particular industry, show you have worked in it for a certain number of years, be sponsored by one (or two or three) of the association's members, and send a copy of your official transcript or diploma proving you have a specific degree. The result is that the members are a very select group, often wealthy or middle-class people, so the association can offer it an excellent health policy. Its insurance company knows what to expect from the group, and knows that most of its members are in a low-risk group.

So spend a little time considering the groups you might be able to join. Ask your friends about professional organizations. The Society for Technical Communication (STC) offers a medical policy, but the STC has open membership, so the policy is not of the same standard as some professional associations' policies.

Note, by the way, that the Kennedy-Kassebaum bill allows the self-employed to set up tax-exempt Medical Savings Accounts (MSA). These accounts allow you to save before-tax funds for use in medical emergencies. You must have an associated high-deductible insurance plan. (The maximum deductible is $4,500, and the maximum out-of-pocket expenses are $5,500 for families.) You can deposit up to 75 percent of the deductible into the savings plan. So if you have family coverage you can put up to $3,375 into this tax-free fund, reducing your tax by almost a $1,000 if you're in the 28 percent tax bracket. When you have medical expenses not covered by your insurance you can pay those expenses from the MSA—in effect paying medical expenses with untaxed income. Talk to your insurance agent if you're interested in setting up such a plan.

Reducing the Cost of a Policy

Once you find a medical policy you like, there are a few things you can do to keep your monthly premiums low. Buy a policy with a high deductible—$500, $1,000, or more. This reduces the premium considerably. If the policy comes with an added life insurance policy, consider removing it. One policy I bought had a $10,000 life policy for $6 a month; I cut it out because I already had enough life insurance, at a cost of only $1 a month for each $10,000 of coverage.

You can also cut costs by purchasing a policy that covers only major medical expenses; if you get the flu and go to a doctor, you pay, but if you get seriously ill and end up in intensive care, the insurance company pays. Omitting maternity insurance also cuts cost. Insuring against pregnancy can be very expensive, and often pays very little, or even nothing, for a couple of years. If you or your spouse are planning to get pregnant within a year, you may pay more in extra premiums than you would get back in benefits; it's only after a year or two that most policies start paying any worthwhile amount. However, discuss this issue with the insurance company before you buy; some policies cover the complications of pregnancy, even if you don't buy the extra maternity coverage itself.

Another option you might consider is a catastrophic-care policy, one with a *very* large deductible. Your deductible may be from $25,000 to $50,000, but your premiums are very low. A $50,000 deductible sounds like a lot, but if you are spending $5,000 to $8,000 a year in premiums for a family policy—and can buy a $35,000-deductible policy for about $500—you may want to consider "self-insuring" yourself for the first $35,000 (in fact many hospitals will write off a large portion of your expenses, effectively giving you a discount, so you may not even have to come up with the full $35,000). Over 30 or 40 years you would save hundreds of thousands of dollars in premiums. So self-insuring for $35,000 per sickness may be a logical choice. Another advantage of such policies is that they are usually easy to join—you don't have to be examined or complete an extensive medical history form—so it may be hard for the insurance company to wriggle out of paying.

Of course there are things to watch for with these plans. The deductible is usually per sickness, so you could end up paying $35,000 several times if you are really unlucky. (Some plans apply only one deductible, though, if more than one family member suffers in the same accident or from the same sickness.) Also, each sickness or accident may be covered for only a limited time (three years, for example). Some insurance agents can sell you these policies, but a lot of professional associations carry them as well.

Whatever you do about medical insurance, do something. The consequences of serious sickness without insurance can be severe, and financial ruin—or even death—is not uncommon. I'm stressing this in such strong terms because I know how easy it is to "let things slip," and I know several freelancers who don't have insurance. But it's just not worth the risk. Buy a book about the subject, and read a few magazine articles. Go to your library and check the periodicals index. You may find that one of the consumer magazines (such as *Consumer Digest*) has recently compared medical policies. If you are at all unsure about your insurability, investigate insurance long before you need it. (The Bibliography lists several books on medical insurance.)

Deducting from Your Taxes

If you are an independent contractor, you can deduct 40 percent of your medical insurance premiums from your taxes on Form 1040 (1997 figure). This deduction has been on the books for a few years now, and the Kennedy-Kassebaum bill extended it to the year 2008. (The deduction is scheduled to increase in steps, up to 80 percent by the year 2006. It'll be 45 percent for 1998 to 2002.) The deduction is not available to you if you are an employee, though. You may also be able to deduct *all* your medical costs, premiums, and out-of-pocket expenses. You'll have to set up a corporation, though, which may be more trouble than it's worth; see Chapter 23. And finally, another way to deduct all expenses is to hire your spouse, then provide a medical policy to him or her (which, of course, would cover you, too).

Disability Insurance

Ever stopped to think about what you would do if you couldn't work? Disability insurance is usually more important than life insurance, because the chance of being disabled in the middle of your career is greater than the chance of dying. Most companies have some kind of disability policy, and many technical-service agencies now have such policies also, usually packaged with the medical policy. If your agency doesn't have one, though, you should start looking. A simple policy paying $2,500 a month after 90 days of disability could cost a 32-year-old man about $85 a month, for instance. My own policy has a 4 to 6 percent cost-of-living adjustment to keep the policy in line with inflation, and the right to increase the monthly benefit (by increasing the premium) at any time, even if I become sick.

Of course the older you are, the shorter the waiting period, and the larger the monthly benefit, the greater the monthly premium. But there are also many "bells and whistles" that can quickly add up. You can purchase a Social Security supplement— a rider to the policy that pays extra benefits if you receive no money from Social Security—though the extra money usually lasts only two years. You also can buy a rider that pays a portion of the monthly benefit if you return to work part time and a rider that pays the monthly overhead expenses of your business office while you are disabled. No doubt there are many other options, but buying all these can quickly double or triple the monthly premium.

You can get a disability policy from many insurance companies and groups. Look for a policy that defines disability as being unable to carry out the duties of your regular occupation (some policies are more strict than this, defining disability purely biologically, with no regard to the type of work you do—if you are fit enough to bag groceries, you are not disabled). Make sure you understand exactly how long the payments last if you are disabled. Some end when you retire, for example, and there are dozens of different permutations; mine would pay me for the rest of my life, unless I'm disabled by sickness after the age of 60, in which case it pays until I'm 65 (if I'm disabled by *accident* after the age of 60, the policy still pays for the rest of my life). I've no idea who thinks up all these variations, but it must take some imagination.

Look for a noncancellable policy; so long as you pay the premium, the company can't dump you up to age 65, and after 65, the insurer can't cancel the policy so long as you are paying the premium and working. A policy with a recurrent disability clause may be worth considering, also. This means that even if you are not off work for consecutive days, as long as the disability is caused by the same accident or sickness and the days are not separated by more than six months, the insurance company will regard them as being the result of the same disability.

Disability policies are complicated, and I can't make recommendations beyond these few simple points. Remember, however, that with any disability policy, you will have a waiting period between becoming disabled and receiving money—another excellent reason to have money in the bank. Incidentally, although you can't use your disability insurance premiums as a tax deduction (except the portion, if any, that pays for business overhead insurance), any benefit you may receive is not taxable, as long as you paid the premium yourself.

Term Life Insurance

If you need a life insurance policy, you usually need more than a typical company policy provides, because $10,000 doesn't go very far. Most employers' policies are nice little extras with little real value, benefits that don't need to be replaced directly, because you have probably bought a large policy independently. Of course, if your employer gave you a large policy—some insure your life for a couple of times your salary—you may not have bought your own. Before you go out and buy a policy, read Andrew Tobias's *The Only Investment Guide You'll Ever Need* or Norman Dacey's *What's Wrong with Your Life Insurance* (both are listed in the Bibliography). Both of these books explain why you need a term life policy, not a whole life or cash value policy. And once you are ready to buy a term policy, don't go straight to an insurance agent.

First, check with your credit union to see if it works with a computerized listing service; these services take your information, feed it into a computer, and then give you a list of five or six policies and companies you can choose from. This is probably the best way to find low-cost life insurance. You can also use SelectQuote (see Appendix F). The service is free, and you can do everything over the phone (which is good if you hate hassling with insurance agents). You can even call and talk to the people at SelectQuote to get information and advice.

Tax-Free Savings Plans

There are several ways to replace your employer's savings plans. What do these tax-free plans do? They allow you to pay money into a pension fund, without first paying income tax on that money, and they allow you to keep all the income made by your pension fund, without paying income tax on it until you begin withdrawing money from the fund.

Your own pension plan has certain advantages over an employer's. Permanent employees rely to a great extent on the employer's contribution. That is part of the bargain: The employee receives less than the employer can afford to pay, but instead the employer puts some of the unpaid money into a pension plan. You may never get that money, though.

These days people seem to move around quickly. Sure, some people work with the same company for 25 or 30 years, but that is becoming less common. I know many people who stick with a company for two years and then get laid off, go to the next company and last 18 months, and so on. But the employer contribution to a pension plan doesn't immediately become your property. Typically you must wait over three years to "own" 25 percent, four years to own 50 percent, and five years to own 100 percent. An independent contractor probably can afford to save more money (because he or she receives more), and controls all the money placed in the account, with no waiting.

Also, many company pension plans are now going broke, and some retired employees are finding that their pensions are now worth only a few percent of what they expected—and what they were originally told the pension would be. In some cases money is being illegally removed from company pension plans; in effect, companies are stealing their employees' pensions.

Independent Retirement Accounts

So, what can you do if you go freelance? First, you still have an Independent Retirement Account (IRA). Although recent tax law changes have placed some restrictions on IRAs, if you are not eligible for any other tax-free savings plan, you can put the maximum amount allowable into an IRA: $2,000 for an individual, or $2,250 for a married couple when only one spouse is working. (By the time you read this book, the maximum amounts allowable may be higher; Congress was talking of allowing nonworking spouses to contribute up to $2,000.)

If you are an employee of an agency, you may be able to use the agency's pension plan. Many agencies now have 401(k) plans or Simplified Employee Pension plans (SEPs) (the next section discusses these SEPs). If your agency doesn't have any kind of pension plan, all you are left with is an IRA, so take advantage of it. Remember, though, just because you don't have a large, tax-free savings plan doesn't mean you shouldn't save for your retirement. One of the major advantages of freelancing is that it allows you to earn more money. Sure, your last permanent employer had a good tax-free savings plan, but did you make enough money to save any?

If you are an independent freelancer, you can open two types of retirement plans: a Keogh or an SEP. (If you work most of the year through an agency but part of the year as an independent contractor, you can still set up one of these pension plans, but your savings are based on your income from self-employment only.) You can set up these plans through a bank, credit union, brokerage firm, or insurance company.

Simplified Employee Pension Plans (SEPs)

A SEP/IRA is an IRA set up to receive larger-than-normal payments from a self-employed person. If you set up an SEP you can deposit up to 13.0435 percent of your income, or $30,000, whichever is less, and you won't pay any taxes on the money put into the plan. (To calculate your income for these purposes, deduct from your business income half of your Self Employment tax, then multiply the result by .130435 to find the amount that you can put into the SEP.) SEPs are very easy to set up, and have the same rules as an IRA. Again, contact your bank, credit union, or brokerage firm.

Keogh Plans

Keogh plans, also known as HR-10 plans, are more complicated to set up than SEPs, but, depending on how you set them up, may allow you to deduct a higher percentage of your income. You may set up a plan into which you can pay a fixed portion of your profits (a profit-sharing plan) or one into which you pay a fixed contribution (a money-purchase plan). You can set up both a profit-sharing and money-purchase plan if you wish. If you have a money-purchase plan, you can deposit up to 20 percent of your income tax-free. (Again, you have to deduct half of your Self Employment income to come up with the number you multiply by 20 percent.)

Keoghs have a couple of advantages over SEPs. When you retire and withdraw money from the Keogh you may be able to "income-average," reducing the amount of tax you will have to pay by calculating your tax as if a single large payment was actually made over several years. Also, if you think you may incorporate at some point, you'll be able to transfer your Keogh money into a corporate pension plan—and you can borrow money from corporate pension plans to, for example, buy a house. (See Chapter 23 for a discussion on incorporating.)

Okay, pension plans look complicated, but they seem worse than they really are because they have so many "ifs, ands, and buts" that won't normally concern you. Go to a bank (better still, a credit union) or a brokerage firm, and ask someone to explain what you need to do. You will find it is reasonably straightforward. Or find a book on pensions and retirement planning, and invest a little time ensuring your financial security.

You've now looked at the most important company benefits that you must replace. These benefits are often the most difficult to deal with. Consider how you are going to replace these benefits some time before you need to do so, because they take time to investigate and set up. Health and life insurance policies are probably the most critical, but don't put off your pension plan. There is never a "good" time to start one, so it's easy to let the pension plan slip—but if you leave it too long, you may live to regret it.

Credit Unions

There is another benefit you may want to grab before you leave permanent employment. If your present employer has a credit union and you are not a member, join before you become a contractor. Credit unions are generally in better financial health than banks and savings and loans, and can provide you with cheap checking accounts, high-interest savings accounts, and low-interest loans. Many even allow you to overdraw your account at little or no cost to you.

Everyone should have a credit union account, but freelancers will find the cheap loans and relaxed attitude about overdrafts especially useful. Incidentally, you may be able to join a credit union even if your employer doesn't have one, or if you don't have an employer. Look in the Yellow Pages, call all the credit unions, and ask who can join. Some allow residents of a particular town to join, or people in a particular occupation. You might also look at the National Association for the Self-Employed, which has a credit union for members (see Appendix D). Many clubs and professional organizations also have associated credit unions.

U.S. banks are pressuring the government to restrict credit unions from recruiting people widely—so get one while you can.

Business Insurance

Another thing you should consider if you reach the independent contractor status is business insurance. You may find, for instance, that your computer equipment is not covered by your renter's or homeowner's policy. One good way to insure computer equipment is through Safeware (see Appendix F). You may also want to get business liability insurance (a General Commercial Liability policy), which covers you if a client is hurt while visiting your home office, or if you trip and stab someone with a pencil at a client's office. Some small-business associations have business liability insurance. For instance, you can get such a policy from the Home Business Institute; see Appendix D.

Work Habits and

Overtime

Personally, I have nothing against work, particularly when performed, quietly
and unobtrusively, by someone else.

U.S. author Barbara Ehrenreich

I know some would-be freelancers who are a little scared of working freelance—not
because they can't handle money, not because they are scared of looking for contracts,
but because they are not sure that they are "good enough" to freelance. Many people
have a misconception about freelancing: They think you have to be experienced and
highly skilled before you can be a contractor.

But this isn't so. I have met freelancers who were close to incompetent, but still kept
themselves employed. Paradoxically, the technical service industry has many people
who don't fit in well elsewhere, but can take advantage of unethical agencies. Because
most agencies don't check references, many freelancers fabricate experience. A friend
of mine, a manager of a technical-writing department, once told me of one writer she
had interviewed. It turned out that both had worked at the same company in the past,
although not at the same time. She asked to see a writing sample, and he brought out
a book he claimed to have written while with this previous employer. "I couldn't
believe it," my friend told me. "It was *my* book!"

Another publications department manager told me, "I used to think contractors were
experienced, skilled professionals. Now I realize that they are no better than anyone
else, they just want to make more money." He wrote a memo to his boss explaining
why he didn't like to use contractors. "They are not the skilled professionals they are
advertised to be," he wrote. "I have grounds to suspect that they are more clever at
marketing themselves and evading objective evaluation than producing good work."

Unfortunately he is quite correct that many freelancers are not very good at their
chosen profession. Don't misunderstand me, I'm not suggesting that incompetent
people should become contractors (though obviously they can do so), nor that all
freelancers are incompetent (I suspect that the average freelancer does better work
than the average employee). What I am saying is that if you are reasonably hard-
working and reasonably competent, there is no reason to think that you can't do well
as a freelancer.

Often, working as a contractor seems just the same as working as a captive. You keep the same hours, do the same work, follow the same instructions—but take home more money. You get invited to the company parties, picnics, and beer bashes. Some companies even include the contractors when they give their employees time off with pay ("Go to the product-release announcement this afternoon, and then go home early").

However, there is often a difference between the way your client treats you and the way your client treats employees. Remember that one reason the client hired you is that you are expendable. Your client can get rid of you quickly and easily, for any reason—if the project is canceled, the project runs low on funds, or you don't do good work. Firing captive employees, on the other hand, is much more difficult, and we all know captives who seem to hold on to a job for years without appearing to do any work. You, though, have a contract that comes up for renewal every few months; your client has to justify the expense over and over again, so if there isn't a good reason to keep you, your contract won't be extended.

Your clients are likely to expect a bit more from you than they expect from their permanent employees (and perhaps be a little less lenient toward you). Also, don't underestimate envy; often you will be paid considerably more than your immediate superior, and this can cause some friction, perhaps even outright resentment.

Often clients are justifiably resentful. One manager referred to the "country club atmosphere" that pervaded his office full of contractors—people on the phone all day, chatting with each other, swapping job leads, comparing rates. One contractor I worked with spent about three or four hours a day on the phone to friends, or just visiting people around the office.

Sometimes clients are partly to blame for these problems, though. Many offices have a very relaxed, laid-back atmosphere, in which very little work gets done. The client brings in a contractor or two, and expects them to do nothing but work. But it is very difficult for the freelancer not to be "infected" with the same lackadaisical attitude that everyone else has, especially when the contractor has to work closely with employees.

Some managers don't much like contractors, and hire them only because they have to. I know one department manager who doesn't think contractors should be allowed to have phones; he would like contractors to work every minute of every hour they bill. Unfortunately, that is just not possible. Very few people can work eight hours straight without a break, and if anyone expects you to bill only for every minute you actually work, you had better increase the hourly rate at least 25 percent. Technical-service contracts usually pay for normal work hours: an eight-hour day including a "normal" number of breaks.

You may find yourself without many of the comforts of the captive employee. Telephones seem especially difficult to get hold of for some reason (even if the manager has no particular objection to you having one). As a contractor you often end up at the bottom of the "to do" list. You also could find yourself moved around a bit, shuffled from one office to another as captives come and go. One company I worked for has a policy that denies contractors door-cards, those credit-card-size electronic "keys" that you hold up to a panel to unlock the door. Company policy stated that contractors would be let in by their manager each morning.

Some contractors have the idea that they are consultants, that they are there to do the best job possible, and have a duty to tell the client the best way to get the job done. This isn't quite true. In the client's eyes you are a temporary employee, not a consultant. You are usually not expected to take over and run things your way. Sure, give your advice to the client, but if the client doesn't want to take your advice, don't get offended; it's the client's prerogative. Sometimes you just have to do things the wrong way, the inefficient way, because that is what the client wants. If you suggest another way a couple of times and the client isn't interested, get on with the job, the client's way. My attitude about per-hour jobs is that I get paid by the hour, not by the finished product. In some situations the client may know it is doing the job the wrong way, but other factors force the client to do the job that way—because the rest of the company does it that way, for example, or because the company lacks the equipment needed to do the job properly.

This, incidentally, is the major difference between a contractor and a consultant. A contractor is paid by the hour, not by the job. The consultant, on the other hand, is paid to get a job done, and may even receive a lump sum for the job. In such a case the consultant must have the right to say how the job will be done, so it can be done quickly and efficiently.

How to Act at the Office

So, how should you act at the company office? The rules are obvious, really.

Be Prompt and Begin Work When You Are Supposed To

Though many employees in your profession may be salaried, you are not, and clients tend to watch your promptness more than that of the captives. Clients pay by the hour for your work, and are constantly reminded of this fact, and of the large sums involved, each time they sign an invoice. They can see their precious budget pouring out of the department, so each time they see you goofing off, all they can think of is money going up in smoke. Of course captive employees cost a lot of money too, but that is more easily forgotten because the client doesn't have a constant reminder.

Avoid Getting Involved in a "Country Club" Atmosphere

Don't spend too much time on the phone or talking with other employees or contractors. One company I worked for allowed employees to close their office doors. The result was small groups of employees and contractors "shooting the breeze" behind closed doors. Avoid these groups. The client may allow it at first, but will grow to resent it.

Do the Best Job You Can

Sure, you can often get away with doing a mediocre job (thousands of contractors do so every day), but the better the job you do, the better your reputation will be. The client will be more likely to extend your contract, give you good references, and hire you again, and you will find it easier to get other contracts. Reputations travel.

Make Sure Your Appearance Is Acceptable to the Client

I hate ties, and avoid them if I can. One vice-president told me he didn't care what I looked like, so long as I did a good job (that is the sort of company I like to work for!). Unfortunately, many companies expect "business dress," which, for men, means wearing a piece of clothing that restricts the flow of blood to the brain. If that is what the company wants, that is what I do (or rather, what I used to do; no more).

Of course, even if you don't wear traditional business clothes, you should always be neat and well groomed. Acceptable dress varies among industries, professions, and companies. It even varies among different divisions of the same company. I once worked for a large telecommunications company that had a separate research division. People in the main company had to wear traditional business dress, while those in the research division wore jeans and sweaters, even though they worked in the same building.

So as much as I dislike business dress, I sometimes have to wear these clothes. I have come up with a good rule of thumb, though: Wear what you feel comfortable in, without upsetting your client. If your client doesn't care, there's no reason you should.

Don't Drag Your Feet

I know contractors who expect the client to wait on them; they want the client to bring the work to them, not to have to get up out of their seats and take some initiative themselves. They have the attitude that "if the client wants me to do something, he's going to have to show me exactly how." But contractors earn a lot of money, and although the client rarely expects them to take over and work miracles, the client deserves, and usually expects, a certain amount of energy and resourcefulness.

In fact, clients often expect you to have more initiative than their captives. After all, you are going to be with the company for a limited time, so the client doesn't want you to spend months "settling in" or "getting the feel of the project." You need to learn quickly—the client's word processing system, work procedures, specialized tools, report requirements, and so on. If you can quickly size up a situation and start producing something the client can see, you'll go a long way toward keeping the client happy.

Also, don't try to drag a job out so that you can keep pulling in the paychecks. A good manager can see what you are doing, and after a while it becomes obvious to even the most trusting boss. Dragging your feet won't do your reputation any good, and if you market yourself properly it shouldn't even be necessary, because you can always find work elsewhere.

Remember That While You Are Working for the Client, You Are Still Selling Yourself

Even after you get a contract, you are always selling yourself. You are working to get the contract extended, the next contract, the good reference, the referrals to other managers, and so on. This doesn't mean you have to be hyped up all the time, acting like a caricature of a used-car salesman, but it does mean you should try to get along with people. Try to avoid conflicts. Be helpful, friendly, and cooperative. Reputations are built not only on competence, but also on congeniality. Consider these two references: "He's good at his job, and he's friendly and easy to get along with," or "He's one of the best, but he's a real pain in the neck to work with." Which would you rather have? I'll bet that the first reference gets more jobs.

Successful freelancers are usually friendly people. It's very difficult for someone who doesn't get along with others to do well in freelancing, because he or she can't build a solid network. Each job you have is a stepping-stone, a way to find a useful contact, something to build on. If you leave behind a company full of people happy to see you go, you've lost an opportunity to make contract-hunting easier.

Don't Talk Money with the Captives

No client wants its employees to know how much it is paying you, because such knowledge just starts the employees thinking "Why doesn't the company pay me more, if it can afford $40 an hour for this guy? Maybe I should quit and work contract." It is likely to lower morale, and won't make your client happy, so be careful. Of course talking money with other contractors is essential, as I've explained elsewhere in this book, but be careful who is listening!

Don't Encourage Captives to Break Free

Your client presumably wants to keep its employees, and isn't going to be happy if your images of the happy-go-lucky freelancer's life persuade the company's employees to try it for themselves. Sometimes it's unavoidable—captives are not stupid, after all (just misguided, the true freelancer would say). Just don't encourage anyone to leave.

The Overtime Debate

By law, certain employees must be paid one-and-a-half times their regular hourly pay when they work more than 40 hours in one week. The law defines two types of employee: exempt and nonexempt. If you are nonexempt, you are not exempt from the law (that is, your employer must pay you the special overtime rate). If you are exempt, your employer does not have to pay this special rate.

A nonexempt employee is one who is paid hourly, or who receives a salary but does not fit within one of the special exemptions (Executive, Administrative, Professional, and Outside Sales). Yet many, if not most, agencies do not pay overtime rates. You get paid by the hour, the same amount for the 50th hour as you get for the first.

The rest of this chapter comprises two articles I originally wrote a few years ago for *PD News* (now *Technical Employment Weekly*), a technical-service industry magazine. (You can find the address and subscription information for this magazine in Appendix B.)

"We Always Pay Time-and-a-Half for Overtime"

" . . . even if the client refuses to pay the extra." How often do you hear that from an agency? Not too often probably, but you may be hearing it more soon. I heard this about a month ago from a representative (I'll call him Mike) of a large national technical service agency. But that wasn't all Mike told me: "It's not a matter of being nice, we have to pay it. It's the law."

That is not a belief shared by many agencies, if my experiences and those of my friends are anything to go by. Most agencies do not pay time-and-a-half for overtime; they believe contracting is a different form of employment relationship that doesn't warrant extra pay for overtime, and, more important, they believe they don't have to pay. They may be wrong.

continues

continued

Before I go any further let me state that this isn't agency bashing. I don't know if contractors do deserve higher rates once they have worked forty hours in a week. I've a feeling most probably don't. I simply want to discuss a problem that the industry is going to have to come to terms with eventually.

Quite simply, the law states that most technical-service contractors are nonexempt employees, and as such have a legal right to be paid one-and-one-half hours' pay for every hour they work over forty hours in one week.

As an employee of the Labor Department told me, "The assumption is that all employees are nonexempt unless it can be shown otherwise." What does nonexempt mean? It means the employee is covered under the Overtime provisions of the Fair Labor Standards Act. In some situations an employee may be "exempt" from the law (that is, not eligible for overtime pay), but most people are not; they are "nonexempt."

The first thing to consider is whether a contractor is an employee. If an agency takes out the contractor's taxes and uses a W-2 form to account to the IRS, then yes, he is an employee. (If he isn't paid in this manner he may still be an employee, but that is another article.)

The next thing to consider is the form of payment. If the contractor receives hourly pay, he is nonexempt. No need to go any further, that's it. Hourly-paid employees are legally entitled to overtime rates.

Now, you may have heard of the Executive, Administrative, and Professional exemptions. They are complicated and confusing, but they only come into play for salaried people. Except for outside salespeople, doctors, lawyers, and teachers (specifically including flight instructors, for some reason), all the exemptions are dependent on the employee being paid "on a salary or fee basis."

Of course most contractors sign a contract that specifies the rate they will receive. By signing the document aren't they waiving their right to overtime rates? No. The law states that "overtime pay may not be waived by agreement between the employer and employee." In other words, even if the employee doesn't want a special overtime rate, the law says the employer must pay it.

Many agencies now pay "salaries." At least they call them salaries. I once worked for one of the world's largest tech-services agencies; I won't name it, but it paid me one of these pseudo-salaries. This is how it works: You agree to a yearly salary and sign a contract with that yearly rate. The agency divides the salary by 2,080 to arrive at an hourly rate. You then report the hours you work and receive that number of hours multiplied by the hourly rate. If you only work thirty hours in a week you are paid for thirty, and if you work eighty you are paid for eighty.

Is this a salary? Probably not. The law says that a salaried employee "must receive (subject to certain exceptions) his full salary any week in which he performs any work without regard to the number of days or hours worked." The employer could deduct money "if an employee absents himself from work for a day or more to handle personal affairs" for example, or, in some situations, when the absence "is due to sickness or accident." But if the employee took the afternoon off, the employer presumably couldn't deduct money (or it wouldn't be a salary). The employer can't deduct money for time spent on jury duty, military duty, or when "there is no work available." (The agency I worked for didn't pay if a contractor was unable to work due to the client company closing for a holiday.)

All this makes the pseudosalary look more pseudo than salary. There may be some loopholes that a clever lawyer could crawl through, but more and more agencies have decided that there aren't any. Even if the agency can defend its "salary," it has only won half the battle. Just because someone is paid a salary doesn't mean he is exempt. The law specifically mentions computer programmers, for example, and states that some "have duties . . . which qualify them for exemption." Only some.

What's the answer? Many agencies and clients no longer allow overtime. (This may not be sufficient, though. The law says that "an announcement . . . that no overtime will be permitted . . . will not impair the employee's right to compensation for the overtime work"—a wonderfully ambiguous statement that Washington should be proud of.) Other agencies pay it, and some are even losing money on overtime. Perhaps agencies will start figuring overtime into the projected costs, paying slightly lower hourly rates to make up for it. But perhaps the law should be changed.

Congress didn't write the Fair Labor Standards Act for us. They wrote it for people on $3.35 an hour, not $33.50. Is a programmer making $80,000 a year being exploited if he doesn't get extra for overtime? I don't think so. The law was intended to protect poor people, not to provide wealthy people with a windfall profit.

The Fair Labor Standards Act is not a new law, but the Department of Labor seems to be applying it to the technical-service industry more often now. Many companies are at great risk, potentially owing millions of dollars in back pay; these companies are going to realize how much they have to lose, and start dealing with the problem. "There is no way out," Mike told me. "Our lawyers have looked at the overtime issue, and all they can say is, 'Pay it.'"

After this first article appeared, someone from an agency wrote to *PD News* to say that agencies can pay people straight time, because contractors came under the professional or executive exemptions; I decided to go into more detail in a second article.

"Overtime, Once Again"

Robert Marmaduke, of APEX Technical Services in Washington, believes that I incorrectly interpreted the Fair Labor Standards Act in my "Overtime" article of August 21. Mr. Marmaduke stated that employees in "non-trade executive, administrative, and professional positions, spending more than 50 percent of one's day in responsible charge or doing professional design," are exempt from overtime rates (**PD News**, Oct. 2). Perhaps I did misread the Act—it's a little confusing in places, and I may not have seen all the relevant documents—but let me explain why I don't believe I did.

You can find the exemptions Mr. Marmaduke wrote of in the Department of Labor WH Publication 1363, Executive, Administrative, Professional and Outside Sales Exemptions Under the Fair Labor Standards Act. This document states that employees' exemptions depend on two factors: "(1) their duties and responsibilities, and (2) (except in the case of doctors, lawyers, teachers, and outside sales people) the salary paid." The document then lists the "tests" for the different categories and states that "all the tests must be met." The last test in each category is the salary test. For example, the Executive exemption depends on the employee being paid "on a salary basis at a rate of at least $155 a week...." In other words, if an employee is paid hourly, it doesn't matter what his other duties are, he is nonexempt.

continues

continued

The law also provides "special provisos" that effectively bypass the tests. The proviso Mr. Marmaduke describes applies only to Executives, and also requires that the employee must be "regularly directing the work of two or more other employees," a requirement that excludes most contractors. However, there are also special provisos for Administrative and Professional employees, provisos that are less restrictive than the Executive proviso. But if you refer to the text of the regulations (see Regulations, Part 541: Defining the Terms "Executive," "Administrative," "Professional," and "Outside Salesman," WH Publication 1281), you find that in each case the proviso specifies that the employee must be paid on a "salary or fee basis," which leaves us just where we started from.

In his letter Mr. Marmaduke stated that "an agency which offers salaries on a prorated hourly basis in lieu of wages may thus escape overtime [rates]," suggesting that if an employee is exempt the employer may pay an hourly rate. This is the wrong way around, though, as the method of payment is one of the determining factors for exemption status. Thus, an employer cannot say, "I don't have to pay overtime on your hourly rate because you are exempt," because there is, by definition, no such thing as an exempt employee paid an hourly rate. Most contractors receive an hourly rate without the agency calling it a salary, so most contractors do not fit the special provisos that Mr. Marmaduke is relying on.

So the only real ambiguity arises when an agency tells the employee they pay a salary, and then pays what appears to be an hourly rate. Because an exempt employee must be paid a salary, the question hinges on what you call a salary. What I call a pseudosalary, and Mr. Marmaduke calls a "salary on a prorated hourly basis in lieu of wages," may or may not be a genuine salary. If it is a real salary, the contractor, if he meets the other requirements, may be exempt, and not eligible for the higher overtime rate. If it is not a salary, the contractor cannot be exempt.

In my "Overtime" article I wrote that the pseudosalary I had received was "probably not" a real salary. I believe it was not a salary. Why? Because it operated like an hourly rate. Being told it was a salary by my employer didn't make it so, any more than being told a duck is a dog changes the animal's species—if it walks like a duck and quacks like a duck, it probably isn't a dog.

However, I'm not a lawyer. There could be occasions when a duck may be legally defined as a dog, in the same way that South Africa occasionally confers the title of "Honorary White" upon blacks. Also, there may be some loopholes that agencies can crawl through.

For example, let's say you receive one of these pseudosalaries, and one week you work only thirty-two hours because the client closed the office. The company you work for pays you the full forty hours, but subtracts eight hours from your vacation pay. Because no law states that an employer must provide vacations, this pseudo-salary is still a real salary. What happens if you miss work once you have used all your vacation? If your employer pays you less than the normal forty hours, they have probably stepped over the boundary into an hourly rate. (If you receive a salary there are two types of lost time: time your employer must pay for—such as when you are available for work but your employer is unable to provide work for you—and time that the employer does not have to pay for. I'm assuming in these examples that the lost time is of the first kind.)

Another thing to consider is what the agency does if you are between contracts. Agencies that pay pseudosalaries usually claim that you are their "employee" in all senses of the word, and that they simply hire your services out to various clients. In other words, the relationship should continue from client to client. I would think that if the agency dumps you when you come to the end of a contract the agency has again stepped over the boundary into an hourly rate. However, it may count in the agency's favor if it continues paying you for forty hours a week even when it has no client for you. The agency I worked for did just that. While I worked for them several people were between jobs for long periods of time, a few months in some cases, I believe. I have no idea what bearing this would have on the employees who were never between jobs, employees who worked for a long time with just one client, or went directly from one to the other. I worked for the agency for only six months, and when I ended the first contract, they had an immediate contract lined up for me (I left the day my first contract ended). Does this mean the agency had paid me an hourly rate while I worked for them, or was I paid a salary because other people were paid while not working? I imagine each employee's case would be examined separately, but I don't know for sure.

I think that most pseudosalaries would not stand up to close scrutiny, loopholes not with-standing. What happens if you work a lot of overtime, for example? The agency normally pays you for the extra time, at "straight time" rates, right? But if you receive a salary you would not automatically receive extra pay for overtime—isn't that one of the reasons you gave up "captive" work in the first place?

By the way, any of you who wish to dig further into this quagmire should refer to the following documents, besides the ones I mentioned earlier: Employment Relationship Under the Fair Labor Standards Act, WH Publication 1297, and Overtime Compensation Under the Fair Labor Standards Act, WH Publication 1325. If you call the Department of Labor, ask for the Wage and Hour Division.

What Should You Do?

Should you turn down a contract that doesn't pay time-and-a-half for overtime? No, at least not for that reason. You should consider the rate and how much overtime you are likely to work, calculate the weekly income, and compare that with other con-tracts. After all, time-and-a-half for overtime may not be worth much if the base rate is low and you're not going to do any overtime.

Since I wrote these articles the law has changed slightly: Programmers and systems analysts are no longer nonexempt employees if their hourly pay is over six times the minimum wage. This change was made with Public Law 101-583 (11/15/91). Section 2 states that the law applies to "computer systems analysts, computer pro-grammers, software engineers, and other similarly skilled professional workers." This is rather ambiguous. Are technical writers "similarly skilled professional workers"? Some might say yes (though most programmers I know would scoff at the idea!). However, at the time of writing, the Department of Labor regulations make it quite clear that these regulations do not apply to technical writers, although the regulations could change (see page 8,250 in Volume 56, issue 39, of the Federal Register [dated February 27, 1991]).

Part III

Step Two: Cut Out the Middleman

Preparing for

Step Two

If we had had more time for discussion we should probably have made a great many more mistakes.

Leon Trotsky (1879–1940)

You've finally found a good contract. You are earning considerably more than you used to earn, but you know what? You don't feel much different from the way you used to. You still come in to work each day, work 8 or 10 hours, then go home. It all feels much the same as being a permanent employee—until payday, that is.

So where do you go from here? There is no rush, of course. You are already making good money, but probably not as good as you could make. It's funny, but when you first get a contract, you're amazed how good the money is. Then, after you get used to it, you start thinking, "Well, maybe I can get $28 an hour." Perhaps you find another agency contract and you do manage to increase your rate a dollar or two, so you are making $28 or $29 an hour. That feels great until, a month or two down the road, you start thinking, "I know people making $32 an hour. I ought to start looking for more money." And $32 an hour does feel good, but after a while you start thinking it's not so much, and wondering whether you can increase the rate a bit. I know this happened to me, and I've learned from talking with other contractors that most go through the same "ratcheting up" process.

I suppose it's the very nature of contracting that encourages these thoughts. The contractor is a mercenary with no "company loyalty," no hopes for a vice-presidency or a gold watch upon retirement. So what is left? Money. While the permanent employee knows his salary is severely restricted, the contractor is playing a game in which pay is the prize. Every six or twelve months the contractor throws the die again to see how much he can make.

One contractor friend of mine had four contracts in one year, and each time he moved, his rate went up. This isn't always possible to do, and it helps if you have experience and a good reputation. One way to make more money, however, is to cut out the middleman, to move to Step Two (see "The Three-Step Method of Freelancing" in Chapter 4) and find your contracts yourself, without the aid of an agency.

129

Unfortunately, finding work without the agencies is more difficult. The agencies have full-time salespeople who know hundreds of companies in your city. Those companies often call the agency looking for contractors. Furthermore, many companies will not do business with independents. Some have a large staff of contractors and would rather let an agency handle all the paperwork and just present the agency with one bill every couple of weeks. Others want to avoid the problems posed by the Internal Revenue Service (see Chapter 19). So you have to put more effort into finding independent contracts. On the other hand, you will sometimes run into companies that prefer not to do business with agencies, perhaps because they have had problems with them in the past.

How do you begin? The chapters in this part of the book describe what you need to do. It's quite simple, just a matter of building your reputation and network and knowing how to look for contracts. The salespeople in the agencies do it, so you can, too. It may take six months or a couple of years to prepare for Step Two (it took me one year from getting my first agency contract to finding an independent contract), but you can begin the process as soon as you start your first contract. There are two main things you must do to prepare yourself.

Build Your Business Capital

The first thing is to begin saving money. I know it's nice to have all that extra cash; if suddenly you go from earning $30,000 to making $50,000, it's tempting to start living a $50,000 lifestyle. But the extra $20,000 is not profit; you are in business, remember, and should earmark a portion of that extra money for "business expansion," to allow you to move on to the next phase of your business. Of course, you can spend a bit more than you used to—taking a longer vacation, or going out to a good restaurant a bit more often. But don't make the mistake that most contractors seem to make.

Contractors get carried away with all the money. But if you don't save enough money to live on for a few months, you are going to hurt yourself in a couple of ways. You are going to make it difficult to move on to Step Two, in which you can make considerably more money, and you can end up in a position in which you have to take a low-paying contract because you don't have the time (that is, the money) to find a better one.

Why do I say you need to save a few months' living expenses? It is not just because you may be out of work for a few months—you may be, I suppose, although many contractors are rarely out of work for more than a week or two—but for psychological reasons. If it takes two weeks to find a contract, it's no good having four weeks' living expenses (two weeks while you look for a contract and two weeks waiting for the first paycheck). After all, you don't know how long it will take to get a contract until you finally sign one. What happens if you are offered a mediocre contract after one week of looking? Do you wait, or do you think, "I'm going to be in real financial trouble if I don't get work within a week," and take the offered contract? I have seen contractors in this position before. I have one friend working for $22 an hour, when he could easily get $28 an hour—all because he didn't save.

If you do save, you have more confidence. You don't think about financial trouble if you know you can last three or six months if you need to. Not that you want or expect to wait that long, but knowing you can reduces the psychological pressure.

You need money to move on to Step Two. In Step Two you are running a business. You will have to invoice the client and then wait for the client's accounting department to pay. On my first independent contract it took six weeks from my first day at work to depositing my first check in the bank. But it's not uncommon for companies to take 60 or even 90 days to pay invoices, even if the terms are actually net 30. Don't let me frighten you, though. You should be prepared for such late payments, but don't expect them. Most of my clients have paid much more quickly. In fact I wouldn't normally allow a client to go that long without paying. The only reason I did was because this was a giant telecommunications company, and it took a long time for the paperwork to grind its way through the bureaucracy (and I was pretty certain that I'd get the money). Usually I make sure I get paid reasonably quickly and on time, so my clients are never too far behind in their payments. Most clients, I've found, will try to get the money to you as soon as they can, if you ask.

When I got that contract, I went straight from an agency contract to the independent contract with only the weekend off between. Imagine if it had taken two or three weeks to find a contract—eight or nine weeks without an income. That is why you must save money. If you don't save, you will be unable to take independent contracts, or be in financial trouble if you do.

Educate Yourself

The other major preparation for Step Two is to educate yourself. Talk to people about the contract market, about who hires contractors and what they pay. Talk about what the other contractors make and what the range of contract rates is in your profession. Working through agencies can help you educate yourself, because more often than not you are thrown in with other contractors. Draw on their experience and learn from their knowledge of the local market. Join their little network groups, which are often nothing more than several contractors who get together for lunch every few weeks. Ask about local professional societies and associations.

Most important, keep records. Keep a card file with the names and telephone numbers of the people you meet—contractors, noncontractor colleagues, and employers. When you go on job interviews through agencies, keep business cards. You will build up a file of names of people you know and people you don't—a list of names that can help you find a contract when you need one.

Read On

Continue reading this book! In the next few chapters you'll learn more about finding independent contracts. You can start using these techniques before you ever leave your agency contract. So after you've got the money saved, after you know the rates in your area, get started on your road to independence.

16

Networking

> Eighty percent of success is turning up.
>
> Woody Allen

Networking. The very word frightens many people. They think of endless hours at seminars and association "events," forcing themselves to smile at people they don't know or even want to know. They think of pushing themselves upon strangers, asking for business cards and going into long explanations of what they do and why the stranger should consider hiring them, or tell a friend to hire them, or tell a friend to tell a friend . . .

Many people think of networking as "using" people, and in a way it is. But it doesn't have to be calculating or dishonest. My friends use me when they are looking for work, and I use them when I am looking. I don't socialize with people I don't like, so the people I go for lunch with or have a beer with after work are not being used; I would be there even if they were of no "use" to me.

This is one of the great misunderstandings about networking, that you have to socialize with people you don't like so that you can get something from them. I regard networking differently: As you naturally form friendships with people you work with, why not use each other's knowledge to help each other?

Networking doesn't have to be hard. To me networking is having lunch with a group of friends—friends who also happen to know what is going on in the job market. There are certain networking techniques that you may not want to try, but that doesn't mean you can't build a network. If you are a normal, sociable human being, you can build a network just by making friends.

First, though, what is it you want from your network?

The Information You Need

There are several things you need a network for, and looking for an immediate contract is only one of them. You want to get a "feel" for your market. You want to know names of companies, other freelancers, and managers. You want to know which companies are hiring, which are laying off, who pays well, and who doesn't. Keep a card file, or a database on your computer, and add this information periodically.

133

You want to know how much money people make. This is often a sensitive question, especially with people you don't know very well. Make the effort to get this information, nevertheless. Ask friends; no one I've asked has seemed to take offense, and friends often volunteer the information, especially if you reciprocate. If you are not quite sure whether you know someone well enough to ask, ask anyway. Remember, *Who fears to ask, doth teach to be denied.* In other words, if you are too modest to find this information, you will be denied the best rates.

Finding out how much money people are making tells you a few things. It tells you what your potential is—if you know less qualified people than you making 20 percent *more* than you, figure you can make at least 20 or 30 percent more than you are making now. You can also get an overview of the market. What is a good rate or an average rate? You can't tell if you know only how much you make, or what one or two other people make.

You also will find out which companies pay the best rates, and will know how much to ask a company for if it offers you a contract. For example, I know of companies that simply don't pay more than $25 per hour for technical writers, but I also know of companies that will pay $37 or $38.

You also want to know what companies are like: which ones are fun to work for, which ones take a long time to pay (or never pay), which ones are likely to be hiring soon, and which ones are in financial difficulty.

The information you need is anything that will help you find work and get a good rate. You may not need work now, but you still need your network, because you can't build a network in a short time, and you can't learn all you need to know about the market in just a few weeks.

Building a Network

This section presents a few tips for building a network. Use the ones you like, and discard the ones you don't.

Make a List

Start by making a list of all the technical writers you know. Then add all the programmers you know, all the department heads you know, all the electrical engineers, and so on. Add anyone to the list who may be able to give you leads about possible contracts.

Keep a Card File

Keep a card file that includes a card for everyone you work with, either in your profession or in related jobs. Include anyone who may have information that could be useful to you. Note the name, telephone number, company, and position, and any other relevant information, or staple a business card to the file card. Better still, use a computer database to store all this information.

Keep in Contact with Other Writers

You're going to be working with scores of writers, perhaps hundreds, if you spend much time as a freelancer. At every company you work with, make sure you add all the writers to your card file or database. Don't forget the department heads, programmers, engineers, and anyone else who might be useful to call when you're looking for work later.

Keep in Contact with "Key" People

You will find contractors who seem to know what is going on just about everywhere. They have networks that keep them informed of new contracts, of companies that may need people soon, of contractors who are about to quit (even though the client doesn't yet know it), of companies that may hire people but are just as likely to cancel the contract early, and so on. Contacting one of these key people is like being invited into an instant network.

Stay Friendly with Some of the Agencies

Even though I try to avoid working through agencies, I still have a few friends in agencies who feed me information—not necessarily information that will get me a contract immediately, but information about companies and other agencies that may provide good background data.

Keep Company Telephone Directories When You Leave a Contract

Many large companies have internal telephone directories. These can be very useful when you are looking for work later. You may be able to call department managers or other writers working there.

Put a Card in Your Card File for Every Company That Interviews You

Each time you interview with a potential client, keep information in your card file or computer database. Staple a business card to the file card. Note how the interview went. Keep this information even when an agency set up the interview. The information could still become useful later. A couple of companies that originally interviewed me through agencies later offered me work. This is advice that I didn't use early enough; I didn't keep records of interviews, so I lost a lot of good information.

Join Professional Associations

Professional organizations provide another way to enter instant networks. For example, the Dallas chapter of the Society for Technical Communication (STC) has over 300 members, all people in companies that use technical writers, an excellent source of contacts. In Boulder the Boulder Writers Alliance has almost 200 members, many of them technical and business writers. These professional organizations are all over the place. Ask colleagues if they know of any. Take a look in local newspapers—for instance, local computer papers often list local events, including meetings of groups, technical writers' groups, Internet consultant groups, computer-consultant groups, and so on.

In his book *The Consultant's Kit*, Dr. Jeffrey Lant suggests that you attend professional association meetings and "go to the bar to meet people. Invest some money in buying drinks for people." You don't need to be so calculating about it; just go to meetings and make friends.

Even If You Are Not a Member of a Local Association, See If You Can Get Hold of the Membership List

Many organizations publish directories or membership lists. Some even mail the lists to local companies to help them find skilled people. They may even put the directory on the World Wide Web, as the Boulder Writer's Alliance has. These lists can help you when you are contract-hunting.

Find Out Which Companies Are Associate Members of Local Associations

Some professional organizations have associate or corporate members. For instance, many STC chapters have corporate members who sponsor various events—in other words, they give the society money. These companies are potential clients.

Go on Job Interviews Even If You Don't Need Work

Jeffrey Lant also suggests going on interviews for captive positions and not revealing that you are a contractor, so that you can find out about the company and make contacts. This may be a good idea in some circumstances, but don't do it indiscriminately.

Find the Local "Job Banks"

The STC has job banks in most large cities, and other associations do also. The leads may be for captive employment, for independent contracts, or for agency contracts. Try to get all the leads; some job banks will try to screen people, so that you get only the leads that they think are suitable for you. There are a couple of problems with that: Even if a company tells the job bank its list of criteria, it may settle for less if it can't find the right person, or it may settle for slightly less experience in the specified area if the person has more experience in a related area. And just because you don't fit the criteria doesn't mean that the company hasn't got other positions better suited to you, or will not have soon.

See Chapter 24, which discusses working online. These days there are many job leads online. Many organizations even have e-mail mailing lists; get yourself onto these lists and you'll have job leads sent directly to your computer every day!

Check Your Local Paper's Classified Ads

Look at your paper's classified ads. You'll find ads from companies looking for full-time technical writers now and again. Very occasionally you'll find ads from companies looking for freelance writers (you'll often see ads from agencies, but you're not interested in those right now).

The companies may be looking only for captives, but it doesn't matter—they may not be able to find a captive, and at least you have the name of a company that may need freelancers one day. I used to collect ads from companies looking for technical writers, so that when I was looking for work I knew who to call. The ads sometimes even have names of the people who handle the hiring, which can save you a lot of time when you are trying to get through to a company.

You may want to send a résumé and business card, with a cover letter explaining that you are a freelancer, to all the companies advertising for your profession. Some companies keep these résumés on file for later use. It's a simple way to build "name recognition." If one of these companies is looking for a contractor at some point in the future and again receives your résumé, your name may appear familiar, and your résumé has a better chance of getting read. By the way, you'll *always* find ads from companies who *use* technical writers, even if those ads don't say so. For instance, you'll find ads for computer programmers and electrical engineers. These companies must be producing something that needs documenting! Keep these ads, too.

Go to Job Fairs

You can hand out your résumé at job fairs. Include a business card, and a cover letter explaining that you are a freelancer. Most companies keep résumés on file, and although companies at job fairs are usually looking for captives, who knows what their needs will be in the future? Chat with people at the job fair. Tell them you are a freelance writer, and that you are wondering if they need any help now, or if they might in the future.

I met one good client at a job fair. He told me to call in a few weeks, which I did. He then kept putting me off for several months; he had nothing yet, he'd say, but try again next month. Eventually I did over $20,000 worth of business with this client.

Talk to People in Your Network About Their Job Interviews

When your friends and colleagues go on interviews, make a point of doing a "debriefing." Ask them which company they visited, and with whom they spoke. Ask what the interviewing company was looking for, and how much it was offering. Then save this information in your card file or computer database.

Get to Know the Personnel Recruiters

When you work at a company, make a point of talking with the personnel recruiters. Keep their names and numbers. They often know which companies are looking for what. One personnel recruiter even gave me a list of recruiters at dozens of local high-tech companies. When you are looking for work, call these people.

Business Lunches Are a Great Way to Meet People in Your Profession

I occasionally go for lunch with friends I met while working on previous contracts. As we all move from contract to contract, we meet different people, expanding our network as we go. We invite new friends to lunch, and introduce them to the other members of the network. This is beneficial to all of us, both new and old members of the network. We learn about new contracts coming up, rates, and all the rest of the information we need to know to keep up on the market.

Have Parties

As a freelancer you can introduce friends to each other, people in the same profession working in different companies. Why not invite friends you have met at different contracts to a party? Not only is it fun to have parties with new people (instead of the same old crowd), but you are doing your friends a favor. (It's also tax deductible!)

Keep in Touch with People

If you move, send change of address notes to companies and friends. I made the mistake of not doing this when I moved, and lost a contract; a company was ready to hire me—but didn't know where I was! Even if you don't move, you might want to do what many salespeople do: send notes or cards to potential clients now and again, to make sure they don't forget you.

Get to Know Other People in the Company You Are Working for

Other departments also may hire people in your line of work, so get to know other department managers. Big companies, especially, often have many departments that need your skills, but the departments have little or no communication among each other. Make a point of seeking out the department heads, explaining that you are working for another department of the same company, and chatting for a while. Get their business cards, and add them to your card file or database.

Save Business Cards

I usually forget to carry my business cards, and rarely give them out, which I'll admit is a mistake. However, as far as business cards go, it is more important to *receive* than to give! Most cards you give away will be lost or trashed within a day or two (that's no reason not to give them, though, because now and again they will be saved—and maybe used one day). On the other hand, you should save the cards you receive. Those cards are an important part of your network, and you shouldn't waste them.

Help People

It's important to help people. (If this comes naturally to you, that's fine; if not, make an effort!) When friends are looking for work I do all I can to help them. I give them the names of people looking for freelancers and information about companies that may be hiring soon. When I was working with the agencies, I used to share my list of technical service agencies so that my friends could mail résumés to the agencies. I don't do this because I expect anything in return. However, I know that because I have helped my friends, they are apt to go out of their way to help me when I'm looking for a contract.

You should even help the technical service agencies. If an agency calls you when you don't need work, don't just hang up. Ask about the job—how much the agency is paying, where the job is, what type of job it is, even the company name (although the agency may not tell you any of this information). This is all good information, of course, but you also should try to find someone to fill the slot. Don't spend too much time on this, but if you know people who are looking or may want to move to a new contract, tell them to call the agency, and ask them to mention your name.

One of my technical-writing friends always helps the agencies. He pulls out his little book of addresses and goes through it looking for the names of people who may be interested. As a result, he gets a lot of calls from agencies looking for contractors, and agencies throughout Dallas know him, something that can come in handy when he is looking for work. The person getting the job is grateful also, and will undoubtedly help him the next time he is looking for a contract.

Remember, helping other people find work is just as much part of your own job search as asking others to help you.

Remember—Keep Records!

Make sure you keep records of all your contacts. You never know when you'll need them. Either keep a card file or a computer database. Record the contact information for every writer you know, every potential client you've ever spoken with, every company asking for technical writers—or related professions—in the classified ads. Keep company phone books and professional-organization directories. With all this information, you'll have a powerful way to find work when you need it.

You'll be collecting a lot of useless information, of course—useless in the sense that most of it will never lead to a job. Only a small fraction of your information will help you find contracts, but the problem is you don't know *which* pieces are the good pieces; if you did, you wouldn't need a network. You don't know where the important information is going to come from, so the more of these methods you use the better.

Salespeople understand that you have to make a lot of contacts to make a sale. Most of those contacts are useless. Most will not lead to a sale. But the salesperson doesn't know which contact will buy, so he or she has to contact 10, 20, or 50 people for each sale. You should remember that you are a salesperson, selling your own skills and services.

You can think of networking as boring and tedious, but I think of it as a kind of game. It's fun to gossip about what's going on in the market, and it's amusing to see people's faces when you give them the inside scoop on a company they have applied to. It helps if you *enjoy* gossiping, of course—most people do—because that is what networking is all about.

Skip to Step Three

If you follow all the advice I've given you, you may soon find yourself offered work that you can do at home, work that you can, perhaps, make a "per-project" bid on rather than a per-hour bid. In effect you've skipped through Step Two all the way to Step Three (see "The Three-Step Method of Freelancing" in Chapter 4). Many writers seem to fluctuate between Step Two and Step Three: one contract is an onsite contract, by the hour; the next couple are per-project contracts at home; the next is onsite, while they do a couple of small contracts at home; and so on.

In fact, I made up this Three-Step program as a simple concept that I could use to explain the process of freelancing. The real world is more complicated, of course, and you may find that you are never in a Step Two situation. You do a few agency contracts, then find a Step Three-type contract, and never work onsite on a contract that you've found without the assistance of the agencies. (I only worked two onsite contracts that I found for myself. During the second contract I found another one that I could do at home in the evenings and—when the onsite contract ended—full time.)

So understand that there's a lot in common between Steps Two and Three. Many of the marketing methods are the same. The only real difference is the type of work you end up with. A Step Two-type contract is just like an agency contract, only without the agency. You'll be working at the client's site, quite likely with a team of other writers, and be paid by the hour. A Step Three-type contract is a little different. You'll be working at home most of the time (maybe you'll visit the client's offices once or twice a week). You may be billing by the project instead of by the hour (we'll discuss that in Chapter 21). And you'll probably be working on a single project by yourself (doing a complete manual, for instance, rather than a chapter or two). You may even be subcontracting work.

Looking for Work

It's true hard work never killed anybody, but I figure, why take the chance?

Ronald Reagan

So, you're ready to look for an independent contract. You have money in the bank, and you've built a good network. How are you going to start? This chapter describes a number of ways to search for work. I suggest you start at the top and work your way down the list. With luck and a good economy, you may not get too far down the list before you find a contract. If you are working on an agency contract now, try beginning your job search about six weeks before the contract finishes, which should give you enough time to find a new one. Of course, if you are actively networking, you may run across a contract offer even before you start looking for work in earnest.

You are searching for leads, information that will lead you to a job. When you find a lead, act on it immediately, before moving to the next step in the list or the next person in your card file. There is nothing more frustrating than hearing a prospective client tell you that you have just missed an opportunity.

When you talk to a prospective client, don't just ask if the client is looking for someone with your skills, but also ask if the client knows of anyone else who may be hiring, or if someone else in the company also hires people in your profession. Note as many names and numbers as possible, and add them to your card file or database. *Don't* forget to ask these questions. You can use this method to multiply your leads dramatically, one lead bringing one or two other leads, just as a professional salesperson does.

After speaking with a prospective client, send a résumé and a thank-you letter, and a business card if you have one. Even if you don't have a chance of being hired right now, the résumé will help the client remember you in the future, and the client may even keep the résumé on file.

The Steps to Your Next Contract

Here, then, are a series of steps you can use to find your next contract. These steps are in the order that you should use them, more or less. The best job-finding methods are near the top of the list, and the least productive (and most unpleasant) are near the bottom of the list.

1. Call the "key" people in your network, the people who seem to know what is going on everywhere. Each of these people can often give you several good leads.

2. Call the professional societies' job banks and ask who is hiring. In many cases, these job banks are recordings. If you get through to a real person, though, ask for *all* the job listings. Don't just ask about contract work, for instance; often companies looking for permanent employees may not be able to find anyone suitable to take the job, or may be hiring contractors as well. And don't let that person "filter" you by asking you questions and giving you only the "appropriate" listings. What the job-bank person thinks is appropriate and what you think is appropriate may be completely different.

3. Check the newspaper classified ads for companies looking for your skills. Don't just check with the ones advertising for contractors, but even those looking for "captives." Call these companies even if the ads tell you not to; you can tell them that a friend told you about the job and that you haven't seen the classified ad. Even if the company address is a post office box, you may be able to track it down. Your library should have a "reverse" telephone directory that allows you to look up an address to find a telephone number; some of these directories also list post office boxes and whom they belong to. (Of course, if the company recently rented the box, or rents a box from the newspaper, you won't be able to find out who it is.)

4. If you are working on a contract, ask your client if any other departments in the company hire contractors. You may be able to transfer to another department. (Remember that if you are working through an agency, the contract you signed—and the one signed by the client—may stop you from working for the client without the permission of the agency. This clause may not be legally enforceable in some states, but may be enough to scare off the client.)

5. Call people in your network: friends, colleagues, people you worked with some time ago, and so on.

6. If you have an Internet account go online and check job listings. Subscribe to job-bank mailing lists, too; many local writer's and consultant's groups have online mailing lists that distribute job leads to members. Immediately follow up on leads you find. (See Chapter 24.)

7. Try "advertising" your services on computer bulletin boards and online services. Again, see Chapter 24.

8. Call companies you have worked for in the past, and people for whom you have "almost" worked (people who have interviewed you or offered you work in the past). These people already know you, so if they are looking for someone, they can save themselves a lot of time and trouble by hiring you. If the person who hired you has left the company, try to find out where he or she has gone; your contact may have transferred to a managerial position at another company.

9. Use the lists of writers you've found. The Society for Technical Communication (STC) publishes a list of all its members, and many local chapters also publish smaller lists. Many other professional societies publish lists, too. Call *everyone*

on the list. (I'll discuss calling people you don't know in the next section, "Not-So-Cold Calling.")

10. Go to the local job fairs, talk to employers, and spread a few résumés around, with cover letters and business cards, explaining that you are a contractor.

11. Go through the classified ads you have collected in the past and call the companies that were hiring writers or "associated" professions (programmers, engineers, and so on). They may have something available soon.

12. Go through your card file or database and call the rest of the people in it—people you may not know well, or at all, but whose names you've added while networking.

13. Look for lists of companies that can use your services. This is very easy to do. Go to your library and ask the librarian for help. You should be able to find a directory that will list all the companies in your area. Your library may have Microcosm, which is a microfiche directory, or the Business Index, which is on a rotary microfiche machine. (One advantage to Microcosm is that you can use a microfiche copier to copy pages; with the Business Index, you need to write down the names and addresses.) In many regions, local publishers issue directories of high-tech companies, a great source of leads. You'll find loads of other business directories, too. Just spend a little time digging around in the library.

You use these directories to pick the companies by zip code, name, size, and so on, to limit the search to the most likely candidates. Note the company name, phone number, and officers' names if included (many of the lists include the president's, vice-president's, and treasurer's names, which may be useful for smaller companies). You also could use the Yellow Pages to find company names, just calling every company in a likely category, one by one. You will get a lot of companies that are not likely to be good prospects, but on the other hand you will save a lot of time in research.

Next, call all the companies you've found. The section "Slightly Colder Calling," later in this chapter, discusses this process.

Not-So-Cold Calling

You'll spend a lot of time on the phone looking for work. In many cases you'll be calling friends and colleagues, which should be relatively easy. The only problem you may find is that it takes you a lot of time to make your calls, because you end up chatting with people you haven't spoken to for a while.

But other calls fall into the "cold calling" category. Cold calling is phoning someone you've never spoken with and asking for something. Most people find "cold-calling" distasteful, if not downright uncomfortable, but it isn't so bad. It's not as if you are calling people to sell aluminum siding or encyclopedias—the type of telephone work that leads to incredible rejection rates. No, you're not selling anything, and in most cases you won't be calling anyone at home; even the STC listings and other professional society listings contain mostly work numbers.

You'll find that few, if any, of the people you call will be rude. In fact you may be surprised to find just how helpful people are likely to be. When you are calling another writer you've found in an association list, for instance, simply introduce yourself, explain that you're a fellow technical writer, that you found the person's name in the association's list, and ask whether he or she has a moment to speak. Most people will say yes—after all, what would you do? There is no threat from this fellow association member, so it's only natural that you would take a moment to talk.

You can then explain that you are a contractor looking for work, and ask whether your contact knows of any companies looking for contractors right now. You may get a lead right away, but even if you do, keep asking questions—don't stop at the first lead. Does this person know of any companies looking for permanent employees? Will your contact's company require someone soon, contract or permanent? Are there people in other companies who you could call and ask? (Remember to add these names and numbers to your list.)

The response you receive will probably be very favorable. People enjoy talking to others in their profession, and people especially enjoy finding a reason not to work for a few minutes. People usually enjoy helping others, sometimes because they hope someone will do the same for them someday. Perhaps one or two of the people you talk to will be unfriendly, and you won't get very far with them. You will know from their tone of voice when not to bother asking more questions. Just thank them for their time and go on to the next person in the list (make a note by that person's name not to bother calling next time).

If you talk to enough colleagues, you will get a clear view of what is going on in your market and find dozens of leads. You also will make many useful contacts for the future. And if someone is especially helpful to you, send a thank-you letter, and include a résumé and a business card. By the way, keep on the lookout for new "key contacts." Some of the people you call may have a wealth of information, so these people should move up the list of "people to call" next time you're looking.

Calling companies who are advertising for writers, or who have at some time, is fairly easy, too. After all, they are looking for writers, why wouldn't they want to talk with you? Even if you see an ad that says don't call, you'll find that few people will be upset or rude if you do (just say you were given a lead by a friend, and hadn't seen the ad). You'll sometimes get straight through to the person doing the hiring. And whatever he or she says, the personal contact *does* make a difference.

Slightly Colder Calling

Here's a colder form of calling: calling people you don't know, and who you have no reason to believe are currently looking for technical writers. For instance, if you get all the way down your list of people to contact (down to numbers 11 and 12) and you still haven't found anything, the next step is to call companies that *may* need writers. For instance, I once used a directory of high-tech companies around Denver. I picked one particular area and started calling all the companies, one by one.

Cold calling can actually be quite easy, if you know the tricks. And I'll admit, I do use tricks. You see, if you call and say "I'm a technical writer and I was wondering if you had any work for me," you'll almost certainly be rejected. So here's an easier way to do it. You call and say something like this:

> "Hi, my name's John Smith, and I'm calling because I heard that you might be looking for a technical writer."

Usually you get one of three different responses:

◆ The person you have reached has no idea whether the company needs a writer or not. This is the most likely scenario. However, this person probably won't just say "no, go away." After all, you've *heard* that the company *needs* a writer, you're not just calling on the off chance. So this person will probably ask someone else, and perhaps transfer you to that other person. You're then back at the beginning, asking the same question of this new person.

◆ The person you have reached knows for sure that the company doesn't need a writer—you may have reached the owner of a small company—and that's the end of it.

◆ The person you have reached either *is* looking for a writer, or knows that a writer may be needed at some point. You may be surprised at just how many calls end up in this situation. I don't remember the exact numbers, but when I did my last little cold-calling session, it was probably somewhere between one call in 10 and one in 20.

Now, there's an obvious question you may find your contact asking: "Oh, you heard that we need a writer? Who told you that?" Ah, tricky. What do you say now?

"Well, I don't remember exactly; someone told me at the last STC meeting" (or whatever organization you're a member of).

Usually your contact won't ask much more, though. If the company needs a writer or soon will, talk will soon turn to the upcoming project—and away you go.

Cold calling can be very effective. But if you've done your homework and have created a good network, you probably won't need to do any cold calling. And if you *do* have to try it, you may find that a day, or even a half-day, is enough to find you work.

Why, then, did I cold call? When I first moved to Denver I found work very quickly and easily. Each job seemed to come without any effort, and so I never really created a very strong network—I didn't need one, the work was too easy to find without it. (Also, by this stage in my career, I was working at home, isolated from other writers.) Then, in the summer of 1993, I went on vacation, with the promise of a contract to come back to. After I returned, though, my client told me the project had been canceled—so there I was, with no contract and a weak network. I used the network to the best of my ability, of course, but I'd soon worked my way through the entire thing and got down to the cold-calling stage. But I spent only a short while cold calling; one morning, I think. I got about five or six great leads, one of which turned into a $16,000 contract (which I managed to complete in about 120 hours—you can do the math yourself!) and a couple of others that didn't provide me with contracts directly, but which provided me with leads that later turned into contracts.

"We Only Use Agencies"

Some of the companies you contact will tell you that they work only with agencies, that they will not hire independent contractors. They do this for a variety of reasons, not the least of which is that they don't want trouble with the IRS. Don't give up yet. Tell the client that you are prepared to work through an agency. Explain that if the client interviews you and decides to hire you, you will find an agency acceptable to the client and work through that agency. Explain that you have contacts in several agencies, and that you can easily find a suitable one. (Many companies have a list of agencies that they work with.)

This ploy may not work, but if you have a reputation in your area, or skills or experience that the client is having trouble finding, you may be able to get the company to agree. And if the client does decide to hire you? Negotiate a rate high enough to pay you well and cover an agency's overhead and profit. Go to several agencies and "sell" the contract to them. You should get a high rate, because you are bringing the work to them. All the agency has to do is process the paperwork to make the money. You have already done the most expensive, time-consuming part of the agency's work for it— finding the contract and lining up a contractor.

Of course you need to get your sums right. The rate the client pays must be enough to pay you well, with enough left over for the agency to pay your employment taxes (10 to 15 percent) and give the agency a small profit. Clients are likely to pay a higher rate to an agency than they might pay an independent anyway, because they understand that there are more people taking a bite of the pie. For example, even though $38 per hour is a good technical writing rate for an independent in the Dallas area, companies often pay agencies $42 or $43 an hour. Remember that your cut doesn't need to be as high as a true independent contract rate; assuming you will be paid as an employee of the agency, you will pay less FICA (see Chapter 7), and the agency may have benefits you can use, such as medical insurance.

On the other hand, you will not be able to deduct most of your business expenses, and you won't be able to contribute to a self-employed person's pension plan—a SEP/IRA or a Keogh. You may be able to find an agency that will pay you on a Form 1099, though—that is, the agency pays you without taking out taxes—so you can retain your independent contractor status (but make sure you read Chapter 19 first).

By the way, some writers attempt to get around this problem by incorporating or by simply going under a company name. These strategies may work now and again. While I rarely sell my services using a company name, I have allowed clients to pay me using a company name. However, I don't think this is a good reason to incorporate. I'll go into detail about incorporation in Chapter 23. For now, simply understand that incorporating is a lot of trouble, and won't always get you around this "we only use agencies" problem. You can incorporate, but anyone with half a brain will realize what is going on—that you are just a writer on your own who incorporated to look like an agency. And in any case, when clients say "we only work through agencies," it's not always what they mean. They often work with only a small list of agencies— maybe just two or three agencies. You can incorporate, but that doesn't necessarily get you onto a client's list!

Chapter 22 talks more about how to deal with clients who say they won't hire independents.

Keep Looking

Here are a few more things to consider while looking for work. First, don't count your chickens before they hatch. Don't stop looking for work just because it looks as if you are about to sign a contract, because the contract will often fall through (remember Sam Goldwyn's comment about verbal contracts not being worth "the paper they are printed on"). Whatever you do, don't tell a client you are unavailable for work until you are absolutely sure, until you have begun working on the contract. If you tell someone that you are available and then the other contract comes through, you will have to tell the second contact that you are unavailable. However, that's business. Few companies would be upset, because they know that until a contract is signed, anything can happen; they could also pull out at the last moment (and often will).

Also, don't be discouraged when people don't call you back. It is hard to take rejection, and it's easy to see rejection when it really doesn't exist. You may think you have a contract coming up any day and never hear from the company again. That's not necessarily an indication that the company has decided that you are not good enough for the job. Perhaps your contact at the company has quit or been laid off; perhaps the company has financial problems, or lost a contract that your contract depended on; maybe the department didn't get approval to hire you, or has been told to wait six months, or perhaps the company even lost your phone number! There are thousands of reasons for people not calling back. It would be more polite for them to do so, perhaps, but it's not necessarily a reflection on your skills or reputation. Don't hang around worrying about why they didn't call you, call *them* and inquire about the contract!

Keep moving and keep contacting people. If you use all these methods and there is work to be found, you will find it.

Taxes for the

Freelancer

We don't pay taxes. Only the little people pay taxes.

U.S. hotelier Leona Helmsley

Most freelancers I know are frightened by taxes. They understand next to nothing about how to file their taxes or what deductions they can take, and much of what they think they know is wrong. Taxes are easy to handle, though, if you are willing to invest a few evenings reading a tax guide.

I don't intend the information in this chapter to be a substitute for a good book on taxes (I use J. K. Lasser's *Your Income Tax*, by the way), or for a computer program (I use Personal Tax Edge from Parson's), but it is an overview, a way to give you an idea of what is involved and where to go next. I'm not going to tell you exactly how to fill in every form you may need, but I will discuss the areas of the tax law that affect freelancers. I also assume that you don't have any employees, so I have not covered tax law relating to employee withholding, employee pension plans, and so on. I've also avoided corporate tax. Most freelance writers are not incorporated (and, I believe, don't need to be). For more information about incorporating your business, though, see Chapter 23.

Why bother to do your taxes yourself? Why not hire someone to do them for you? There are several reasons. First, if you hire someone to do them, you have to give that person all your records, in some semblance of order. Record-keeping is 90 percent of the work involved in doing your taxes, however, so you may as well finish off the last 10 percent and save some money. This is especially true if you have your own computer. You can buy very good, inexpensive programs that compute taxes for you, so why not just plug the numbers into the computer and let it do the job?

Another reason not to use tax preparers is that they often don't know what they are doing. You've probably seen newspaper and television reports by journalists who took the same tax records to 10 different tax preparers and got 10 different results. I've also spoken with freelancing friends who have received incorrect information from their accountants. If you want to make sure your taxes are done properly, you will have to do them yourself.

Yet another reason to do your own taxes: If you understand how your taxes are calculated, it's easier to make sensible financial decisions. If you don't know the effect of a decision on your taxes, how can you decide properly? For example, I know people who have bought houses to "save money on their taxes," not realizing how little they were really saving. In some cases you may need to decide whether to invoice a client or wait a few weeks to push the income into next year. If the extra income would push you into a higher tax bracket, you might consider waiting a few weeks to invoice the client and paying a few bills early.

What about all the changes in the tax law, though? Isn't it almost impossible to keep up? Well, the rates change, of course, but the manner in which the tax is calculated mostly remains the same. Most changes occur deep in the tax code, so deep that the average person never sees them. I believe that the complexity of the tax system has been exaggerated for political reasons. For most people taxes are really not particularly complicated, and don't change much.

Note that the tax information in this chapter is for the U.S., and is related to the 1996 tax year. Although the tax laws discussed may change slightly, this chapter will still give you an idea of how to file your taxes. For more up-to-date information, refer to a current tax guide or to Internal Revenue Service (IRS) publications.

I'm going to begin by discussing certain controversial aspects of the tax law. I suggest you read the tax information booklets I mention for more information.

Is Mileage Deductible?

Some freelancers believe that they can deduct a certain sum from their taxes for each mile that they drive while on business. This belief is quite correct, of course; in 1996, you could deduct 31 cents for each mile driven, or deduct a portion of the actual vehicle costs (gas, insurance, maintenance, and so on). The real question is, *what is business-related mileage?* Most freelancers seem to think that driving to work is business-related mileage. After all, they are freelancers, they say, so they are in business for themselves (even many freelancers who are, strictly speaking, technical-service agency employees use this reasoning). Some agencies even pay mileage as an extra benefit. For example, if the contractor drives 35 miles to the client's office and back each day, the agency might pay the contractor $10.85 (35 miles times 31 cents). Some agencies regard this amount as a business expense, so taxes are not normally withheld.

Some contractors that also maintain an office at home reason that driving to work is not commuting, but rather traveling from one business location to another. If a contractor works mainly at a client's office, however, the IRS is unlikely to accept such an argument. As J. K. Lasser's *Your Income Tax* puts it, if a home office is not "your principal place of business or a place in which patients, clients, or customers meet or deal with you in the normal course of your profession or business," then it is not a valid office.

Driving to work and back is a "commuting expense," the IRS says, and so it is not deductible. If an agency pays an extra sum based on the commuting mileage, that sum is ordinary income and is itself taxable. What then is the difference between commuting and business-related driving?

The answer is very simple. We all know what commuting is: traveling to work each day. It doesn't matter if you are a captive employee or a freelancer with several different contracts during a year, commuting is commuting. If you work in the same office for several months and travel to and from that same office each day, the IRS regards that as commuting. The IRS states: "You cannot deduct the costs of driving a car between your home and your main or regular place of work, (even if) you are employed at different locations on different days within the same city or general area." Now, if you were to drive to an agency office, pick up an assignment for the day, then drive to that other location, the drive from the agency to the location is a valid business expense. This is rare in the technical service industry; more commonly, you work at the same location for months or even years.

I've been told that some agencies falsify records, to make it look as if the contractors come into the agency office each day before going out on assignment; the agency can then deduct the mileage rate paid to the contractor as a business expense rather than as salary (if it is salary, the agency should withhold taxes and pay its portion of the taxes as well). Some independent contractors claim that because they have a home office, any driving they do is deductible. One contractor told me that if the IRS audits him, he will say that he goes into his office each morning before driving to work. I don't believe the IRS would accept that; all an IRS auditor has to do is examine his invoices or interview his clients to find that he works in the client's office almost every day, for at least eight hours. In such a case the IRS may disallow the home office because it is not his "regular place of business."

The IRS allows deductions for only these types of commuting:

◆ If you are out of town on a business trip. I discuss what constitutes a business trip later in this chapter.

◆ If you use your car to carry tools. However, the IRS lets you deduct only the expense directly related to carrying the tools. For example, if you didn't need your tools, you could pay to take public transportation. Because you need tools, you have to drive your pickup and incur $3 mileage expense a day. The extra $2 is then deductible. In any case, this is a rare situation for technical writers!

◆ If you commute to a temporary job location that is outside the area in which you normally work, or if the location's within the area in which you normally work but you have another primary place of work. If you work for a company on contract for six months, at the client office, then the office is your principal place of work. If the client wants you to work in another city for a few days, the commuting expense is deductible.

The situation is different if you work at home or in your own office and occasionally visit the client. If your home office is *truly* your principal place of business, then a trip to the client once a week is a justifiable business expense.

Per Diems and Business Travel Expenses

Many agencies pay a *per diem*, usually to road-shoppers, contractors who travel from other areas of the country to take a contract. *Per diem* means per day, of course, but as I've mentioned elsewhere, the technical-service industry doesn't seem to know that. If an agency quotes you a rate and then tells you that it will also pay a $150 per diem, don't get excited; they mean $150 per week, not per day.

Anyway, most contractors assume the per diem is a nontaxable reimbursement for travel expenses, but most contractors are wrong. While there are some situations in which this may be true, usually the per diem is taxable income.

One contractor once stated that "when one is working on the road, away from one's home overnight, expenses may be deductible." The writer didn't explain exactly what he meant by "away from home overnight," but if he meant that when someone travels to another town on business and stays overnight (or even a day or two), then the expenses are deductible. But if he was referring to the road-shopper, the contractor who usually jumps from location to location and has no regular workplace, then the commuting is not deductible. The following comes from my response, published in *PD News*.

Most of this talk about how to deduct expenses and report per diem is irrelevant. Most contractors working away from what they regard as their home are probably not eligible to deduct travel and living expenses. Even if they receive a per diem, it should be reported as taxable income. Why? Because usually the IRS will regard where you work as your tax home. I don't believe most contractors' work situations fit the criteria laid down by the IRS for claiming living expenses.

The IRS intended travel and lodging expenses to be deductible for people temporarily out of town, away from their "home." So the question comes down to, "where is your home, and are you away from it?" Most "temporary" stays are a few days or weeks, but could be as long as two years (if, for example, a company you work for asks you to work temporarily in a subsidiary in another town). However, most contractors are not in this position. As J. K. Lasser's *Your Income Tax* says, if you "do not have regular employment where you live . . . the IRS will disallow the deduction on the grounds that the expenses are not incurred while away from home: The temporary home is the tax-home."

Many contractors, especially single people, do not maintain houses or apartments in their home towns: "Bachelors will find it difficult to get the deduction because they often do not keep regular residences," writes Lasser. Some contractors have trailer homes, and move their homes with them. In such a case, "you move from project to project and you have no other established home . . . each location becomes your principal place of business and, therefore, you are not 'away from home.'" This would apply even if you didn't physically move your home with you, but still traveled from job to job around the country.

Even if you maintain a house or apartment in your home town, you may still not be eligible to deduct expenses. Even if your spouse or children live in your home town, you may still be out of luck, especially if you have not recently worked there.

The IRS considers several circumstances when determining tax homes. The more of the following factors that fit your case, the less chance you have of getting the IRS to accept your deduction:

- ◆ You have no regular employment in your home town.
- ◆ You do not maintain a home in your home town.
- ◆ You move from job to job in different locations.
- ◆ You have no spouse or children living in your home town.
- ◆ Your present contract is indefinite, or scheduled to last one year or more.

◆ You did not work in your home town before the present contract.

◆ You don't intend to return to your home town after your present contract.

◆ You are not continuing to seek employment in your home town.

Scan through a copy of *Technical Employment Weekly* or *Contract Engineer Weekly* (see Appendix C) and look at the Length of Contract listings. If a listing is *indefinite* or over a year, the per diem is not tax-free (perhaps the agency doesn't withhold taxes from it, but the IRS regards it as taxable). "An assignment lasting more than one year is indefinite if you realistically expected it to last that long when you started the assignment, and you may not deduct your living costs of such an assignment," says Lasser, so a per diem would be taxable. In fact even if the assignment lasted only a few months, if you realistically expected it to last a year—or to be of indefinite length—then living costs are not deductible.

Does all this mean that you cannot deduct mileage driven to work, or that you must pay taxes on per diems? No. After all, many contractors throughout the country do deduct mileage, and don't pay taxes on per diems, and get away with it for years. What it means is that if you get audited by an auditor who knows the law, you will lose the deduction and may have to pay penalties.

Many contractors get away with bending the rules slightly, or even breaking them completely. They take advantage of every gray area, and the fact that the IRS can't know their exact work situation unless it audits them. So you will find contractors who tell you the points I have raised are wrong (because they've seen so many others deducting these expenses), or that it doesn't matter, because you won't get caught.

But taking every liberty with the tax system possible may be, as one contractor put it, "killing the goose that laid the golden egg." Too many contractors have avoided paying taxes, or taken illegal deductions, so the IRS—and even state regulators—is out to clean up the mess. The easiest way is to remove the people causing the problem—to stop independent contracting, and force the contractors to work as employees of agencies or of the clients. Many individual states have already clamped down on independents, making it more difficult to find a company that will risk an independent contract. The agencies have reaped a bonanza, and often support the IRS's efforts. If independents went by the letter of the law, the IRS would have no incentive to go after them, though this may be wishful thinking—it's probably too late. [But read Chapter 19; there are still things you can do to avoid legal problems.]

The Home Office—How Much Can You Deduct?

The IRS has tightened up regulations related to home-office deductions in recent years. You can only deduct business expenses related to part of your home if that part is regularly and exclusively used as your principal place of business or as a place for meeting clients or customers in the normal course of business. The IRS wants to make sure that you really are using that part of your home for an office, and not just calling the den your workplace so you can save a few more dollars on your tax bill.

If you file Schedule C, you must now state if you are claiming expenses related to a home office. Checking the Yes box may be a good way to get audited, especially if you don't have much self-employment income. (Note, however, that there's some talk about changing the law to make it easier to take a home-office deduction if you use your home office for administrative or managerial activities and have no other location to carry out such activities.)

Most contractors do not fit the IRS's criteria for home-office use. I even know some contractors who do maintain home offices but don't claim deductions because it is a "gray area" and they don't want the hassle of an audit. But if you are using part of your home for an office and fit the IRS's criteria, you can deduct a portion of real estate taxes, rent, mortgage expense, maintenance, utilities, and insurance. You'll fill in Form 8829 describing your use of your home. See IRS publication 587 for more information.

Filing Your Taxes

How you file your taxes depends on your freelancing status. Most freelancers working through agencies are technically employees; the agency withholds taxes and gives the freelancer a W-2 form at the end of the year stating how much it paid, and how much tax was withheld (this is often known as being "paid on a W-2"). If you are an independent contractor—that is, if a client or agency pays you without withholding taxes—you should receive a Form 1099 from each client showing how much money it paid you.

The Freelance "Employee"

As an "employee" of an agency, you file taxes in much the same way as a captive employee of a company. You must complete Form W-4 for your agency, showing how much tax it should withhold; then, by the middle of April following the tax year, you must file your tax forms. You will normally file Form 1040, 1040A, or 1040EZ. If you have enough itemized deductions, you can file Form 1040 along with Schedule A. The only major difference between the freelance employee and a true captive employee is that the freelancer may be more likely to have deductible business expenses. Remember, though, that the IRS regards both types of employee as the same. There are no deductions that apply to you as a freelancer working for an agency (paying on a W-2) that do not also apply to captive employees.

The expenses you may be able to deduct are "unreimbursed business expenses" and the "expenses of producing income." By *unreimbursed*, the IRS means valid expenses that your employer does not pay you for.

Read the following list to get some ideas on what you may be able to deduct. These items are from a variety of IRS publications (see a tax guide for details of when and how you can deduct these items):

◆ Airfares

◆ Auto club membership

◆ Books used on the job

◆ Business machines

◆ Business use of part of your home—but only if you use that part exclusively and on a regular basis in your work and for the convenience of your employer

◆ Car insurance premiums, if you have a valid business reason for using your car; commuting doesn't count

◆ Christmas gifts

◆ Cleaning costs

◆ Commerce association dues

◆ Commuting costs when out of town, while carrying tools, or at a temporary job site

◆ Convention trips

◆ Correspondence courses

◆ Depreciation

◆ Dues to professional organizations and chambers of commerce (remember your STC dues)

◆ Educational expenses required by your employer or by law or regulation to keep your present salary or job, or for maintaining or improving skills you must have in your present occupation

◆ Equipment

◆ Fees to employment agencies, and other costs that you incur while looking for a new job in your present occupation

◆ Foreign travel costs

◆ Furniture

◆ Garage rent

◆ Gasoline

◆ Gifts

◆ Home-office expenses

◆ Hotel costs

◆ Instruments

◆ Jury duty pay handed over to the employer

◆ Labor union dues

◆ Laundry

◆ Legal expenses

◆ Magazines

◆ Malpractice liability premiums

◆ Meal and entertainment expenses

◆ Medical examinations

◆ Parking fees, tolls, and local transportation

◆ Passport fees

◆ Pay from the previous year repaid to your employer

◆ Physical examinations your employer said you must have

◆ Safety equipment, small tools, and supplies needed for your job

◆ Subscriptions to professional journals

◆ Telegrams

◆ Telephone calls

◆ Tips

◆ Travel expenses while away from home

◆ Typewriter

◆ Vehicle expenses

Other deductions may be allowed, too. Of course these deductions are valid only if they are genuine business expenses. Incidentally, you cannot deduct expenses for meals during regular or extra work hours, the expenses of going to and from work (as discussed earlier), or education needed to meet minimum requirements for your job or to qualify you for a new occupation (as opposed to education required to keep your job).

The way you file these expenses has changed in recent years, and it seems to be getting harder for a freelancer employed by an agency to deduct much. There are two parts to this puzzle. The first part is your business expenses and the second part is the amount, if any, that your agency reimburses.

If an agency reimburses you, perhaps in the form of a per diem, try to make sure that the reimbursement does not appear on your W-2 form. You can do this by adequately accounting to your agency for your expenses, and making sure that the reimbursement does not exceed the expenses. Of course this requires the agency's cooperation, and is more work for them. However, if you don't do this the agency is supposed to report the reimbursement on Form W-2 as part of your income.

According to a recently changed law, once reimbursements from the agency appear on your W-2, the IRS regards it as income and it cannot be removed. Your only option is to deduct the expenses on Schedule A, the Itemized Deductions form. (There are certain expenses that you can deduct directly from your income, but they don't usually apply to technical writers. For example, a performing artist can deduct expenses in this way, and a disabled person can also deduct certain work-related expenses.)

Here's the procedure for deducting expenses. First, fill out Form 2106. This shows your expenses and how much the agency reimbursed you, including any sum the agency listed on Form W-2 as income. You deduct the reimbursements from your expenses, leaving the unreimbursed amount, or the excess reimbursement.

If you have an excess reimbursement, more money paid to you than you spent in expenses, you must report it on Form 1040. The reimbursement in excess of the expenses becomes taxable income. If, on the other hand, your employer reimbursed you less than your expenses (or if you received no reimbursement), claim the excess expenses on Schedule A.

Now you arrive at the catch. Having kept all the records and messed with Form 2106, you may find you can't deduct the unreimbursed expenses anyway. They are deducted as Miscellaneous Deductions on Schedule A (Itemized Deductions). Unfortunately many people can't use Schedule A, especially people who don't own a home. All taxpayers have the option of either filing Schedule A or taking a standard deduction. For example, a married couple filing jointly can either deduct $6,700 from their adjusted gross income or can file Schedule A. Of course, if their itemized deductions are less than $6,700, there is no point using Schedule A, and unless the couple owns a home, gives a lot of money to charity, or loses a lot of property to fire or theft, they are unlikely to exceed the $6,700 level.

But even if they do file Schedule A, only the amount of the Miscellaneous Deductions more than 2 percent of their adjusted gross income is deductible. For instance, if they have an adjusted gross income of $50,000 and $1,500 of Miscellaneous Deductions, only $500 will be deductible (2 percent of $50,000 is $1,000; $1,500 minus $1,000 is

$500). Depending on where on the tax table their other deductions put the couple, the $1,500 in expenses may end up saving only $75 to $160 in taxes.

Moving Expenses

Although many of the expenses of living away from home may not be deductible (because, as I've explained, the IRS may regard you as being in your "tax home"), some of those expenses may be deductible as moving expenses. You can deduct these expenses only if you itemize on Schedule A, but they are not limited by the 2 percent floor; you can deduct the entire sum. You have to use Form 3903 to report the moving expenses, and then deduct the sum on Schedule A.

There are a couple of rules regarding moving expenses. First, the distance from your new job to your old home must be more than 50 miles greater than the distance from your old job to your old home. In other words, if you stayed in your old home, you would add 50 miles or more to your one-way commute by taking the new job. Second, you must stay in the new area and have full-time employment for at least 39 of the next 52 weeks. So if you move to area A for a contract, and then move to area B after six months, you won't be able to deduct the moving expenses. (If you are self-employed the rule is stricter; you must spend 78 weeks of the next two years in the same place.) However, there are various waivers. If you lose your job for any reason other than willful misconduct or resignation, the 39-week limit can be waived, but I don't know if that would be applied to a contractor in a limited-duration contract.

So, what exactly can you deduct? The direct expenses of moving are fully deductible (travel and lodging while en route) as are the cost of moving your personal effects and household goods. Most other expenses—the cost of pre-move house-hunting trips, temporary living quarters for 30 days, and the cost of selling, buying, or leasing accommodation, for instance—are currently not deductible.

If you cannot deduct living expenses as business travel expenses (or don't want to risk an audit), look at the possibility of using moving expenses instead. Since they are not subject to the 2 percent floor, they may be more profitable anyway.

The Independent Freelancer

The independent freelancer, called a *sole proprietor* by the IRS, has a few advantages and one big disadvantage, as far as taxes go. As an independent, you can deduct expenses directly from your income, before paying Self Employment or income tax. Because the expenses are coming directly from your income, you don't need to use Schedule A, so you are not caught in the "2 percent of adjusted income" trap. Also, although the employee of an agency may be able to deduct some expenses, he or she has to pay FICA first. The independent freelancer, though, deducts expenses *before* calculating Self Employment tax.

The big disadvantage as an independent, though, is that you will pay much more FICA and Medicare insurance, in the guise of the Self Employment tax. Employees pay 7.65 percent on the first $61,200, and 1.45 percent on everything above that. The independent freelancer pays 15.3 percent and 2.9 percent.

However, as you learned in Chapter 7, there are a couple of factors that reduce that amount you actually end up paying. First, self-employed people calculate the income on which Self Employment tax must be paid by deducting 7.65 percent from their self-employment income. So, if you earn $100,000, you pay Self Employment tax on $92,350. And once you've figured out how much Self Employment tax to pay, you can then deduct 50 percent of your Self Employment tax from your income before calculating income tax. For a complete example of how this works, see Chapter 7.

Independent freelancers also file taxes differently from employees. Because no one is withholding taxes, you have to do it yourself. The IRS requires you to estimate your taxes for the year and then pay an equal sum every three months.

As of 1996, you are required to pay 90 percent of the tax you owe by the middle of the January after the end of the year. In theory you are supposed to make four equal payments on the four estimated-tax dates (the middle of April, June, September, and January), but if your income fluctuates during the year you can pay less early in the year and catch up later. You must pay the final 10 percent before the middle of April of the following year.

There's a loophole, though. Make sure that by January 15 you have paid 100 percent of what you paid in the previous tax year, even if it is far less than 90 percent of the tax you will owe for the current tax year. Then pay the rest by the middle of April. (If your adjusted gross income is over $150,000, make sure you pay 110 percent of the previous year's tax.)

Don't worry about getting your estimated income exactly right at the beginning of a year (you never know for sure how much you will make during the year). Just re-estimate during the year, and amend your estimated payments correspondingly. You file your estimated tax payments on Form 1040-ES.

When you file your final tax return you must fill in these forms: Form 1040, Schedule C (Profit or Loss from Business), Schedule SE (Self Employment Tax), and Form 4562 (Depreciation and Amortization) if you bought an expensive piece of equipment for your business. A self-employed person cannot use Forms 1040EZ or 1040A.

Schedule C

Unlike freelancers working as agency employees, an independent contractor can deduct *all* valid business expenses on Schedule C. These are the major categories that are relevant to freelance writers:

- ◆ Advertising
- ◆ Car and truck expenses
- ◆ Commissions and fees
- ◆ Depreciation and section 179 expense deduction (from Form 4562—see "Form 4562: Depreciation and Amortization," later in this chapter)
- ◆ Insurance
- ◆ Interest
- ◆ Legal and professional services
- ◆ Office expenses
- ◆ Rent or lease of vehicles, machinery, equipment, and other business properties
- ◆ Repairs and maintenance
- ◆ Supplies

◆ Taxes and licenses

◆ Travel, meals, and entertainment

◆ Utilities

◆ Other expenses—any expense that is directly related to your business yet doesn't seem to fit into the other categories.

All the expenses listed earlier in this chapter fit in one of these categories. Also, you can deduct 40 percent of your medical insurance premiums straight from your gross income on Form 1040 (you can include the rest with your itemized medical deductions on Schedule A).

You have two types of accounting you can use on Schedule C: *cash* or *accrual*. Use the cash method of accounting. With the cash method you report income in the year you receive the money, and expenses in the year you spend the money. With the *accrual* method you report income in the year that you earn it, regardless of when you get the money, and expenses when you incur them, even if you don't pay until the next year. The accrual method is much more complicated, with more stringent reporting and accounting requirements, and is unnecessary for most freelancers.

Some of Schedule C does not apply to your business. For example, businesses that manufacture or purchase goods for sale use the "cost of goods sold," but few freelancers need to worry about this part of the form. Otherwise the form is quite simple. In Part I you list your gross income. In Part II you list all your business expenses and then subtract the expenses from your income to arrive at a profit or loss. You then report that figure on Form 1040.

Deducting Insurance and Medical Costs

A freelancer cannot automatically deduct personal insurance—medical, accident, or disability—or medical expenses. You *can* deduct 40 percent of your medical-insurance premiums on Form 1040 (that deduction will rise to 45 percent for the years 1998 to 2002), and the rest on Schedule A (subject to the 2 percent limitation). You can't, however, deduct your insurance premiums on Schedule C, though you'll see an Insurance category on that form. Use that category to deduct insurance on your business property, such as your computers.

There are two ways that you may be able to deduct your medical insurance and other costs, though. The first way is to employ your spouse, and provide your new employee with a medical plan that insures him or her and pays all out-of-pocket medical expenses, and which also covers your employee's spouse—you. This is not as simple as it sounds, though. You'll end up paying taxes on this employee—unemployment tax and a slightly higher FICA. In fact, you might even pay a much higher FICA rate than your Self Employment tax rate (if you earn a lot of money you'll be taking money off the top of your income—money that would be paid at 2.9 percent Self Employment tax rate if you didn't employ your spouse—and giving it to your spouse to be taxed at the full 15.3 percent FICA rate). You may have to pay worker's compensation, too. In fact this scheme may end up being more expense and trouble than it's worth.

The other way to deduct medical expenses is to incorporate—a "C" corporation, not an "S" corporation. You can then set up a medical plan under which your corporation pays all your medical expenses. But as you'll see in Chapter 23, this scheme also may cause more expense and trouble than it's worth.

Form 4562: Depreciation and Amortization

If you have purchased some kind of asset that you use in your business, you must complete Form 4562. An asset is an item that is expected to have a life of more than one year—vehicles, computers, tools, telephone equipment, and so on. Of course, if you buy an inexpensive tool like a screwdriver, you don't need to fill in this form (just claim the expense under "Supplies" on Schedule C). Use Form 4562 for goods costing hundreds or thousands of dollars.

You can choose to depreciate the item, or deduct the first $17,500 of your depreciable purchases using the Section 179 deduction. If you choose to deduct the cost, you must still fill in Form 4562 but then deduct the expense on Schedule C. If you want to depreciate the expense, you must decide what type of equipment it is and over how many years it will be depreciated. "Depreciation" simply means deducting the expense over several years.

For example, suppose that you buy a computer for $8,000. You can use the Section 179 deduction and claim the entire sum on Schedule C—reducing your taxable income by $8,000 that year—or you may decide to deduct a portion of the cost in each of the next five years. Refer to IRS publication 534 for more information.

The Section 179 deduction is a boon to new freelancers. Without it you wouldn't be able to deduct the full cost of that new computer you bought to start your business. Thanks to Section 179 you can deduct the full cost, and reduce your taxes right away.

Forms You Need

Here is a list of some of the tax forms you may need:

Form	Title
1040-ES	Estimated Tax for Individuals
1040	U.S. Individual Income Tax Return
1040A	U.S. Individual Income Tax Return (an easier form than 1040, but you can use it only if your income is less than $50,000 and you don't use Schedule A—and you can't use it if you are self-employed)
1040EZ	Income Tax Return for Single Filers with No Dependents (same restrictions as for 1040A, plus some more)
2106	Statement of Employee Business Expenses
3903	Moving Expense Adjustment
4562	Depreciation and Amortization
4782	Employee Moving Expense Information
8829	Expenses for Business Use of Your Home
Schedule A	Itemized Deductions
Schedule C	Profit or Loss from Business or Profession
Schedule SE	Computation of Social Security and Self-Employment

Tax Books and Publications

Get a good tax book, such as J. K. Lasser's *Your Income Tax* or *The Consumer Reports Books Guide to Income Tax Preparation*. These will answer many of your questions. (Many of the tax books seem little clearer than the IRS's own publications, but they have the great advantage of putting all the information you are likely to need in one place.) You also can get the following publications from the IRS:

Publication	Title
17	Your Federal Income Tax
334	Tax Guide for Small Business
463	Travel, Entertainment, and Gift Expenses
505	Tax Withholding and Estimated Taxes
508	Educational Expenses
521	Moving Expenses
529	Miscellaneous Deductions
533	Self-Employment Tax
534	Depreciation
535	Business Expenses
560	Retirement Plans for the Self-Employed
583	Taxpayers Starting a Business
587	Business Use of Your Home
589	Tax Information on S Corporations
590	Individual Retirement Arrangements (IRAs)
917	Business Use of a Car
936	Home Mortgage Interest Deduction

You can call the IRS and have it send you the booklets and the forms you need (call (800) 424-3676). Or you can go to your public library and refer to the books and forms there, and make copies of the parts you need. And you can find these forms and publications online, too. Use your Web browser to go to these pages:

◆ The IRS's main page (http://www.irs.ustreas.gov/)

◆ Forms and Publications (http://www.irs.ustreas.gov/prod/forms_pubs/index.html)

You can also subscribe to the IRS's *Tax Tips* newsletter, a free publication intended for small businesses. Call (800) 829-1040. The person who answers may not know what you are talking about; ask for the Taxpayer Education Coordinator. You'll probably then be given a local number to call.

If you have a computer, you should get a tax program. Get one that allows you to do "what if" experiments (most do), so you can plug in different numbers and see what effect they have on your taxes. These programs help you estimate your taxes during the year, and make it fairly simple to handle your taxes yourself, without the assistance of a tax accountant. Some of the program publishers also maintain Web sites with links to useful information. For instance, try these two sites:

◆ Parson's Technology 1040 Online(http://1040online.parsonstech.com/)

◆ The Quicken Financial Network
(http://www.qfn.com/index.html)

Also, you may want to get *How to Keep Your Hard-Earned Money: The Tax Saving Handbook for the Self-Employed* by Henry Aiy'm Fellman. This describes a variety of tax-saving strategies you can use, in very simple terms.

This chapter may have convinced you to do your own taxes—or it may have scared you off and convinced you to find a good accountant. You've got enough problems without this tax nonsense, and you may not want to spend the time and energy learning the tax law, but a few evenings spent reading will teach you all you need to know, and after the first year it is just a matter of keeping up with a few small changes.

Are You Really an

Independent

Contractor?

The man who goes alone can start today; but he who travels with another must wait till that other is ready, and it may be a long time before they get off.

U.S. philosopher Henry David Thoreau (1817–1862)

The IRS seems to dislike independent contractors. Too many contractors have avoided paying taxes in the past, and too many companies have avoided paying their share of taxes by claiming that their employees are contractors. Furthermore, if a contractor defaults on taxes, the IRS may have trouble getting the money, although if a large company defaults, the IRS probably will have more luck. It's easier for the IRS to keep an eye on a few thousand companies rather than hundreds of thousands of contractors. An independent contractor is more likely to try to "slip by" without paying than is a company that the IRS can easily find.

So the IRS trains its agents to determine whether people claiming to be independent contractors are really independent, or whether they are, in fact, employees. If you are an independent, then your client can continue paying you all your money, without withholding any taxes. You are then responsible for paying those taxes. If you are not independent, the client has to withhold taxes, and the IRS may make the client pay back taxes that it should have withheld earlier, and penalties too. In addition, you may lose your self-employment income pension plan. Until recently the IRS had a list of twenty questions it used to determine employment status, but starting in 1996 it did away with this system. It now uses a system that is not quite as easy to describe, yet which actually makes it easier to be classified as an independent contractor.

The New IRS Employment Status-Criteria

The areas now considered by the IRS are broken into three groups: *Behavioral Control, Financial Control,* and *Type of Relationship.* There are eleven facts to be considered:

Behavioral Control

- ◆ Instructions the business gives the worker
- ◆ Training the business gives the worker

Financial Control

- ◆ The extent to which the worker has unreimbursed business expenses
- ◆ The extent of the worker's investment
- ◆ The extent to which the worker makes services available to the relevant market
- ◆ How the business pays the worker ("An independent contractor is usually paid by the job. However, it is common in some professions, such as law, to pay independent contractors hourly.")
- ◆ The extent to which the worker can realize a profit or incur a loss.

Type of Relationship

- ◆ Written contract describing the relationship the parties intended to create.
- ◆ Whether the business provides the worker with employee-type benefits, such as insurance, a pension plan, vacation pay, or sick pay
- ◆ The permanency of the relationship
- ◆ The extent to which services performed by the worker are a key aspect of the regular business of the company

Publication 15-A: Employer's Supplemental Tax Guide

The following text is from **Publication 15-A, Employer's Supplemental Tax Guide, page 4,** and provides more detailed information.

2. Employee or Independent Contractor?

An employer must generally withhold income taxes, withhold and pay social security and Medicare taxes, and pay unemployment taxes on wages paid to an employee. An employer does not generally have to withhold or pay any taxes on payments to independent contractors.

Common-law rules.—To determine whether an individual is an employee or an independent contractor under the common law, the relationship of the worker and the business must be examined. All evidence of control and independence must be considered. In any employee–independent contractor determination, all information that provides evidence of the degree of control and the degree of independence must be considered.

Facts that provide evidence of the degree of control and independence fall into three categories: behavioral control, financial control, and the type of relationship of the parties as shown below.

Behavioral control.—Facts that show whether the business has a right to direct and control how the worker does the task for which the worker is hired include the type and degree of—

- ◆ *Instructions the business gives the worker*. An employee is generally subject to the business's instructions about when, where, and how to work. Even if no instructions are given, sufficient behavioral control may exist if the employer has the right to control how the work results are achieved.

◆ *Training the business gives the worker.* An employee may be trained to perform services in a particular manner. Independent contractors ordinarily use their own methods.

Financial control.—Facts that show whether the business has a right to control the business aspects of the worker's job include:

◆ *The extent to which the worker has unreimbursed business expenses.* Independent contractors are more likely to have unreimbursed expenses than employees. Fixed ongoing costs that are incurred regardless of whether work is currently being performed are especially important. However, employees may also incur unreimbursed expenses in connection with the services they perform for their business.

◆ *The extent of the worker's investment.* An independent contractor often has a significant investment in the facilities he or she uses in performing services for someone else. However, a significant investment is not required.

◆ *The extent to which the worker makes services available to the relevant market.*

◆ *How the business pays the worker.* An employee is generally paid by the hour, week, or month. An independent contractor is usually paid by the job. However, it is common in some professions, such as law, to pay independent contractors hourly.

◆ *The extent to which the worker can realize a profit or incur a loss.* An independent contractor can make a profit or loss.

Type of relationship.—Facts that show the parties' type of relationship include:

◆ *Written contracts describing the relationship the parties intended to create.*

◆ *Whether the business provides the worker with employee-type benefits, such as insurance, a pension plan, vacation pay, or sick pay.*

◆ *The permanency of the relationship.* If you engage a worker with the expectation that the relationship will continue indefinitely, rather than for a specific project or period, this is generally considered evidence that your intent was to create an employer-employee relationship.

◆ *The extent to which services performed by the worker are a key aspect of the regular business of the business of the company.* If a worker provides services that are a key aspect of your regular business activity, it is more likely that you will have the right to direct and control his or her activities. For example, if a law firm hires an attorney, it is likely that it will present the attorney's work as its own and would have the right to control or direct that work. This would indicate an employer-employee relationship.

Incidentally, it doesn't matter what your client calls your position or status. The contract may state that you are an independent contractor, but if the IRS decides that the facts show otherwise, the contract is irrelevant. The contract is just one piece of evidence that the IRS can use to determine your status, but by no means an overriding piece of evidence.

The Safe Harbor

Now, how does all this affect you? If the IRS decides you are an employee, it will most likely ask the client, not you, for back taxes. The client also may have to pay the same sum as a penalty. The client also will have to treat you as an employee, and some clients may decide to get rid of you instead (although as your employer, a client may have to show good cause, depending on the state you work in). Furthermore, if the IRS decides you are an employee, you are not eligible to have a self-employed person's pension plan (an individual 401(k), SEP, or Keogh plan) and lose your Schedule C (Business Profit and Loss) deductions.

Some companies may try to protect themselves. And how can they protect themselves? By hiring through technical service agencies, of course! The Tax Reform Act of 1986 allows companies to treat contractors as nonemployees if they were hired through a technical agency that employed the contractor. This means that as more companies get audited (and fined or assessed back taxes), fewer independent contract positions will be available.

There is a "safe harbor," though. Section 530 of the Revenue Act of 1978 provides protection in cases where the IRS decides that the company was incorrectly treating an employee as a contractor. If the company meets certain criteria, the IRS cannot assess penalties or back taxes. First, the employer must have consistently treated the contractor as such; the firm must not have changed the contractor's status from that of an employee. It must have paid this person as a contractor, and it must have given the contractor work that differs in some way from that of its employees.

Second, the company must have filed the correct tax forms, in particular Form 1099MISC. And third, the company must have had a reasonable basis for treating the contractor as such—perhaps an IRS precedent treated others in that profession as contractors, or maybe it is a common practice in that industry.

Incidentally, an amendment to Section 530, Section 530(d), makes this "safe harbor" applicable only for independent contractors under contract to the client they are working for, not to those with technical service agency contracts. So if a company hires an agency to provide a contractor, and the agency pays the contractor on a 1099, as an independent, the safe harbor is no longer available, to either the agency or the client. Thus, since the IRS may find the client liable—in addition to or instead of the agency—companies can find themselves at more risk hiring through an agent than if they had hired an independent contractor! If you wish to read more on the subject, see "Determining Employee or Independent Contractor Status" in *The Tax Advisor* of October 1989. Your library may have a copy. Also, see the IRS Publication 1976, *Independent Contractor or Employee: Section 530 Relief Requirements*.

So Is It a Problem?

Is there really a problem here? No, not much of one. There will be companies with which you can't work because they're scared of the IRS. There'll be just as many who don't really care.

For years now contractors have been talking about an IRS crackdown on contractors, but it never seems to come. In fact some legal analysts are saying that the changes the IRS made in 1996 to the manner in which it determines employment status makes it *easier* to qualify as an independent contractor. The IRS seems to be more interested in going after companies using a lot of independent contractors first, such as construction firms and companies using independent sales people. (Microsoft has recently got into trouble with the IRS, too, but they had large numbers of people working on-site, for extended periods, in situations that seemed to make them employees rather than independents.)

There was also at one time a rumor in contractor circles of a new law or ruling that would state that any client paying a contractor more than 51 percent of his or her income would be regarded as the contractor's employer; in effect he would have an employee/employer relationship with that client, and a contractor/client relationship with the other clients. It now appears that it was mere rumor, nothing more. However the law changes, don't worry; it's not the end of the road for independents. There are a number of things you can do to protect yourself.

There will still be some contract jobs that are quite clearly and unambiguously independent contractor or consultant jobs—contracts in which you work at home and use your own computer equipment, for example. If you set your own hours and are not supervised or controlled in any manner, for example, you will be okay.

You can also do everything possible to get as close to independent contractor status as possible: Avoid having to provide the client with status reports; arrange a "flexi-time" schedule that allows you to set your own hours; try to do some of the work at home; regularly solicit work from other companies; and try to do several contracts each year, even if you have one main client and several other small contracts. Avoid working for one client for an extended time (of course, this is a double-edged sword; you don't want to be seen as a contract hopper, nor do you want to leave long, profitable contracts). Set up a home office and use it as a business place. Get a business name, business cards, and even a brochure, and mail them to potential clients.

Don't make it difficult for companies to hire you, though. I know freelancers who tell clients that they must be allowed to work flexi-time and to work a significant part of the time at home, that the client mustn't expect progress reports, and so on. This is fine in some circumstances, but most contract jobs are with clients who require someone in the office, working with their equipment and employees, during regular business hours. Don't scare off these clients.

Some clients will accept contractors, but put them on their payroll as temporary employees; the company withholds all the taxes mandated by law, but doesn't provide any of the usual employee benefits. In one company that does this, the contractor makes his deal with the department manager, then the accounting department adds 10 percent to that rate and withholds taxes. Also, some clients are still willing to take chances or remain ignorant of the law, especially small companies that don't use many contractors and so don't attract much attention.

Become a Consultant

You may also be able to become a true consultant, by moving on to Step Three (see "The Three-Step Method of Freelancing" in Chapter 4). By *consultant* I mean someone who is more than simply a temporary employee, someone who comes to the company and provides specific skills for a specific project. The consultant typically charges a set fee, and may even have his or her own staff, or subcontract for the project. I discuss consulting in more detail in Chapter 21.

Start Your Own Agency

You might also consider starting your own technical service agency; I know a few writers who have done this, though most seem to find plenty of work without bothering. Find a few independent contractors and a good accountant, and incorporate. You can then use the company as a vehicle to sell your services. The client pays your company, rather than paying you on a 1099, and you arrange for the account to be paid jointly by all the contractors (the owners). All the money passes through the company in the form of salaries, with each contractor getting what his clients paid to the corporation, minus expenses. Another advantage to setting up such a company is the benefits that you can provide, particularly medical insurance. Your company may be able to get a much more favorable policy than you can get independently. Of course, a problem arises if one of you wants to buy capital goods, such as a computer; if an individual buys the goods, the purchase is only partly deductible from his or her taxes, but if the corporation buys the goods, the purchase belongs to everyone.

Set Up a Corporation

Another alternative is to set up your own corporation. Find an accountant, or incorporate yourself using one of the many books or computer programs, perhaps using a Subchapter S corporation. Unfortunately this scheme may not work. According to *The Tax Advisor*, an amendment to the Tax Reform Act of 1986 stops contractors from forming Personal Service Corporations to bypass the effect of Section 530(d)—that is, in order to avoid being classified as an employee. If you want to set up your own corporation, find an attorney who is familiar with this aspect of the law. And read Chapter 23, which discusses incorporation in detail.

Join an Agency

If you don't want to incorporate yourself, you might be able to find another freelancer who has a small agency and is willing to take on your contract and pass all but a small amount back to you. I wouldn't advise you do this unless the freelancer has an accountant and is willing to do all the taxes and paperwork, rather than pay you on a 1099. After all, you may as well handle the contract yourself if you are going to be paid as an independent. Calculate exactly what it will cost the freelancer to do this (in accountant's fees and payroll taxes) and then add a dollar or two profit. If the freelancer doesn't think that is enough, point out that he or she won't have to do anything for the money that you are paying the accountant.

I have a programmer friend who is working through a "front" corporation like this, but it pays him on a 1099. The client thinks it is free of all responsibility, but is wrong. The IRS recognizes "joint employment," so if it assesses the agency with back taxes or overtime pay, and the agency cannot pay, the client could be dragged in.

Finally, the most important thing you can do is to pay your taxes promptly and correctly. Many contractors invite the wrath of the IRS by "forgetting" to pay taxes (for five or six years) or claiming ridiculous deductions. Once the IRS starts auditing you the auditor may decide to question your employment status. Audits are annoying, expensive things, even if you "win" (I know, I've won one), so do your best to avoid them. If you lose your audit, you may lose the right to your pension plan and bring the IRS down on your client. If you don't pay your taxes properly, you are doing both yourself and your client a disservice.

These schemes all sound a bit drastic, but you'll probably never have to use any of them. I've included this information because you need to be aware of it, but it's actually far easier to work as an independent contractor than many people—the agencies and even some other freelancers—seem to want you to believe. But there are still many independent contracts available. Many companies have stopped using independents, but many haven't, and I don't know of anyone who has been audited for employment status. So go looking for those contracts. They are well worth it.

Finding More Information

If you'd like more information about this subject, you should get the following forms and publications, all but one of which can be downloaded from this book's associated Web site (http://www.mcp.com/mgr/arco/techwr/), and all of which are available directly from the IRS (call 800-424-3676; in the case of the last document write to the specified address):

Publication 15-A, Employer's Supplemental Tax Guide, page 4
A good overview of the process.

Form SS-8, Determination of Employee Work Status for Purposes of Federal Employment Taxes and Income Tax Withholding.
This form is submitted to the IRS, which will tell you whether or not the specified work situation is an employee or contractor relationship.

Publication 1779: Independent Contractor or Employee...
A small trifold pamphlet that provides an overview of the way in which the IRS determines employment status. You can order this directly from the IRS (it's not available at the Web site). You might want to order a few of these to give to your clients, to assuage any concerns about whether or not working with an independent contractor will lead to problems with the IRS.

Publication 1976, Independent Contractor or Employee: Section 530 Relief Requirements
A short document that describes the Section 530 Relief ("Safe Harbor"). It's typically provided to a company that's employment practices are being examined. This form specifies that in some circumstances an employer will not owe back taxes for an employee even if the employer paid the employee as if the employee was an independent contractor.

Training Document 3320-102, Independent Contractor or Employee: Training Materials
A detailed (*very* detailed) description of how IRS agents are supposed to decide whether you're an independent contractor. Available at the Web site or from:

Douglas Izard
Dean, IRS School of Taxation
M;CD;TX
2221 South Clark Street
Arlington, VA 22202

More on Contracts

Verbal contracts are not worth the paper they're written on.

Samuel Goldwyn

If you work as an independent, you will need some form of contract. Never work without some form of written agreement. Samuel Goldwyn said that verbal contracts "are not worth the paper they are written on," and he was right. Putting your agreement on paper is not implying you don't trust the client, you are simply making sure that both parties know exactly what their obligations are. In fact I'd be very suspicious of a client who refused to enter into a written agreement. A written contract not only helps you avoid problems later, when memories of what was agreed upon begin to fade, but may be essential if you ever need to take legal action to recover what a client owes you.

Contracts don't need to be complicated, and don't need to begin with "Know all men by these presents," as one contract I've seen does, or contain terms such as "hereinafter set forth." They can be in clear English and simply explain what the client wants you to do and what the client must do in return.

Many companies, particularly large companies, already have a boilerplate contract they use with contractors. Read through it carefully to make sure there is nothing unreasonable before signing and don't be afraid to offer your own clauses. Some companies insert clauses that protect company secrets, patents, and copyrights, and restrict the contractor from directly competing with the client (or using information gained while working for the client to help one of the client's competitors). These seem reasonable aims, but make sure the wording is not too restrictive; it would be unreasonable for the contract to stop you from doing any work for one of the client's competitors, for example, or to claim the right to any patents you receive while working for the client (as many permanent employment contracts do).

Payment Terms

If you are doing a set-fee project—a project in which you are paid an agreed-upon sum for the project, regardless of how long it takes—make sure you get some money up front. For example, if the project is a short one, you might ask for a third of your pay before you start, a third halfway through, and a third when you finish. If the project is a longer one, you might ask for a monthly payment—for example, 10 percent a month for seven months, and the rest when you finish.

Also, make sure the terms of payment are acceptable. Ensure that the contract provides a reasonable payment period (30 days after you invoice the client, for example), and that both you and the client agree on how often you will be paid. You don't want to wait until the end of a three-month contract for your money, for instance; invoice every week or two instead. Also check that the contract doesn't contain any punitive conditions for unsatisfactory work. For example, make sure that the contract doesn't allow the client to stop payment on all unpaid invoices; if the client doesn't like your work, he or she should end the contract quickly, not let it drag out for weeks and then refuse to pay. Some contracts even state that the contractor is liable for any expense the client may incur purchasing the services of other contractors in the event that you "default" on your contract.

If your client doesn't have a standard contract, you might just type a letter of agreement. All the letter needs to state is the length of the contract, how much you will be paid, how often you will be paid, and how the contract may be terminated. Write a simple letter, addressed to the person who is going to sign, such as the following (just replace *COMPANY* with the company's real name):

Date

Name

COMPANY

Address

City, State Zip

Dear *Name*,

This letter confirms our contracting agreement, as we discussed when I visited your office yesterday.

We agreed that I would provide my services to *COMPANY* for the period between January 15 and June 15, 1998. I will write the User Manual for the new product (*xxx*) that *COMPANY* is developing. I will work approximately 40 hours a week, more if necessary and if *COMPANY* approves the extra hours.

For my work *COMPANY* will pay $40 an hour. I will invoice *COMPANY* every two weeks, and *COMPANY* agrees to pay the invoice within 15 days of receipt.

This agreement may be terminated by either party at any time upon five days' written notice. Upon termination, *COMPANY* will pay me for any hours I have worked for which I have not already invoiced *COMPANY*, plus any unpaid invoices.

If this is your understanding of our agreement, please sign and date one copy of this letter and return it to me.

I look forward to working with *COMPANY*.

Sincerely,

CONTRACTOR

Accepted:

COMPANY

By:

Title:

Date:

A written letter of agreement of this type is a perfectly legal contract, and many clients will be quite satisfied with it. Still, if your client wants a more formal document, try something like this:

THIS AGREEMENT, made and entered into on this the _____ day of _____, 19__ by and between *COMPANY NAME* (CLIENT) and *CONSULTANT NAME* (CONSULTANT), is to witness the following:

The parties agree as follows:

1. TERM

The term of the agreement shall be from the _____ day of , _____19___ until the ___ day of ___, 19__.

2. SERVICES

CONSULTANT agrees to prepare a User Manual for CLIENT'S new product. The manual shall conform to the guidelines set down by CLIENT and shall be completed to CLIENT'S satisfaction. CONSULTANT shall work approximately 40 hours a week; if more hours are required to complete the work, they must be approved by CLIENT.

3. CHARGES

CLIENT agrees to pay CONSULTANT $40 per hour for each hour of work performed by CONSULTANT. CONSULTANT will invoice CLIENT every two weeks, and CLIENT will pay each invoice within 15 days of receipt.

4. TERMINATION

This agreement may be terminated at any time before the completion of the agreement upon five days' prior written notice. Upon termination of the agreement by either party, CLIENT shall pay CONSULTANT for any hours worked for which CONSULTANT has not already invoiced CLIENT, plus any unpaid invoices.

5. CONFIDENTIALITY

CONSULTANT agrees not to disclose information relating to the products, trade secrets, methods of manufacture, or business or affairs of CLIENT that CONSULTANT may acquire in connection with or as a result of any work performed under this agreement. CONSULTANT will not, without prior written consent, publish, communicate, divulge, disclose, or use (except in the performance of the work specified in this agreement) any such information. This obligation of confidentiality shall not apply to information that:

1) becomes publicly known through no fault of CONSULTANT

2) CLIENT approves for disclosure in a written document

3) CONSULTANT rightfully possessed before disclosure by CLIENT, or

4) CONSULTANT independently develops without use of confidential information.

IN WITNESS WHEREOF, each party has caused this agreement to be executed by its duly authorized representative on the date first mentioned above.

CLIENT warrants that it has full power and authority to enter into and perform this agreement, and that the person signing this agreement on CLIENT's behalf has been duly authorized and empowered to enter into this agreement. CLIENT and CONSULTANT further acknowledge that they have read this agreement, understand this agreement, and agree to be bound by this agreement.

Signed by CONSULTANT_____
     CLIENT_____

Name_____
    Name_____

Title_____
    Title_____

The client may ask you to add certain clauses. For example, in the termination clause the client may prefer this:

> This agreement may be terminated at any time before the completion upon five days' prior written notice, or immediately upon unsatisfactory performance.

This clause seems quite reasonable, although it isn't in your interest. You also may wish to omit the Confidentiality clause unless the client requests it. There are some other clauses you might want to consider. You could add a clause stating that your performance depends on being given adequate information and an up-to-date version of the product, for example. If you are documenting a product that is not yet finished, you might specify a "freeze date," the date by which your client will give you a finished product (so you don't have to complete a book one week after the product is finished).

More Advanced Contracts

If you are simply cutting out the agency and working at a client's site, the contract will probably be fairly straightforward. It will cover the number of hours worked, how much you get paid, and when you get paid. When you move to Step Three, however, the contract's likely to get more complicated (see "The Three-Step Method of Freelancing" in Chapter 4). Let's look at what happens in these more complicated contracts.

In *The Complete Guide to Consulting Success*, Howard Shenson lists the following types of contracts:

- ◆ Fixed-price
- ◆ Firm fixed-price
- ◆ Escalating fixed-price
- ◆ Incentive fixed-price
- ◆ Performance fixed-price
- ◆ Fixed-price with redetermination
- ◆ Fixed fee plus expenses
- ◆ Daily rate
- ◆ Time and materials
- ◆ Cost reimbursement
- ◆ Cost contracts
- ◆ Cost plus fixed fee (CPFF)
- ◆ Cost plus incentive fee (CPIF)
- ◆ Cost plus award fee (CPAF)
- ◆ Retainer

It is rare for contractors and consultants to use these contracts, however, except for the fixed-fee and daily rate contracts (the daily rate is just a permutation of the hourly rate contract).

The fixed-fee contract states that the contractor will deliver a finished product, or do the specified work, for a stated fee; it doesn't matter how long it takes you to complete the work, you still get the same money. Nevertheless, you should sign this sort of contract only if you have a good idea of how long it will take to do the job, or you might end up making very little money for your time. You may be able to renegotiate the contract once you realize you have underestimated the work (especially if the client also miscalculated), but don't count on it. Always avoid this type of contract if the project is not clear-cut and easily estimated. For example, if a client wants you to document a product that is so far from completion that it is hard to estimate how much information you would have to put in the documentation, you should be wary of a fixed fee. In such a situation you will have difficulty accurately estimating the amount of work involved, and because the time that it will take to complete your work depends on the client's employees meeting their deadlines.

However, if you know exactly how long a job will take, a fixed fee may be a good way to go. Clients like them because they know what their final cost will be, and they know there is no incentive for you to "drag the work out." Shenson believes such contracts are very profitable. According to a survey he conducted in 1978, consultants who charged fixed fees had profits that were 95 percent greater than those of their colleagues who charged daily rates. This type of contract is especially beneficial if your skills or experience allow you to complete a job in considerably less time than most other people in your profession. While clients may balk at an hourly rate twice the norm, they will be happy to pay a fixed fee that is close to their estimate of the costs—not knowing that you will finish the job in half the time.

Robert E. Kelley, in his book *Consulting, The Complete Guide to a Profitable Career*, lists 12 factors to consider in signing a contract:

◆ Responsibility of each party: What do you and the client agree to?

◆ Time agreements: When will you do the work and when will the client meet its obligations (such as providing you with necessary information)?

◆ Financial arrangements: How and when will the client pay you?

◆ Products or services to be delivered: How will you deliver your work?

◆ Cooperation of the client: Will the client be required to provide cooperation in the form of information, access to employees or company facilities, or raw materials?

◆ Independent contractor status: State that you are an independent contractor and do not have employee status or obligations.

◆ Advisory capacity: If applicable, state that you will not be making decisions for the client, only giving advice.

◆ Client responsibility for review, implementation, and results: Make sure that the client determines the quality and result of your work. Reviews can be especially useful, because they ensure you don't complete a project and then have the client tell you he or she doesn't like the result.

◆ Your potential work with competitors: If you may be working with the client's competitors, you may need to state this or agree to limitations.

◆ Authority of client to contract for your services: Some corporations restrict employees from entering into contracts, so the client should state that it is authorized to do so.

◆ Attorney's fee clause: If you find it necessary to use an attorney to collect your fees, this clause establishes who will pay the attorney's fees.

◆ Limitations: State any special limitations, such as limited liability after a certain date.

Kelley is addressing an audience of people who intend to consult rather than contract. Most technical freelancers contract, and such contracts may be much simpler; you are providing your services by the hour, so the relationship is not as complicated as if you were promising to deliver a product for a fixed sum.

More Things to Consider

Here are a few more things you should seriously think about including in your contracts. I haven't used all these in every contract I've ever written—but I wish I had. In at least one case it would have helped me avoid a rather nasty argument with a client.

Specify That the Client Is Responsible for Technical Accuracy

It's a good idea to have a statement to the effect that the client is responsible for reviewing your work and correcting any problems. I regard this as a form of liability protection. If the client is ever sued for something written in the document, you can say that the client alone is responsible for the accuracy of the document. If the client doesn't like this clause, state that it's normal for *any* technical document to be reviewed by the people with the most knowledge about the product, and that while you are sure there won't be many problems with the document, you simply want to ensure that the finished product is absolutely correct in all ways.

Specify Who Will Review the Document

Once you've stated that the client will review the document, have the client say who will review the document; use actual names. On one project my book was being reviewed continuously, and my contact at the company kept telling me how much he liked the book. I specifically asked if the style was okay, for instance. Yes, he said, it was great. Once the book was finished, though, he gave it to his boss, who disagreed. She was of the old "if it's technical it should be stodgy" school of thought, and went through the book changing all sorts of things. If I'd had a clause like this in the contract (I didn't!), I could have billed the company for the changes she demanded.

Note in the clause that the reviewer or reviewers will return a signed and dated copy of the document to you. You might also name one reviewer as the lead reviewer; if you have several people disagreeing on what the document should say, it helps if it's clear who has the final say.

State an Early Review Date

It's a good idea to state in the contract that the company will review your work fairly early on in the contract. The company should make sure that you are creating the sort of document that it wants, and that you are using a writing style that the company likes. I've heard of companies complaining about the standard of work at the *end* of the contract; that's an issue that should have been resolved early on.

When you have the early review, get the client to sign and date a statement. There's no need to make this sound like the client is signing a second contract. Rather, when you submit a review copy, include a cover sheet with a simple statement like "I have reviewed this document and have found that x is writing in a style that is suitable for this document, and that his/her work is acceptable to us." Then have a line for the reviewer's name and signature and the date.

Specify Conditions for Extensions

As you'll see in Chapter 21, I recommend that eventually you should work per-project contracts rather than per-hour contracts. The earning potential is much higher in such contracts. But if you're paid by the contract, you will occasionally run into a problem: The work, through no fault of your own, will take much longer than you realized. For instance, if you are documenting software the project will probably be delayed; virtually *all* software projects take longer than the programmers project. (There are two basic rules of programming. The first rule is that the project will always take 20 to 50 percent longer than originally anticipated. The second rule is that there's no way to circumvent the first rule by overestimating 20 to 50 percent.)

It's a good idea to add some kind of clause that makes the company pay more if it extends the deadlines or adds features to the project. You might state that the contract is based on a particular software delivery date, and based on the beta software that you've been shown (keep a copy of the software), and that if the project changes greatly you will renegotiate. Some writers add clauses saying that they can drop the contract if the dates slip too far. In most cases companies fully understand that you might need to be paid more when they change the ground rules.

Specify Overtime Rates

If you are being paid by the hour, you might want to charge time-and-a-half for overtime. I've never done so myself (but then, I haven't done many per-hour contracts, preferring per-project contracts). However, other writers say that it's quite possible to bill for overtime. Simply write into the contract that you will charge time-and-a-half for all hours worked over 40. (Note that this may be tricky if you're working off the client's premises, though, as they'll have no confirmation that you really are working overtime.)

State That Payments Be Timely

Some writers, to make sure they get paid on time, clearly state in the contract that if payments are not made within a certain period they will stop work. For instance, one writer sent me a contract that included this:

> I will present an invoice to _____ every two weeks. Payment is due upon presentation of said invoice. In the event that payment is not received promptly, work on the project will cease until such payment is made. At the writer's discretion, an additional deposit may be required in the event that _____ defaults on a scheduled payment.

Be careful with such a contract, particularly the last part about the additional deposit. Some large companies probably won't accept the clause, though it looks like a good one if your sales skills are sufficient to convince the client that it's fair.

Cover Expenses

Some writers also charge for expenses, though I think this is rare. The writer whose clause you've just seen also had this clause in her contract:

> All expenses incurred by the writer for the sole purpose of completion of this project, including, but not limited to, shipping, long distance calls, faxing, travel, food, lodging, entertainment, computer equipment and software, photographic expenses, office supplies, etc., will be reimbursed within 30 days from presentation of receipts. Receipts and expense statements will be presented with invoices.

This writer told me that she charges for all equipment purchased for a particular project, regarding only her computer and basic software (word processing, accounting, and so on) as overhead costs not billable to the client. Again, you might have trouble getting clients to agree to this clause, but if a project looks like it might entail certain unusual expenses, you should definitely consider it.

Specify Client Responsibilities

You might want to add a clause that makes quite clear that you are dependent on the client providing certain things, such as information and facilities. The writer whose contract you've just been looking at uses this clause:

> In the event that work is being performed at the client site, suitable facilities and resources must be made available to the writer to allow timely completion of the project.

You might also state that the client is responsible for providing access to the client's employees so that you can find the information you need, and for delivering the latest version of the product (which is particularly important for software documentation). If you find, early on in the contract, that you are not getting access to the people you need to talk to, go to the person you negotiated the contract with and make clear that you must have access to a "subject matter expert" (SME). That is, someone who really knows the product well, and can answer all your questions.

Whatever you do, *don't* let a company restrict your access to the people who have the information you need. Some companies will tell you that the people who are creating the item you are writing about are too busy to talk with you. But that's okay, they'll tell you, just write down any questions you have and they'll pass them onto the SME. This is a completely ridiculous situation, but one that I've run into a few times. It's okay, I guess, if you're being paid by the hour with no performance criteria in your contract. But if you're being paid by the project to produce a manual, such a situation is completely unacceptable. There's no way you can produce a decent document in a reasonable amount of time under these conditions, and it's completely unreasonable for the client to expect you to do so.

Nor should you allow your SME—the programmer or engineer—to stall you with claims that he or she will answer your questions by e-mail. Some people will tell you they don't have time to talk with you, but will answer written questions, as if some-how it would be quicker than just sitting with you and chatting. It won't. You shouldn't accept those conditions—except, of course, if you're being paid by the hour without regard to what you produce.

Who Owns the Copyright?

There are copyright issues that you should consider when entering into an agreement with a client. Copyright law states that when you write something you own it, *unless* you've signed away the rights to it in some manner. If you are an employee and you are clearly writing the work for your employer, then the work is clearly a "work for hire" and belongs to the employer. But if you are a freelancer, the situation is different—and few clients understand it. If there is no statement in your contract about work for hire or copyright transfer, then you own the work.

It's generally accepted that the client has the right to use the work for what it was obviously intended. If the work is a software manual, for instance, the client can obviously send the manual out with the software; there's an implied agreement to the effect. However, there are many things the client *can't* legally do with the work. The client can't modify the work, for instance, nor extract pieces and use them in another manual for another product. You own the copyright, and the client has only a limited right of use.

If the contract states that the work is a "work for hire," the work belongs to the client lock, stock, and barrel; the client can do anything with the book. The client owns the copyright. If the client inserts a statement to the effect that the copyright will be transferred, the effect is the same: The client ends up owning the copyright.

Now, I want to be quite clear about this, because you'll run into people who won't believe it. I've excerpted the following from *Circular 9 Works-Made-for-Hire Under the 1976 Copyright Act*, available from the Copyright Office or on the Internet (the next section includes contact information for the Copyright Office).

> Section 101 of the copyright law defines a work made for hire as:
>
> (1) a work prepared by an employee within the scope of his or her employment; or
>
> 2) a work specially ordered or commissioned for use as a contribution to a collective work, as a part of a motion picture or other audiovisual work, as a translation, as a supplementary work, as a compilation, as an instructional text, as a test, as answer material for a test, or as an atlas, *if the parties expressly agree in a written instrument signed by them that the work shall be considered a work made for hire.* (Emphasis added.)

The document defines the term *supplementary work*, then continues:

> DETERMINING WHETHER A WORK IS MADE FOR HIRE
>
> Whether or not a particular work is made for hire is determined by the relationship between the parties. This determination may be difficult because the statutory definition of a work made for hire is complex and not always easily applied. That definition was the focus of a recent Supreme Court decision (Community for Creative Non-Violence v. Reid, 490 U.S. 730 [1989]). The court held that to determine whether a work is made for hire, one must first ascertain whether the work was prepared by (1) an employee or (2) an independent contractor.

We're not interested in the employee, so let's see what the document says about an independent contractor:

If a work is created by an independent contractor (that is, someone who is not an employee under the general common law of agency), the work is a specially ordered or commissioned work and part 2 of the statutory definition applies. Such a work can be a work made for hire only if (1) it comes within one of the nine categories of works listed in part 2 of the definition and (2) *there is a written agreement between the parties specifying that the work is a work made for hire.* (Emphasis added.)

This piece of information may come as a complete surprise to you; I know that few writers I've spoken with understand this. So, let me restate this quite clearly: *The fact that a client has paid you to create a document does not mean the client owns the document. Unless you have signed a written agreement transferring all rights in some manner, you still own the document and are only giving away limited rights to the document.*

This is the law in the United States, but copyright law is similar throughout much of the world, thanks to international treaties. If you are working in a country outside the United States, check with that nation's copyright authorities.

Register Your Copyright

This copyright information is well worth remembering, because it may help you if you ever run into problems with a client that won't pay. If the client uses the document without paying, it has broken copyright law. In fact, if you think you are running into problems with a client, you should probably register the work as soon as it's finished (it costs $20). If the work is not registered, all you can be awarded is actual damages—the money the client hasn't paid you. But if you register within three months of publication, or before the client has had a chance to use the document and infringe your rights, then the client will also be liable for statutory damages (in effect, a fine) and attorney fees. You can find more information from the Copyright Office (which will tell you how to register, though it won't give legal advice):

> Copyright Office
> Library of Congress, Washington, DC 20559-6000 (202) 707-3000
> Web: http://lcweb.loc.gov/copyright/Gopher: marvel.loc.govTelnet:
> marvel.loc.gov (login as *marvel*)
> Telnet: Locis.loc.gov

So how does all of this affect your contracts?

Avoid All Mention of "Work for Hire" and "Copyright "

Ideally, you should make sure that the contract doesn't mention the terms *"work for hire"* or *"copyright."* That gives you the most power, because until the client has completely paid for the work, the client has no right to use it. And even once the client *has* paid for the work, he or she still has only limited rights. The client cannot modify the work, for instance.

I've never used the copyright law as a weapon against a client. In fact, once I hand over a document to clients, I allow them to do what they want with it. I've never said, "Nope, you can't modify that, that belongs to me!" Usually, my clients have come back to me for modifications, anyway. However, if a client refused to pay, I could use the fact that the work belongs to me as leverage against the client.

Use "*Copyright*" Rather Than "*Work for Hire*"

What if the client demands some kind of statement to the effect that the client owns the work? Currently few clients understand copyright law, so few will put anything in the contract—and there's no need to educate them! Still, if the client tries to insert a clause saying that the work is a work for hire, suggest that you remove the clause and instead use a copyright transference clause—something like "When the contractor has received the final payment for services, the copyright for the document will be automatically transferred to the client."

Why transfer copyright rather than work for hire? If you work for hire and then have a dispute with the client, the client can argue that he or she owns everything you've done so far. With a copyright transfer at the end of the project, you own the entire thing right up to the point at which the copyright is transferred, putting you in a much stronger position.

More Information

If you or your client decide that you need a more complicated contract, talk with an attorney, or at least have an attorney review the contract before signing. In fact if you feel a little unsure of the whole contract issue, have an attorney review your first contract.

For more information on contracts see both Shenson's *Complete Guide to Consulting Success*, Jeffrey Lant's *The Consultant's Kit*, and Robert E. Kelley's *Consulting, the Complete Guide to a Profitable Career*. (See the Bibliography for more information about these books.)

There are also a couple of useful Web sites you might want to see. First, check out the National Writers Union Grievance Assistance & Contract Advice site, which has links to a variety of documents: http://www.nwu.org/nwu/grv/grvhome.htm. There's also a site created by attorney and writer Ivan Hoffman. This site has lots of articles related to how the law affects writers. See http://home.earthlink.net/~ivanlove. (Use the Helpful Articles for Writers and Publishers link.) You'll find that many of these articles are related to computer-book publishing (see Chapter 25), but you'll also find articles on subjects such as work-for-hire contracts.

Part IV

**Step Three:
Consulting**

Step Three—

Technical Writing

Consultant

Adam was not alone in the Garden of Eden, however, and does not deserve all the credit; much is due to Eve, the first woman, and Satan, the first consultant.

Mark Twain

Steps Two and Three often merge together (see "The Three-Step Method of Freelancing" in Chapter 4). I consider Step Two to be working at a customer's site, but without an agency paying you. You've cut out the middle man. I consider Step Three to be a more consultant-like situation; much of the time you won't be working at the customer's offices—you'll probably be working at home. And you may not be charging by the hour; to increase your income you will have to learn to charge by the project.

These two steps merge together, though, in the sense that while you are seeking one, you may run across the other. The marketing techniques for Step Two often bring you into contact with clients who don't want you in their office, or who would prefer to pay you for the entire project rather than by the hour. On the other hand, in Step Three, when you are actively seeking consulting work, you may use more "advanced" techniques. That's what we'll be looking at in this section of the book.

By the way, I've been asked now and again how one gains the "courage" to start doing independent contracts that you can do at home, to jump to true consulting. I don't think it's courage, really. I think it's a matter of having everything come together at the right time. You have a network and the marketing skills you need to find the potential clients. You have the résumé and list of references that will persuade clients to give you the job. You have money saved up so you don't feel the need to have a long-term, full-time contract. And you have the knowledge of your local market necessary to ask for a high rate without completely pricing yourself out of the market. When everything comes together at the right time, finding those consulting contracts is quite easy.

What Is a Consultant?

So far this book has explained how you can work like an employee but get paid like a consultant. Many contractors like to use the word *consultant* when people ask them what they do, but they are misusing the word. A contractor fills a job slot temporarily, perhaps for a week or two or maybe a year or two. He often does the same work as an employee; in fact in many situations you will work side by side with the client's employees, doing the same work in the same conditions. Contractors remain cogs in the machine (though well-paid cogs).

A true consultant, on the other hand, is in a different position. Consultants may have to create their own positions, using their marketing skills to convince a client that they should be hired to deal with a special problem, a problem the client company does not have the resources to deal with. Consultants work independently, and are not controlled or supervised by the client. Consultants may even hire other people to work on the project, and supervise them. Also, consultants often receive a set fee, because they are selling the solution to a problem or a finished product, not their time.

Some contractors may wish to continue down the road to consulting. Consulting sometimes requires much more marketing, and more sophisticated marketing, than mere contracting. It also may require more experience and ability. Consultants traditionally charge much more than contractors, but may also bill for less time, having to work more at selling themselves and handling administrative tasks.

Is it worth it? Successful technical-writing consultants can do very well, making $100,000 a year or more. But those who don't sell themselves well are often no better off than their contracting cousins, who may be working as cogs in the machine but are also free of much of the hassle involved in consulting. And a few contractors are making $100,000 or more, too. If you can work as a contractor and make $80,000, $100,000, or even $150,000 a year, you may find little incentive for becoming a true consultant.

In *The Complete Guide to Consulting Success* Howard Shenson provides a table showing the average pretax income of consultants in a variety of disciplines. For example, the average engineering consultant makes $96,311 while the average data processing consultant makes $81,008. Shenson believes the average income of all consultants to be about $91,102. Healthy though these incomes may be, they are within reach of many technical writers who are contracting rather than consulting. A contract writer in New York, for example, making $50 or $60 an hour and working 1,800 hours a year, will make $90,000 to $108,000.

In many areas of the country, though, rates such as these are rare for a contractor. I've met one contractor in the Denver area who earned $150,000 in his best year, for instance, working on a government contract. That's very unusual for the Denver area, though. Most contractors are making between $45,000 and $55,000. To push their incomes above $100,000, these writers would have to become consultants.

Charge by the Project

I try to make my projects pay between $100 and $150 an hour. That presents a problem, though. What would happen if I asked a prospective client for $130 an hour? That person would be neither prospective nor a client. Quite simply, I'd lose the contract. When other technical writers in my area are asking for $35 or $40 an hour, I can't ask for three or four times that sum, however good I may be.

I can, however, ask for $20,000 or $30,000. The nice thing about asking for a large sum like this is that the client has no idea how much I'll make per hour, and I certainly have no intention of volunteering the information. In fact I don't believe it's any of the client's business to know how much I earn an hour. After all, I'm not selling my time, I'm selling a product. When you buy a car, do you ask how much time it took to create the car? No, you base your decision on the worth of the car by comparing it to other, similar, cars.

Estimating Projects

Before you can charge by the project, though, you have to figure out how long a project will take you. And before you can do that, you have to figure out how long it takes you to do other jobs. I learned how to do that by logging my hours while working on my computer books (see Chapter 25). I used a stop watch, turning it on when I sat down to work, and off when I stopped—whether to take a break, answer the phone, or go to the bathroom. Later I began logging all my projects. Even now, I keep track of all the hours I spend on a project. As I write this sentence, I have a stop watch program running in the background, keeping track of the time I've spent working on this book.

Try this for yourself, and after a while you will find out how quickly you work, and be able to estimate how long a project will take. I don't mean that you will be able to say, "This book will take 320 hours." What you will be able to say is "This book will probably take 320 hours, but if it turns out to be a lot more complicated than I imagine, it could take as much as 400 hours." That's a big range, but it doesn't necessarily matter, because you can charge a much higher set fee than hourly fee, if you work quickly.

Here's how I figure all this out. I talk for a while with the client, trying to figure out exactly what is wanted. I always ask how big the book will be, and whether the client wants online help, too. You have to get the client to come up with an estimated page count. It's possible to write 50 pages about a product, or 250 or 500 pages about the same product. How much detail does the client want? That's a decision that the client must make, and most clients are quite willing to come up with a general page count, if only because they want to limit the size (and cost) of the document. (By the way, a paper document can be turned into a good online help system very quickly, often in a week or less. It can be turned into a mediocre online help system in an few hours.) I'll also take a look at the product, and try to estimate, based on previous projects, just how much work is involved.

Now, based on the page size, and what I've seen of the product, I'll try to figure out how long it should take to write the book. I try to figure out how long it will take *me* to do the work. But I also try to estimate how long it would take a technical-service agency to do the same book. Then I can do a few sums. For instance, if I figure that it would take a technical-service agency 400 to 500 hours to do the job, I may bid $30,000, which is what a technical-service agency might end up charging. I know, however, that I'll probably get the job done in 200 to 250 hours, bringing my hourly rate to somewhere around $130. What if I'm wrong, though? What if it takes me 300 hours? I still make $100 an hour. What if it takes me 350 hours? I still make $86 an hour. I should note, however, that I've never been that far off in my estimations, and with practice, there's no reason you should be, either.

I'd like to tell you that there's a magic formula that you can use to estimate projects, but there isn't. I once attended a Society for Technical Communication (STC) talk given by several documentation managers. They were explaining how they estimated projects. It was all very interesting, but at the end of the evening I don't think anyone in the audience really came away with a technique he or she could use. There were so many variables, so much variation and rules of thumb and guessing, that I'm convinced my method is just as good. Track your performance for a few months or a couple of years and eventually you'll be able to take a "guess" and get just as close as you can using any other method.

On the other hand, many technical writers do try to be more "scientific" about this process; in fact if you are managing a team of writers, you almost certainly have to. For information about estimating projects you might read *Managing Your Documentation Projects* by JoAnn T. Hackos (John Wiley and Sons). Hackos also sells a project-estimation program called PUB$ Estimator. You can read a review of this product on the World Wide Web, at http://stc.org/region2/phi/n&v/soft0196.html. And you can purchase the product through Hackos' company, Comtech, which is listed in Appendix C.

Another way to figure out prices is to bid a per-page price. A commonly stated price is $100 a page. What a page is, I'm not exactly sure, but that's a sum you'll often hear. For example, suppose that you have talked with the client and decided that the book will be 300 pages long, and you feel that in your area $100 a page is a reasonable fee. So you propose a fee of $30,000.

Of course whatever you propose, the client may come back and tell you that it's too much. Then you'll have to figure out how much lower you can go and still make it worthwhile, whether the project provides other benefits that will be useful (such as experience with a particular technique or technology that you know can help you earn money later), and just how badly you need the work. Of course you may want to pad your first bid a little to leave a little negotiating room.

Negotiating a contract like this is an art, not a science. There are no set rules to follow; a lot of it is simply a matter of having a "feel" for the situation—a feel for how quickly you can do the project, a feel for how long it would take your competition to do the job, a feel for how much the client can afford to pay, and so on. The more you do this sort of thing, the better you'll get—though you'll still screw up now and again. The thing I really hate to hear from a client is "Oh, that price sounds very reasonable." If it sounds reasonable to the client, you bid too low! You want to ask for just a little higher than the client is willing to pay. Either the client will agree to pay slightly more than originally intended—as one client told me, "I'm not going to quibble over a few dollars"—or force you down to the top rate.

A lot of writers base their fees on what they want to make per hour. That's the wrong way to do things, because what they want to make is usually based on the hourly fees they are used to making as contractors. One consultant, for example, told me that she estimates how long the job will take and then multiplies by $35 an hour. She's guaranteeing herself a low rate that way. Your fee should be based on "what the market will bear." Try to figure out how much the client would pay if it hired somebody from a technical-service agency. Agency rates can be as high as $60 or $65 an hour, sometimes more (this is the amount that the agency charges the client, not the amount the agency pays the writers).

Several years ago the manager of a programming consulting firm in Denver told me that the firm typically asked clients for $60 an hour for any writers they provided—and the firm was experiencing absolutely no problems with that price. The companies were paying without question, and getting average-ability writers. Rates will vary around the country, but remember that you are interested in the high rates, not the low rates. Compare yourself to the *best* writers, and don't try to sell yourself cheap.

Not only must you figure out the rate a technical-service agency would charge, but you have to figure out how long the agency's writers would take. Remember, though, the client is paying for time that the writers spend taking breaks, getting back late from lunch, talking to coworkers, sitting in unproductive company meetings, tracking down supplies, flirting with the receptionist, talking with friends and lovers on the phone, and so on. (I'm not exaggerating. Take a stopwatch to work with you and time the hours you and your colleagues spend in productive work; you might be surprised.) The client pays for both the productive and unproductive time.

Of course there's a catch: As you can see, you can make a lot of money by completing a job more quickly than most other writers, while charging the same that an agency would charge. This means that you will work harder than you would normally—but after all, nothing's for free!

Incidentally, there's one way to make a lot of money *without* charging by the project: You can lie. In other words, you tell the client you are billing $35 an hour, but you really bill $70 or more. I'm not advising that you do this, and I don't like the idea, but some writers work this way. As one writer told me, "I work more quickly at certain tasks than most writers, so when I carry out those particular tasks I bill the client two hours for every hour that I work." I don't like the dishonesty of this method; I'd rather be upfront and charge by the project. I can make good money, and I don't have to lie.

Managing Extensions

How do you protect yourself, though? What happens if the client keeps adding things to the project? I'll admit that there are some projects that simply can't be bid in this manner, projects that are so vague and open to interpretation that you'd be crazy to commit to a fixed sum. I haven't run into many projects like that, though. Usually it's quite clear what the client wants to produce, even if it isn't yet clear exactly which features the product will have.

I haven't yet run into a project that hasn't had additions and changes. For instance, when you start on a project documenting a computer program, you are given the program. As the project proceeds you get updates to the program. And the program changes. By the time the project is finished, you'll find that some of its original features have gone, new features have been added, and most features work slightly differently. (Here's a software-project tip: Don't bother taking snapshots of the computer program while you are documenting. Take the snapshots right at the end of the project. If you take them early, you'll only have to replace them anyway.)

In most cases I assume that there will be changes, and include those changes in the estimate of how long the project will take and how much I should charge. Sometimes, though, projects do change so much that you end up doing much more work. In such a case you can renegotiate the contract—though you should make sure you have something in the contract that allows you to do so (see Chapter 20), such as a clause stating that if the client adds more modules to the program or if the book will have to be larger, you can renegotiate.

Remember, though, that the idea of bidding by the project is to earn much more per hour than you would otherwise. If you screw up now and again, and the project takes longer than you thought it would, you may find that you are still earning much more than your old hourly rate.

Explaining the Price

Here's how I explain my prices to my clients. When the client asks how much I charge, or asks something like "What's your hourly rate?" I'll say something like this:

> "I don't charge by the hour. I prefer to work by the project. That way you know up front what the project will cost you, and I get paid a reasonable sum for my skills."

I've found most clients like the idea of paying by the project. Often they've worked with other writers who had a reasonable hourly rate, but who billed, and billed, and billed. If the client needs more explanation, though, I say something like this:

> "I really don't know what an 'hour' is. Do you? I know writers who will tell you one price, then bill for more hours than they actually work. And anyway, one person's hour is worth more than another person's. If I come in here and tell you that I'll charge you $45 an hour, what does that mean, exactly? Does that mean the project will cost you $15,000? $20,000? $50,000? You've no idea, right? If I bill by the project, then that's a solid figure you can work with."

Sometimes a client will ask me how I came up with my price. I usually say something like this:

> "Well, I try to figure out how much a technical-service agency would charge you to do the same job—not for an entry-level writer, but for one of the agency's top writers. I'm not trying to undercut anyone's price, I'm not trying to work cheaply, because you'll get a much better product from me than you will from a technical-service agency. But I still try to keep my price competitive with a technical-service agency."

Note that I don't sell myself as a cheap solution to the client's technical-writing problems. I never tell a client that I can do the job cheaper than anyone else; I have no intention of competing with $15- or $20-an-hour writers. I do, however, tell the client that my prices are competitive with the technical-service agencies, and I point out that I'll do a better job than the agencies. Remember, this is all linked to my other sales techniques, which we'll discuss in Chapter 22.

By the way, you'll sometimes run into a client who figures you are making a lot of money, and wants to know more. You might get a comment like "You'll do pretty well out of this contract, won't you?" or "So how long is this going to take you, then?" I respond with something like this:

"It's really difficult to estimate projects like this. Sometimes they take much more time than I figure, sometimes less. I win some and I lose some, and it balances out in the end. As for time, I'm not exactly sure how long it's going to take. I have to overlap projects, so at the beginning of your project and at the end I may be doing a few hours a week on something else; it's difficult to figure out actual hours. Anyway, I'm selling you a product, not my time. I base my costs on what it would cost you to get this done somewhere else. The only difference is, you'll get a better product if you use me."

How to Work Quickly

To do really well in freelance technical writing, you must be able to work quickly. I generally bid my projects based on how long I figure it would take a technical-service employee to do the project—then I complete the project in half the time. Here are a few tips for working quickly:

◆ Learn how to use all your tools correctly. It always amazes me how little most people know about the word processor they work with every day, for instance. Figure out all the little tricks that can speed up your work.

◆ Learn to type quickly. If necessary, buy a typing program that will help you increase your speed.

◆ Work with a word processor, not a desktop-publishing program. Most technical documentation can be created in a word processor far more quickly than with a desktop-publishing program. Word processors contain all sorts of tools to help you place words on paper more quickly, and they also contain basic desktop-publishing tools. Very few user manuals, for instance, require a desktop-publishing program to produce.

◆ Learn to use your word processor's macros. You'll often run into repetitive tasks that you can accomplish much more quickly by creating a simple macro. I've been able to cut a day's work into an hour or so by creating a macro to speed things up.

◆ Learn to use your word processor's "glossary" or "auto-text" features. These can drop large blocks of text into your documents with just one or two keystrokes. Save commonly used text as boilerplate that you can quickly insert at any time.

◆ Don't fix typos. You can waste a lot of time backing up and fixing typos. It's often quicker to use your spell-checker to fix them later. Also, many word processors can now automatically fix spelling mistakes for you; you can often add mistakes and their corrections to the list of automatic fixes during the spell-check.

◆ Use a programmable keyboard, mouse, or toolbar. Not all the programs you work with will have a macro feature. You can still automate actions by using a programmable keyboard (which allows you to program a number of keystrokes onto one key combination) or a toolbar utility that allows you to add program-mable buttons and keyboard shortcuts to any program. You can also buy programmable mice, which allow you to add operations to keyboard and mouse button sequences, or even to create custom pop-up menus.

◆ Keep on the lookout for software that can help you. There's an awful lot of bad software around, but now and again you'll find a program that really can help you work more quickly and run your business more efficiently. For instance, you need a good address book or personal information manager to store information about your clients.

Give Value for Money—Produce a Good Product

Not only can you make more money by working more quickly, but you can increase your income by becoming the sort of writer for whom companies are willing to pay more. In many cases contract (and full-time) technical writers work for months or years and produce little or nothing. I know writers who jump from job to job making good money, without doing anything worthwhile for their clients or employers. Many companies have lost tens or even hundreds of thousands of dollars by hiring bad technical writers. You can improve your consulting career by proving that clients can trust you to deliver high-quality, timely work. While some companies operate in the "warm body" mode—they hire the cheapest writer they can find—many actively seek writers with good reputations and are willing to pay more rather than take a risk with an unknown commodity.

Juggle Projects

Consulting work has a major drawback. You can never be sure when a project starts or ends. Consequently most technical-writing consultants I know work more than one project at a time. They rarely turn down work, and usually follow up on leads, even if they are busy. How, then, do they manage all this work?

They juggle, that's how. There's no easy solution. Sometimes they are working one project, at other times they have four or five going at a time. Occasionally they may find themselves in a crunch, with two or three projects ending at about the same time. Somehow they manage it! You may subcontract some of the work (for instance, you might hand over the completed text of a book to someone who can do the final layout, pagination, table of contents, and index), or you may end up working *very* long hours for a few weeks. That's just one of the occupational hazards.

One writer told me this: "To handle the glut, I have five people working for me part time to do the grunt work. I've told all clients that turnaround will be a little slower. And I'm working double shifts (9–6 and 9–2) plus between 12 and 20 hours on the weekends."

There's another reason for juggling projects. Many projects, particularly software projects, are extended dramatically. A six-month software project can easily extend to a year or 18 months. There are a couple of ways to handle this. You might try charging a retainer for the extended months. Or you might assume that every project will be extended and work multiple projects at once. That's what I've always done. I don't think I've ever worked on a software project in which the software was delivered on time. So when a client tells me a delivery date, I know that the program won't be delivered then; it'll be at least several months later.

Some writers are very specific about dates in their contracts. They state in a contract that if the contract stalls, then the contract becomes null and void, or may be renegotiated. This may work well for people billing by the hour, but if you're billing by the project it may be a little different. My attitude is that whether I do the work now or do it six months from now, I'll get paid for my work, so I don't walk away from contracts.

However, once or twice, when a contract has been stalled for several months and all of a sudden the client has wanted it completed, I've put that contract "on the back burner" while I've finished something else. I think I have an obligation to deliver a product on time, but a client that stalls a project can't expect lightning-fast turnaround a few months later. As one writer told me, "Failure on the part of the client to meet its deadlines may mean that it will have to wait for me when the product is finally ready."

Another writer likened writing software documentation to "changing a tire on a moving car." The software is always changing, and the deadlines are always extended and never met. It's just one of the problems that goes with the business. However, things seem to work out one way or the other. A friend told me recently that she'd been really worried about several projects she had. It looked like all of them would come together at once, and there would be no way that she could do them all. Somehow, though, she ended, "it seems like you manage to do it all one way or the other."

Just-In-Time Learning

I'm a great believer in what author William Horton has called *just-in-time learning*. I don't believe you should run out and learn everything you can, just in case you run into a client who wants a particular skill. Don't waste hundreds of hours learning every word processor and desktop-publishing program on the market, or learning HyperText Markup Language (HTML), WinHelp, and Java. Don't try to stuff yourself full of every little technique and trick that might ever be necessary in your business. It will cost a lot of money and, more importantly, take up a great deal of time—which could be better spent in marketing yourself.

Instead, quickly learn the skills that you need, when you need them—just in time. In most cases, you can learn each skill in just a few hours. HTML authoring is actually quite easy, for instance (HTML is the system used to build World Wide Web pages). You can learn the basics—enough to create multiple linked pages, with inline images, lists, a variety of different text styles, links within pages, and so on—literally in a couple of hours.

Now, that's not to say that you shouldn't learn a few basic skills and technologies. You should know how to use at least one of the major word processors (Word for Windows is the most used Windows word processor in the corporate world, for instance) and a desktop-publishing program. And (as you'll see next), you may want to go out and learn a particular skill if you want to target a particular niche. But trying to learn everything you possibly can is counterproductive.

Building a Reputation

To build a good consulting business you need to build your reputation. So how can you build your reputation? The first step, of course, is to do a good job for all of your clients. The next step is to build your network, and let people know who you are and what you can do. But you can do more. Write a few magazine articles and publish a book or two. Write a column for a local paper or computer magazine. You may not make much money—although if you do the right computer book you could make quite a bit—but having published work will help you build your image as a professional writer.

Find a Niche

If you can pick a well-paid niche and concentrate on it, you can push your income higher and make finding work easier. For instance, a few years ago I got the contract to write the user manual for a product called ForeHelp, a Windows-Help authoring tool. (In other words, this product is used to create the Windows Help files that most Windows programs include.)

At the time I knew nothing about Windows Help itself, though that really wasn't a problem. This contract was like any other—I had to learn the program, then write about it. Of course by the time I had finished the contract I knew a lot about creating Windows Help files. I also had a free copy of an excellent authoring tool (you can find more information about this tool at http://www.ff.com/), and had discovered that very few writers understood how to create Windows Help files. In fact when companies started looking for someone to create their online help, they had a lot of trouble finding anyone.

So I started selling my services doing online help. The work was fairly easy to come by, rates were pretty good, and it made a nice change from doing paper documents. In fact I could now sell an extra service to my clients. If I ran into a client who was creating a Windows product, I could offer to do the paper documentation *and* the online help. Furthermore, because few writers knew how to create Windows Help files, I could even sell my services online. (Chapter 24 explores in more detail how you can sell your services online.)

What sort of niche should you pick? I don't know how "hot" Windows Help is right now. I suspect there is still a shortage of good Windows Help authors, though I haven't done any myself for some time. Here are a few other areas you might consider, though:

Creating Web pages with HTML:	This is a hot area right now, but it's also one that *many* writers have latched onto. Though it's a newer technology, it may actually be more competitive than WinHelp work, because so many people are getting into it. You can find HTML classes everywhere. I've heard of writers getting $70 to $100 an hour creating Web pages, and know one writer grossing almost $200,000. I suspect rates are dropping quickly, though.
Java and JavaScript	I've heard writers suggest that these will be good technologies to learn. I'm sure they will, but they are really programming languages. (These are systems used to create programs that can be linked to World Wide Web pages.) There's a great misunderstanding about Java and JavaScript at the time of writing. JavaScript is simply difficult to use, while Java is *very* difficult to use. Yes, you can learn Java, but you won't be a technical writer anymore—you'll be a programmer.

ent response rate (which is pretty good for direct mail). One respondent asked
rite a magazine article, one asked me to begin work on a 400-page manual
tely, and one asked if I could write a computer manual for him. (I didn't take
the big projects, though, because by the time I received the offers, I was
l with work.) The other responses ranged from "We may be interested later"
e got something soon." I've now worked for several companies that I've
hanks to this mailing.

mail your résumé to 5,000 companies, however; you may get a few job
t you won't get consulting work. Before you produce a direct-mail piece, do
arch. In particular, read Jeffrey Lant's *Cash Copy*. You have to give your
npanies a reason to respond, not just say, "Here I am, come and get me."
art to direct-mail marketing, so before you invest a lot of money in
make sure you can produce a reasonable mailing piece. My mailing cost
0 for 1,000 pieces, though mailing rates have gone up since then. You can
g lists, build your own from directories you find in your local library, or
ts of advertisers in magazines.

ct direct mail, even if done expertly, to flood you instantly with contract
sider direct mail as just one way to help beef up your network. If you're
you might find something immediately. You're more likely, however, to
contacts that can prove valuable in the long run, contacts that lead to
onths or a year later.

tacts

ight you sell your work? Contact consulting programmers and begin a
relationship; for every program produced, there is a manual waiting to be
k to local printers and find out if they can recommend you to companies
ting manuals. Try advertising in industry-specific publications. (Shenson
ot an efficient way to find business, so I would call other consultants who
publications and go ahead only if they had a good response.) You might
or work using the Internet and the CompuServe computer network (see
teach a technical-writing course, produce a newsletter for local compa-
freelancing seminar at your local STC chapter. Shenson claims the most
chniques are using references from previous clients, giving seminars,
es, and publishing newsletters.

lting work is another book's worth of material, so if that's what you
ad Bly, Shenson, and some of the other business authors listed in the

ier!

of space in this book explaining how to find work. Here's the good
asier. If you do a good job for your clients, and you build a good
urself, eventually you can almost give up looking for work. The work
u. Many experienced writers almost never look for work; they are too
nd turning down job offers. The work comes to them. You may find all
a lot of work right now, but you should understand that if you do the
you can relax a little tomorrow.

| Multimedia authoring | I think this could b
There's not much n
work around comp
but there's a shorta |
| Software testing | A good writer coul
business doing "h
that is, sitting dov
program, playing
and then giving a
are a number of
blown testing lal
budgets of most
testing business
to a small comp |

Keep your eyes open for niches. New technologies emerge
to predict what will be "hot" a year from now, let alone
World Wide Web, for instance, didn't really start until la

Finding Consulting Contracts

How can you find the high-paying consulting projects?
techniques in this book, you will already be meeting pe
consultant. My first "set fee" project was with a compa
hire me on an hourly rate. I said that I would rather d
convinced the company that the benefit of knowing fr
would cost outweighed the disadvantages, if any, of ha
projects can be done away from the customer's site; se
that is available only there. But many projects can be
to getting this work is to recognize the opportunity ar
home. Remember, nevertheless, you are selling somer
sound as though the customer will benefit. And prop
do so.

If you become known throughout your network as a
you may get offers out of the blue from companies
Most writers don't want to work on a set fee—they
if you are known to work like that, you will someti

How else will you find consulting work? Read *The*
Success by Howard Shenson and *Secrets of a Free*
contain many good ideas. One method I can vouch
After one of my articles appeared in *Software Ma*
of work, one from a local company and another f
were at-home, set-fee projects). You can also try
online—and all the networking and job-hunting
this book.

Use Direct Mail

Few technical writers use direct mail to find wo
can work. A mailing of 1,000 pieces to comput

2.6 perc
me to w
immedia
either of
swampe
to "We'
reached

Don't jus
offers, bu
some rese
target cor
There's ar
mailings,
about $73
buy mailir
compile lis

Don't expe
offers. Cor
very lucky.
make a few
work six m

Make Cor

How else m
professional
written. Tall
that are prir
says this is r
advertise in
try looking f
Chapter 24)
nies, or give
productive te
giving speech

Finding cons
want to do, r
Bibliography.

It Gets Eas

I've spent a lo
news: It gets e
network for yo
will come to yo
busy working
this marketing
job right today

Sales Basics

Bold knaves thrive without one grain of sense, But good men starve for want of impudence.

English poet John Dryden (1631–1700)

I've been very lucky in my writing career. After getting laid off from the oil business, I spent over a year in a variety of sales jobs. First I tried running my own import/export business, bringing handicrafts into the U.S. from Latin America; I sold a couple of hundred thousand dollars worth of items from Colombia, Peru, Ecuador, and Mexico. But I didn't have the working capital I needed, nor the experience or knowledge of the business.

For a while after that I sold encyclopedias. I did okay; I almost got the nationwide "rookie of the month" award, but missed by just a handful of sales after my wife had to go into the hospital during the last week of the month. Still, it wasn't making me rich, and I moved on to selling telephone PBXs, burglar alarms, and photographic business cards.

Now, all this may not sound like good luck to you! In fact at the time I didn't *feel* very lucky. To do really well in most sales jobs you have to be exceptionally good at selling, and I wasn't. I think I was *good*, but that's not enough. Still, looking back on my experience, I realize that I learned things that help me now in my writing career, things that the average writer never really figures out. So, to help those of you not as fortunate as I, I've decided to explain a few of the basics of sales.

A Handful of Leads Is Not Enough

Many writers go after one contract at a time, or maybe two or three at a time. That's a lousy way to sell yourself. Any good salesperson knows that the real secret to good sales is to contact a lot of people. In fact while the general public has the idea that the truly successful salesperson is somehow too slick, many of the really top salespeople are not like this at all; their real secret is that they are very persistent and work very hard. The really important thing to know about sales is quite simple: The more leads you get, the more prospective clients you contact, the more sales you'll make! This is a variation of Woody Allen's claim that "80 percent of success is turning up." One might say that 80 percent of sales success is turning up—again, and again, and again.

Many writers go after one job at a time, and once they are working they stop looking. I've heard people say things like, "Thanks for the lead, but right now I've got my résumé out at a couple of places." You should *never* turn down leads, *never* turn down the chance to contact someone who's got a project you want.

You Are Always Looking for a Sale—Even When Working

Never give up looking for work. You should always be looking for the next contract, even when you don't need work right away. You can't afford to give up looking until you are out of work again, or you'll have lots of time out of work.

Even if you are working on a project, you should still follow up on leads. Just because a company is looking for a writer right now doesn't mean that the contract will begin immediately. These things have a tendency to drag out, and you may find that the contract begins in two or three months, just when your current contract is ending. Contracts often take weeks or months to develop. I've had leads that led to work over a year later. (In any case, most successful freelancers tend to juggle several contracts at once.)

A Sale Is Not a Sale Until the Contract's Signed . . .

. . . and even then you can't be completely sure. Maybe it's better to say that a sale is not a sale until you begin writing! Don't rely on promises, projections, or even verbal agreements. I once had a contract promised to me, though only verbally. I went on vacation for a month, not worrying too much about how I'd make money when I got back. I had a contract to come back to, after all. But during the month I was away, the contract was canceled, and I came back to nothing! (What did I do? I tried an afternoon of cold calling, which led to tens of thousands of dollars of work; see Chapter 17.)

On another occasion I had a verbal agreement to start work on a project. I spoke with the documentation manager at a small software company on Wednesday, and we arranged that I'd start the following Monday. Nothing was signed, because this was the first meeting I'd had with her; I said I'd bring a contract with me on Monday. She was going to be in a meeting Monday morning, though, so we arranged that I'd call her that morning and we'd figure out a time for me to come in. Knowing that this contract would keep me *very* busy for a few months, I decided to take the rest of the week off.

On Monday I called, but couldn't get through to her. I left a message. I called again a couple of hours later—and later that afternoon, and the next morning, and on Wednesday morning too. I did finally get through to her; she told me that her boss had told her to talk with another writer he knew before she made a commitment, but that she would call me back the following morning. It's been four years now, and she still hasn't called!

The moral of these stories is to keep looking for work all the time, even if you've been promised a job.

Play Up the Positives, Play Down the Negatives

It amazes me sometimes how freelancers manage to put their feet in their mouths, and raise irrelevant issues that may confuse or mislead the client. Remember always to "accentuate the positive" and forget about the negative. For instance, if your client asks if you know how to use the PageMaker desktop-publishing program, what do you say? Do you say, "Well, I did, sometime ago—well, it's been a while"? Or do you say, "Sure"?

Why waffle around and put doubt into the client's mind? Do you want the job, or not? If not—if you think you can't do the job—say so, thank the client, and move on. Otherwise, simply state what you *can* do, and don't seed the client's mind with doubt.

When discussing the project and how you can help, lead the discussion around to your strengths; that's the point of your visit, to show the client how good you are. If one of your weaknesses is somehow discussed in the meeting, don't linger. "Yes," you might say, "I haven't used PageMaker, but I've used Ventura, Quark, and FrameMaker; I don't think it will take long to pick up PageMaker."

Have You Used This Program?

Clients often get hung up on particular programs. If you haven't used program x, they think, maybe they should find someone who has. If you run into such a problem with a program, where the client is really concerned about how much you know, there are several ways to deal with it:

♦ Tell the client how many programs you *have* used. Most freelance writers eventually work with a whole bunch of different programs. Explain that you've used so many that you can pick up new programs quite quickly.

♦ Point out that you'll be working on the project for a long time—weeks or months. The time it takes to pick up the program is insignificant compared to the total project.

♦ Explain that there's a lot more to technical writing than being able to use a computer program. Who would they prefer to work with: a writer who knows the program but can't write, or a very good writer who needs to spend an hour or two picking up the program?

♦ As a last resort, offer to work the first day or two for free, while you learn the program.

A friend once told me she thought that a company was going to offer her a contract, but there was just one problem: She had to know how to use Samna, a simple word processing program that she'd never seen. "How many word processing programs have you used?" I asked. "Dozens," she replied. "And you don't think you could learn Samna?" "Well, of course I can!" I suggested that she go to a bookstore, buy a book on Samna, and read up on it. She did so. She then told the client that she could use the program (no lie, really). She got the job, and never was her competency with Samna an issue.

By the way, this technique was discussed in the TECHWR-L Internet mailing list (see Chapter 24) a year or two ago. One or two members of the list expressed anger that anyone would do such a thing. However, most responses were from writers agreeing that they would do the same thing—that they *do* do the same thing. Unfortunately many clients have a checklist mentality when they are hiring technical writers. They don't really know what makes a good writer, so they look for the things that they *do* understand: Has the writer got writing samples we can see? Has the writer done this sort of work before? Can the writer use WordPerfect, Word for Windows, PageMaker, or whatever? This mentality is very frustrating, as many writers really can pick up these programs very quickly, and it really makes no sense to exclude writers because they haven't used a particular word processor; far more important are the writer's research and writing skills.

Many writers think that if they can learn a program quickly, they can justifiably say "yes" when asked if they can use the program. If you follow suit, just make sure that you really *can* learn quickly.

"Assume" the Sale

Salespeople are often taught to "assume" sales. They act, to some degree, as if they have already sold the product to the client, and all that remains to be done is figure out how to deliver. When you talk with your clients you can use this technique, too. You talk as if you assume that the client would want you to do the job. For instance, you talk about what you *will* do, not what you *can* do on this project. You ask, "Do you want me to" do this or that? not, "Will you want the writer you hire to" do this or that?

No, assuming a sale won't guarantee a sale. But when you talk like this, the client can soon come to imagine you doing the job. Of course you have to assume the sale in your *actions*, not just your words. Which brings us to the next point.

Be Confident

The meek shall inherit the earth—but they'll find it difficult to find a technical-writing contract. It's important to be confident in all interviews, but much more important when you are selling your personal services as a consultant or independent contractor. Why? Because you have to convince the client that you can do what the company needs done, and that you can do it quickly and efficiently. Give the impression that you *might* be able to do the job, or that you can do the job if the client helps you, and you probably won't get the contract. I don't know how to teach you to be confident during meetings with clients. All I can suggest is that you get to meet plenty of clients; practice makes perfect.

Think About Why the Client Needs *You*

What's so special about you? What is it that you can do that other writers can't? When you visit a client, you are in competition with other writers. You have to think of a reason for the client to hire you instead of someone else. *Don't* try to sell yourself as a generic technical writer. "Hi, here I am, I'm a technical writer, hire me!" You have to be more than that. You have to be a consultant. You have to convince the client that you know *more* than the average technical writer, that you do a better job than the average technical writer. Actually you have to go further than that: You're not just better than the average technical writer, you're better than most.

There are a variety of ways to do this. Here are several things that I do:

◆ I show my magazine articles and books (see Chapter 25). I instantly set myself apart from other writers, because I'm published, and most aren't.

◆ I give a list of references to the client, and mention the list several times. I say something like "I'd really like you to follow up on my references, because they are very important to me."

◆ I raise an important issue in my prospective client's mind: How good are technical writers? We'll look at this issue next.

Bring Objections into the Open

An important technique taught to salespeople is to bring objections (that is, reasons that the client may not want to buy from you) into the open. You bring the problem out before the client has a chance to discuss it, then answer it and move on.

When you are selling your technical-writing services the client has a problem, though one that may not be mentioned. The simple fact is that many of your prospective clients have very little respect for technical writers—and that includes you. As I discussed earlier in this book, the standards in technical writing are very low. Ask your clients, and you'll find out just what sort of opinion people have of technical writers.

I've been asking my clients for a few years. Here's how it works. At some point during the meeting, usually fairly early on, I'll ask something like, "Have you worked with many technical writers before?" In most cases my clients say "yes," or "a few," or something similar. I'll then ask, "What did you think of them?" I've heard reactions such as these:

◆ "Not a lot."

◆ "They weren't a lot of good."

◆ "They all seemed to be cut from the same mold." (This was *not* meant as any kind of praise, I can assure you.)

◆ "They didn't seem to do much."

Remember, it's not your job to defend your fellow technical writers; you're there to find work. In fact if you do try to defend your fellow writers, you risk losing the contract, because in the client's mind you are now linked to those other (awful) writers. Instead you have a great opportunity to set yourself apart from (and way above) other technical writers. I say something like this:

> "It doesn't surprise me. I know standards in technical writing are very low. I've worked with hundreds of writers, and seen all sorts of shoddy work. There *are* good writers, but you have to look hard for them."

Now, there's one problem with this: It's nothing but my words. It does work to some degree—by admitting that standards are low in technical writing I've caught the client's attention, and I've set myself apart. After all, if I *don't* recognize the mediocrity in technical writing, I'm probably producing some of that mediocrity. Still, it begs an unspoken question from the client: "What's so special about you, then?"

For this technique to work properly, you must have a follow-up of some kind. So I usually continue by saying this:

> "That's why my references are so important to me. My clients ask me back because I give value for money—I do a good job and charge a fair price." I give the client my list of references at this point. "I hope you call them, because I really do rely on those references a lot."

Think about the effect of this statement: I'm not avoiding giving references, I'm not providing them and hoping the client doesn't call them. I'm right up front with the client, *encouraging* such calls. Even if the client never does call—and clients often don't—the client still will notice those references and my attitude toward them.

Now, I know this little sales technique shocks some technical writers. But there are two things to consider. First, it's very effective if used correctly. Second, *you (and I) didn't create the situation in which most clients have a low opinion of technical writers!* Those other writers did that. When I use this technique, I'm not misinforming my clients, I'm not brainwashing or tricking them. In most cases, all I'm doing is bringing the client's opinions out into the open and using them as a springboard to a sale.

Sell Solutions, Not Your Skills

I hate the word *solutions*; it's so overplayed that it's become a cliché, so I use it with some trepidation here. Still, it's a basic sales principle that customers don't buy products, they buy solutions to their problems and needs. For instance, you don't buy a book or video tape, you buy entertainment. Sure, you pay your money and the salesperson hands over a book or video tape, but what are you paying for? A few hundred sheets of paper between two glossy covers, a plastic molding with a plastic tape inside? No, you are buying the entertainment (or education, or whatever) that is held by the paper or plastic.

Now, this may sound like just so much sales hype, but until you understand this principle, you'll never fully understand what you are selling. When a prospective client starts looking for a writer, what does the company want? A writer? Of course not; what good is a writer? Can the company sell the writer? No, the client wants a particular document, of a particular format and standard and by a particular date. The writer the client is looking for is merely a means to an end. In fact if possible, the client would pay the janitor to produce the document—assuming, of course, that the client was sure that the janitor could deliver what the company needed. (In fact this is how so many secretaries get into technical writing. They're in the right place at the right time, when a boss figures anyone who can type can also write a user manual.)

So think about what you are selling. When I visit a client I certainly discuss my skills and experience, but I'm always looking for ways to convince the client that I can do what the client needs done. I'll try to focus on the project, not on what I've done in the past. When I do talk about what I've done in the past, I try to find parallels between my earlier projects and this new one.

I also want my client to believe that I can deliver a book without wasting too much of the client's time. Most clients want someone to go away, write a book, and come back when it's finished. Your prospective clients are very busy, and if you can take this hassle off their hands, if they can trust you to do the job without too much input from them, they'll be very grateful.

Ask for a Lot . . . and Accept Your Losses

If you ask for a low hourly or per-project rate, you guarantee one thing: You'll get paid a low rate. You must learn to ask for a lot of money. Many writers are intimidated by negotiating, and the very worst part for them is when it comes time to talk money. All too often they chicken out and ask for a low rate, because they'd be embarrassed if the client thought they were asking too much.

Part of negotiation is preparation. You need to know how much it would cost this company if it were to go elsewhere to get the job done. *Don't* compare your cost to the cost of the project if the company were to use a $12 an hour writer. There's no point being in this business if you plan to compete with writers making next to nothing. I've told companies that have offered ridiculously low rates that I just wasn't interested, and so should you (the more of us that send these companies packing, the higher rates will be for all of us). One client got quite offended when I told him I couldn't work for what he was offering. "Well, there are plenty of writers who *will* work for that," he said. "Oh, I'm sure there are," I replied, "but I don't have to work for that kind of money, and I don't plan to." I lost that client, but there's no way I wanted that project anyway.

You've got to accept that you'll lose some and win some—actually, that you'll lose most, at least early in your career. That's part of the game, and there's nothing wrong with it. In fact, you *want* to lose some sales, because some sales will come at such a cost to you that they are not worth taking. You want work on your terms, not the client's. For instance, I've heard freelance writers say "but if you charge that much, you are going to lose jobs!" Well, yes, I will and I do. But I don't *want* low-paying jobs. I'd rather work for 100 hours at $100 an hour than 333 hours at $30 an hour. You're not interested in finding jobs, you are interested in finding well-paid contracts that are interesting.

In fact some clients won't respect you if you ask too little, anyway. As one freelancer told me, "If you ask a really low rate, clients don't think much of you; they assume that you are worth as little as you are asking for." This freelancer also told me that on a couple of occasions she'd asked for more money than the client wanted to pay, wouldn't back down far enough for the client to offer her the work—and then had the client call back a week or so later asking her to do the job at her price, simply because the company couldn't find anyone else it trusted to do it as well.

Remember, you don't want to sound reasonable when you ask for money—you want to sound just a *little* unreasonable, you want to ask just a little more than the company wants to pay. Not so much more that the company won't even bother talking to you, but just high enough for the company either to go ahead and pay you, even if you are a little more expensive than it expected, or to negotiate your price down just a little. (By the way, you'll find that you aren't the only one who is not comfortable negotiating prices; many of your clients will be uncomfortable about this, too, and will often pay a higher price than they want to just because they feel awkward trying to bring your price down.)

To judge your price you need to understand the market you are working in. Accept that some companies will always look for a cheaper way to get the job done, and won't hire you. Just move on to the next contract.

Practice, Practice, Practice

I can't teach you sales success in one chapter. It's really something that takes practice, more art than science. You'll find that the more clients you talk to, the more comfortable you'll become and the more successful you'll be. How successful? I think most freelance writers have to visit several clients for every contract they get. In the last few years, though, I've successfully sold my service to *most* of my prospective clients. In other words, I knew that when I went on a sales call, the client would *probably* hire me. That's a much better feeling than going to visit a client and thinking that you've only got one chance in five or 10 of getting the work, and it's a feeling that you can achieve, with practice.

Remember also that you'll probably start with low rates and have to work your way up to higher rates. There's no need to feel bad because you don't get the very highest possible rates. As you get a better feel for what clients in your area will pay, and as your experience, skills, reputation, and sales ability grows, you'll earn more.

The Incorporation Issue

The next chapter looks at incorporation—whether you should or shouldn't incorporate. There are good reasons to start your own corporation, and good reasons not to. But you'll sometimes hear writers claim that you *must* incorporate, or you'll get turned down by too many clients.

Will you run into potential clients that won't give you a contract because you are not incorporated? Sure, it may happen. It probably won't happen often, though. There are lots of reasons that you'll lose prospective clients. The lack of corporate status is just one of many, and not a very important one at that. I've spoken with people who see this as a serious problem; I just can't get excited about it. And anyway, there's a technique you can use to avoid the problem in many situations, as I'll explain in a moment.

Incorporating to avoid this problem is like using a chainsaw to open a letter; it's overkill. Especially when incorporating often won't be enough for many of the companies that want you to be incorporated. Even if you are incorporated, they still won't hire you, because these companies usually have their list of approved technical-service agencies that they work with. If you're not on the list (and you probably won't get on the list), it doesn't matter how you've structured your business, you won't get the work.

Rather than spending time and money incorporating, apply the same resources to marketing, and you'll more than make up for clients lost to this problem. After all, each time you lose a job because you don't have a particular skill or knowledge of a particular program, should you blindly run out and get that skill, or learn that program? Not if you've got any sense. First you'll ask if it's worthwhile learning that skill or program, whether there's much call for it. You shouldn't assume that if you lose one contract because of that lack, you'll lose many more. And the same goes for incorporation.

I've rarely run into the lack-of-incorporation problem; contrary to popular opinion, there are *many* clients who are not concerned. I've recently done work for Mac Tools (you've seen their trucks driving around, visiting garages and selling tools),

MasterCard, and Amgen (a big biotechnology company), all without being incorporated. Few if any of my small clients express any concern. And why should they be concerned? If you are working as a true independent contractor (see Chapter 19), the client has absolutely no reason to worry.

Let's suppose that you are visiting a potential client who raises this issue. "You aren't incorporated, are you? Won't we have problems with the IRS?," he asks. You might reply to the client as follows:

> "It's really not a problem, though I know a lot of people worry about this. The IRS has a set of guidelines that help determine a person's status, whether he's an independent contractor or an employee."

You can make a copy of the information listed in Chapter 19 and show it to your client, or even give your client a copy of **Publication 1779: Independent Contractor or Employee...** (a small flyer available free from the IRS; see Chapter 19 for more information), which looks a little more official. (Do I carry copies of this document? No, because I think this whole thing is pretty much a nonissue, and have never really run into serious problems. But so many people are concerned about it; I'm just suggesting that you *can* do this if the problem really worries you.) Continue talking with the client in this general vein:

> "Take a look at those guidelines; you won't find the word *corporation* or *incorporation* anywhere in that list. As long as I satisfy these guidelines, there's absolutely no reason to worry about the IRS. It doesn't matter if a person is incorporated or not. Even if someone *is* incorporated, if he *doesn't* satisfy the guidelines, that person *and* the client are still in trouble. The IRS can still define the person as an employee of the client.
>
> "Corporations are a red herring. A lot of technical-service agencies encourage the belief that only corporations can protect you, because the agencies benefit. Every time they scare a company away from an independent contractor, that's one more contract for the technical-service agencies. But if a technical-service agency doesn't act correctly, its clients can still get in trouble with the IRS; the fact that the agency is incorporated is no protection.
>
> "What really counts is that I will be working in such a manner that the IRS will not be able to question my status. I won't be working on site all the time; I'll be using my own equipment; I'll still have other customers; I'll still keep my marketing going; and so on. There's no real reason to worry about the IRS."

Of course presentation is everything. If you deliver the preceding speech nervously, as if you aren't sure of yourself, it will count for nothing. If you deliver this speech confidently, you can often win the client over to your side.

Sometimes a client is willing to use a company name on the invoices and contracts (rather than your personal name) and to forget about the incorporation issue. You don't need to incorporate to use a company name; simply register one with the state (it usually costs around $10).

A couple of times I've solved this incorporation issue to my clients' satisfaction simply by providing a company name. In most cases, though, I use my own name, and the client doesn't care. I can't think of any contracts I've lost because I wasn't incorporated.

c h a p t e r **23**

Should You

Incorporate?

I see it all perfectly; there are two possible situations— one can either do this or that. My honest opinion and my friendly advice is this: do it or do not do it— you will regret both.

Danish philosopher Søren Kierkegaard (1813–1855)

This chapter discusses incorporation in some detail, because as you progress in your freelancing career you'll probably meet other writers who inform you that you must be incorporated. That's quite simply, and demonstrably, untrue; many successful freelancers are not incorporated. However, it may be true that at some point in your career incorporating will be beneficial. Or it may not. There's so much misinformation about the subject that it is worthwhile to examine the issue closely.

Note that this chapter discusses the advantages and disadvantages of incorporating your business. It's intended as an introduction to the issue, not as the answer to all your questions. Before you make a final decision about whether incorporating is beneficial for you, talk with your tax and legal advisors.

If you ask proponents of incorporating for details about just how incorporating can help you, they waffle. They often can't answer; they claim a general benefit, but can't give you specifics. So, here are a few examples of statements I've heard from a number of people (including "experts"), statements that are incorrect or misleading:

"If you incorporate, you won't pay FICA on corporate income, but you will pay it on all your income if you are a sole proprietor; the government doesn't care what your business expenses are." (This piece of "advice" comes from someone who claims to have been a chief financial officer for large corporations, and currently runs a company advising new businesses.)

This is nonsense. The first part is correct: Corporations don't pay FICA (Self Employment tax) on income. Of course, they *do* pay FICA on the wages paid to their employees (that's you, if you incorporate). As for the second part, it's completely incorrect. A sole proprietor subtracts business expenses from business income and *then* pays FICA.

continues

continued

"As a sole proprietor, you can deduct business expenses only if you have declared that you are in business." (The chief financial officer again.)

I suppose this is true, but it's also meaningless. You "declare" that you are in business by filling out Schedule C at tax time. You deduct your business expenses on that form. Of course, unless you fill out Schedule C, you can't file your business *income*, either, so this comment is meaningless.

"If you incorporate, when you travel, you can deduct hotel and meal expenses."

Argument: "You can do that if you are a sole proprietor."

Response: "Oh, but you can deduct a higher percentage if you are incorporated."

(This advice comes from the writer of a nationally syndicated business advice column, in a private discussion.)

Rubbish. A business expense is a business expense. You can currently deduct 50 percent of your business-related meals and entertainment costs—whether you are incorporated or not.

"Anyway, it's easier to deduct expenses if you are a corporation."

Argument: "Why?"

Response: "Well, it just is; you are obviously a business."

(The same nationally syndicated business advice writer.)

If you file Schedule C, you are obviously in business, and you can deduct the same things that you could if you were incorporated (with the exception of several important items that you learn about in the section "The Advantages of Incorporation," later in this chapter). Perhaps the IRS looks more closely at freelancers than corporations; indeed, the IRS audits freelancers more often than S corporations (I discuss the different forms of corporation a little later), according to Henry Aiy'm Fellman, author of *How to Keep Your Hard Earned Money: The Tax Saving Handbook for the Self-Employed*. But the difference in audit rates is generally small, perhaps a fraction of 1 percent, or perhaps as much as 1 or 2 percent.

"As a corporation, you can deduct *tangential* expenses." (The nationally syndicated business-advice writer again—to a private group, not in print!)

The clear implication of this comment is that you can deduct expenses that are not really business expenses if you are incorporated. Of course, you don't need to incorporate to commit tax fraud! I'll concede that it may be easier in some situations to carry out fraud on a larger scale if you incorporate, but I think you'll have to have a larger business to make such fraud worthwhile anyway. And in any case, I'm assuming that you are *not* planning tax fraud, and I don't plan to provide any advice on this subject!

Double-taxation doesn't exist, and is a myth. "You won't be taxed twice on the same money." (Judith H. McQuown, in her book *Inc. Yourself.*)

Not all corporations run into the double-taxation situation, but it most certainly *does* exist, and if your C corporation is profitable, you *will* experience double-taxation. This chapter explains this in more detail later (and explains the difference between a C and an S corporation).

"For most people, [medical deductions] can wipe out over $5,000 in medical bills every year." (McQuown again.)

How can you make incorporation sound good? Exaggerate the benefits. While a corporation can pay your medical bills, having the corporation pay $5,000 of your medical expenses is not the same as *saving* $5,000. The actual saving is the amount you'd pay in taxes on $5,000 if you weren't incorporated—probably somewhere between $1,350 and $1,600, a long way from $5,000.

"It's easier to deduct expenses for a corporation."

Argument: "Why?"

Response: "I don't know, I don't write the tax laws!"

Argument: "I mean, in what manner is it easier to deduct expenses?"

Response: "Oh, I don't know, I leave that up to my accountants. All I know is, I pay a lot less tax."

(This gem was from the small-business advisor again.)

How can I answer this? *It's easier to deduct expenses…I don't know why, my accountant deals with that.* It's hard to argue with imprecision. As I've just mentioned, a business expense is a business expense. If you spend money, and you can show that the expense is related to your business, it's a deductible expense, whether you are incorporated or not. There are several important things that you can deduct as a corporation—medical expenses and life insurance, for instance—but the day-to-day operating costs of a business are deductible to both sole proprietors and corporations.

"My friends will stop rolling their eyes when I say I'm not incorporated."

Sorry, not a good reason to incorporate! Of course, if your friends plan to pay the expenses involved . . .

continues

continued

"It instills discipline."	You need discipline to run a business, incorporated or not. Of course, you'll need more discipline to run a corporation, because you have to comply with a lot of regulations.
"It shows commitment."	To whom? There are cases in which incorporating is essential, in which the only way a business can grow is to show that it's a real business. But if you don't plan to grow, if you want to remain working by yourself, incorporation is rarely necessary.
"I eventually found it useful to be incorporated."	I'll admit that there *are* good reasons to incorporate. We'll look at them later in this chapter. But I don't think it's a good idea to incorporate *now* just in case it might be useful *later*. Incorporate when you need to, not before.
"It makes it easier; as an employee of your corporation, you don't have to file quarterly taxes."	You, personally, will have to file fewer tax forms, that's true. But you, as a corporate official, will have a far more complicated tax picture to deal with. There's no way that incorporating *simplifies* your tax paperwork!
"I'll save enough in taxes to pay the cost of incorporation in a couple of months!"	If you think you're really going to save that much money, you have a shock coming!
"If you are incorporated, you can get jobs with clients who won't normally work with freelancers."	Maybe, maybe not. Probably not, I believe, or at least not often enough to make incorporating worthwhile.

So many freelancers push incorporation as a Good Thing, without understanding the ramifications. All too often they use the age-old cop-out: "I don't know why, but my accountant/lawyer/teacher/friend/mother told me it's true."

How can you tell when someone is giving you bad information about incorporating? Well, it's very difficult. If you don't understand business taxes, for instance, some of the "advice" in the preceding table may sound quite rational. "Oh, I can deduct a higher proportion of my travel and entertainment expenses; I can deduct other expenses, too, ones that I couldn't as a sole proprietor." This advice is probably nonsense, of course (with a few exceptions that we'll look at in a moment), but if you don't understand taxes, you might accept such advice as the truth.

Don't rush into incorporating. Do your homework, ask for specifics, and don't be afraid to challenge statements that don't ring true. If you really want to benefit from incorporating, make sure the benefits are not just dreams and misunderstandings.

How can so many people be so sure that they are benefiting from their corporations in ways that they are *not*? In many cases it's the only form of business they have ever had or understood. I think that many people understand only corporations, have heard how good corporations are, and thus assume that sole proprietorship is a real problem. Also, many people are in businesses that most certainly *should* be incorporated. As you'll learn later in this chapter, there are very good reasons for incorporating. But there are also very good reasons for *not* incorporating, and those are often forgotten. People often assume that "If I'm incorporated, and it's good for me, it must be good for everyone else." Not so.

Finally, many people didn't understand their tax and liability situation before they were incorporated, don't understand it now that they've incorporated, and thus have no good way to compare the two situations.

"Incorporate Yourself" Books

The waters have been muddied by the "incorporate cheap" writers. At your local bookstore, you'll find books with titles such as *Inc. Yourself: How to Profit by Setting up Your Own Corporation*, *The Complete Book of Corporate Legal Forms*, and *How to Form Your Own Corporation Without a Lawyer for Under $75.00*. The basic premise of all these books is that incorporating is a Good Thing, a Profitable Thing, and that you can do it by yourself. Many of the books are little more than detailed descriptions of which forms to fill in; there are a few pages at the front telling you all the wonderful things you can do once you are incorporated, then the rest of the book is filled with sample forms and instructions.

But as easy as incorporating can be, actually *running* the corporation is a different matter. There are as many disadvantages as advantages, and you really have to understand both sides if you want to figure out whether the advantages outweigh the disadvantages. Unfortunately these writers are incorporation zealots; their books sell on the basis that it's a good idea to incorporate. Few of these books explain the disadvantages in anything but the most cursory detail, and some are downright misleading. Take the claim that double-taxation doesn't exist, for instance.

Double-Taxation Is *Not* a Myth

Inc. Yourself is one of the most popular incorporate-yourself books. It's sold hundreds of thousands of copies—over 400,000 the last time I looked! The premise of the book is that you can use incorporating as a way to get rich, and that virtually anyone can benefit. But the author spends little time discussing the disadvantages, and seems to misrepresent certain facts.

Under the heading "The Myth of Double Taxation," for instance, the book blatantly misrepresents the corporate tax situation. In a section that should, surely, discuss double-taxation, it doesn't; instead, the book states that your salary will be taxed at your personal rate, and any income to the corporation that is not paid out is taxed at the lower corporate rate, thus saving you taxes. The writer leaves the reader thinking that double-taxation really is a myth, but she hasn't even discussed double-taxation.

Here's why double-taxation is *not* a myth. The author of *Inc. Yourself* is quite correct about the two tax rates. She's quite correct that the money left in the corporation will be taxed at a lower rate. What she fails to point out is that the money left in the corporation *isn't your money!* It's the corporation's money. You can't use it to buy groceries, to pay the rent or mortgage, or to buy a car, clothes, or vacations. At some point, then, you have to get the money out of the corporation. In fact, if you accumulate too much money in the corporation, the IRS can assess a penalty and *force* you to take the money out as dividends.

At some point, then, you must take the money out. What happens at that point? You are taxed on it. This money is the corporation's profits, money that has already been taxed once within the corporation; when you take it out, it will be taxed again. Hence the term *double-taxation*. Double-taxation *does* exist.

The Advantages of Incorporation

So much for the misinformation. But for all the nonsense, there really *are* good reasons to incorporate (though they're often not quite as good as the proponents make out). This section takes a look at them.

Lower Taxes on Money Not Removed from the Corporation

Corporate tax rates are lower than the personal tax rates you are likely to be paying. But remember, if you don't take the money out of the corporation, you can't spend it; it's not your money, it's the corporation's. When you take the money out of the corporation it will probably be taxed, as you'll see in a moment.

Limited Liability in Some Circumstances

One of the most important reasons for incorporating is to protect yourself from legal liability. If your business somehow harms someone who then sues, your business takes the rap, not your personal finances. However, this may not always work well for freelancers, as we'll see later.

Deductible Medical Expenses

You can have your corporation pay your medical insurance and medical costs, and deduct the costs as a business expense. (Note, however, that if you are married, you can do this as a sole proprietor; you can employ your spouse, then pay his or her medical insurance and costs, and make the plan also cover your spouses' spouse—that's you.)

Deductible Disability Insurance

You can also have the corporation provide a disability insurance policy.

Deductible Life Insurance

The corporation can provide a life insurance policy of up to $50,000 for you, tax free. It can also buy more life insurance, though you'll be taxed on the value of the insurance.

A Pension from Which You Can Borrow

You can set up a pension fund that allows you to borrow money from it; you could borrow to put a down payment on a house, for instance.

Stock Profits Are Mostly Tax-Free

Money left in the corporation can be invested in stock; the profits from this stock are taxed at a greatly reduced rate. You can also turn over stock to your corporation, and allow the stock dividends to accumulate at a fairly low tax rate. However, there are limits to how much stock the corporation can hold. If 60 percent of your corporate income comes from stocks, the corporation automatically becomes a personal holding corporation, and is taxed at a higher rate. If you think this advantage may be one you can take advantage of, talk to a tax account.

A $5,000 Death Benefit to Your Family

The corporation can pay your family $5,000 when you die, and deduct the cost as a business expense. (Wow, that's one advantage to look forward to!)

Getting Money Out

How can you take money out of your corporation? There are basically four ways:

- *Salary.* There's no tax benefit here. You'll end up paying higher taxes on money paid to you as salary, because there are some taxes that employers have to pay that freelancers don't, and the FICA rate is slightly higher.

- *Dividends.* If you take money out as dividends, you'll pay the current capital gains tax—which currently is the same as your income-tax rate—to a maximum of 28 percent for long-term capital gains, perhaps more for short-term. If tax law changes and dividends are made nontaxable, as some lawmakers are calling for, then the incorporation picture will change entirely. (I'm not betting on it happening!)

- *Loans.* Your corporation can make you a loan, but you'd better be careful, as the IRS may get suspicious. And you'll have to pay it back, anyway, with interest, so you'll still have to get the money out some other way eventually.

- *Liquidation.* When you close your corporation down (when you retire, for instance), you'll have to pay tax on the profit, the money in the corporation over and above the money and other physical assets that you invested into the corporation. Of course, when you liquidate, you may be in a lower tax bracket than before. And you *may* be able to average out the income from the liquidation over several years. Talk with a tax accountant about this.

Disadvantages of Incorporating

There are a variety of disadvantages to incorporating that seem to get lost in all the hoopla about what a wonderful thing it is. Here are a few things to consider:

- *Higher taxes.* You'll pay a slightly higher rate of tax on your salary, because employers have taxes that most freelancers don't have to worry about— unemployment tax, workers compensation, and a slightly higher FICA rate, for instance.

- *Corporation tax.* Money you don't take out as salary isn't taxed as salary and doesn't have FICA taken out. But you still pay a corporation tax, though probably at a lower rate than your personal income tax.

- *Double-taxation.* As you saw before, the money you take out of your corporation as dividends is taxed twice: once under the corporation tax, and once when you declare your dividends on your personal income tax.

- *The IRS can force you to take money out.* If you retain too much money in the corporation, the IRS can force you to take money out as dividends, and tax you on those dividends. If you are really unlucky, the IRS can also assess a penalty on the excess accumulation. The IRS can fine you 27.5 percent of the first $100,000 excess accumulated income, and 38.5 percent of everything over that. And that's after the corporate income tax you will already have paid on that money, and before the taxes on the dividends that you'll have to pay when you take what's left over out of the corporation.

◆ *The IRS can kill your corporation for tax purposes.* If the IRS decides that the only reason you incorporated was to avoid taxes, it can tax you as if you were not incorporated. Note that *you cannot legally incorporate for the sole purpose of lowering your taxes!* The IRS doesn't like that, and has the power to declare that your corporation must pay taxes as if you were a sole proprietor. I'll admit, though, this probably doesn't happen too much.

◆ *The IRS can declare that your salary is too low.* If you pay yourself a salary that's obviously much too low (lower than you would earn if working for someone else's company doing the same work), the IRS can force you to take a higher salary, negating some of the tax benefits you were trying to obtain.

◆ *The IRS can declare that your salary is too high.* If you pay yourself a salary that is clearly much higher than you would earn with another company, the IRS can force you to take a lower salary, leaving the excess money in your company and making you pay corporate tax on that money. Of course you can't leave that money in your company forever. When you take the money out as dividends, you'll have to pay tax on it again.

◆ *Corporations are complicated.* Running a corporation is complicated (as you've probably already noticed). You've got loads more paperwork, and running it improperly can cause many problems. You'll need professional help—which will cost you money.

A Question of Liability

You can pretty much forget limited liability as far as bankruptcy goes. One writer wrote in the TECHWR-L mailing list (see Chapter 24) that incorporation protects you if your "business fails messily." Just how messy could it get? Freelance technical writers simply don't require much business debt. What debt you do run up—office supplies, software, maybe even computers—is probably going to be *personal* debt, even if you are incorporated. If you take out loans to buy equipment, you may find that bank officers aren't willing to give the loan directly to the corporation; they know you are really a freelancer. Rather, they'll make you take personal responsibility for the loan. Freelance writers do not usually find themselves with much corporate debt, however much personal debt they have. (If you are in a situation in which you plan to run up a lot of debt—perhaps you plan to start a technical writing agency, with employees, office space, and so on—you are in a special situation, and incorporating may be a good idea for you.)

What about the risk of being sued? Corporate status may not help much. As attorney and tax account Henry Aiy'm Fellman told me, "Incorporation can protect you from someone else's negligence, but not from your own." In other words, if you have an employee who harms someone's person or property, your corporation can be sued, but you personally may not be sued because you don't employ this person—the corporation does. But if *you* hurt someone, your corporation can be sued and you can be sued, too. (Fellman is also the author of *How to Keep Your Hard Earned Money: the Tax Saving Handbook for the Self-Employed;* see the Bibliography.)

There's also something called *piercing the corporate veil*. It means that even though you have a cooperation that is intended to place a *veil*, a division, between you and the outside world, that veil can be pierced, and the outside world can come in and get you. How? If you don't run the corporation absolutely by the books, or if your legal opponent can find any small way in which you run your corporation more like a sole proprietorship than a corporation, the corporate veil can be pierced and you personally must take complete responsibility for your corporation.

Personally, I don't think technical writers have much risk of being sued, anyway. (How many technical writers do *you* know who have been sued for damages caused by their writing? I don't know any.) Although suits can happen, even if they do, being incorporated probably won't protect you.

By the way, you may want to try to protect yourself in a couple of other ways. Buy business liability insurance; that will protect you if a client visiting your home office falls down the stairs, or if you trip and drop your laptop on someone's toes at the client's office. (Some of the small business associations in Appendix D, such as the Home Business Institute, have business liability insurance.) You can also make sure your contracts include a clause making the client responsible for reviewing the accuracy of your work (see Chapter 20). And you may want to include a disclaimer in all of your publications; many clients will ask you to include a disclaimer in their books anyway.

If you plan to build a technical-writing agency, and employ other writers to work for you, or if you often subcontract work to other writers, you should consider incorporating to protect yourself.

How Much Can You Save?

So how much money might you save from incorporating? I'm not going to bother discussing the fact that you'll pay less tax on your corporate profits; you've got to get this money out eventually. (However, I'll agree that this may be beneficial to free-lancers nearing the end of their careers, if they can leave as much money as legally possible in their corporation until they stop working, then liquidate the corporation and pay income tax on the realized profit at a lower rate because they no longer have any other income. This is all very complicated, though, and something you should talk about with a tax lawyer.)

But there are definitely some other financial advantages. To explore the advantages and disadvantages, this section uses the example of a typical technical writer. This example won't match everyone, but you can increase or lower the sums I'm using to match your own case. I'm also going to assume that our example writer remains alive, so I can ignore the $5,000 death benefit. Here, then, are the deductions a corporation can make:

◆ *Medical insurance deduction.* You can get the corporation to pay your medical insurance. In this example the insurance is $4,800 a year (because that's what I currently pay). But you can't count this entire sum as the amount saved; even if you are not incorporated, you can deduct 40 percent of your health insurance (on Form 1040). So the real benefit, the sum that a corporation could deduct that a freelancer could not, is 60 percent of the medical insurance, $2,880. (The health insurance deduction will increase to 45 percent soon, then even higher, further reducing the benefit to the corporation.)

◆ *Medical expenses deduction.* Unlike the freelancer, the corporation can pay other medical expenses, too, and deduct the costs. Let's suppose that the example writer has $1,000 of medical expenses on top of his insurance premiums. (On Schedule A, freelancers can deduct medical expenses over and above 2 percent of their adjusted gross income. In most cases, that limit effectively kills the deduction, so we'll ignore it.)

◆ *Disability insurance.* I pay $1,200 a year for disability insurance, so we'll use that sum. There's a drawback to having a corporation pay your disability insurance, though; if you ever use the insurance, any benefits paid to you are taxable. If a freelancer buys a policy, any payments made on the policy are *not* taxable.

◆ *Life insurance.* Life insurance really isn't worth a lot for most people. I'm paying $1 per $1,000 of coverage (see Chapter 13 for information on getting good life insurance rates), so $50,000 of coverage is worth only $50 a year for me. And although the corporation can buy more insurance for our writer, the corporation has to declare "imputed income." In other words, for every x thousands of dollars of life insurance that the corporation buys for the writer, it has to determine how much that insurance is worth (according to tables provided by the IRS . . . isn't this fun) and then declare that value as income. For instance, an additional $100,000 of life insurance for someone between 35–39 inclusive is worth $132 (according to the tables). But our example writer may be able to buy insurance cheaper than this, anyway, so I'm ignoring the value of additional insurance over and above the $50,000 level.

What do these deductions add up to?

Deduction	Dollars
Medical insurance	2,880
Medical expenses	1,000
Disability insurance	1,200
Life insurance	50
Total	5,130

So, the writer has $5,130 in deductions. These deductions are not benefits, but simply the sum the example writer can deduct from his taxes (that he wouldn't be able to deduct if he were not incorporated). So let's see how much tax the writer would pay on this money if he were *not* incorporated; *that's* his savings.

The tax he'd pay on this sum depends on his tax bracket, of course. If our writer is in the 28 percent tax bracket, he'd pay $1,436 on $5,130. If in the 31 percent bracket, he'd pay $1,590. There's also the Self Employment tax to consider, though the amount may not be much, probably somewhere between $125 and $700, depending on total income. Then there's state income taxes. Suppose that the writer lives in Colorado, where state tax is 5 percent. That's $257 in state taxes.

What does the writer end up with? Depending on his income, the writer will probably save somewhere around $2,000—not so much, really. Still, every little bit counts, and it's nice to save even this amount—except that he hasn't really saved this amount, because we haven't considered the cost of running the corporation. The writer pays slightly more FICA on a salary than he'd pay Self Employment tax on self-employment income. He may have to pay state franchise taxes, too, along with corporate income tax, unemployment tax, and workers compensation. And he'll definitely be doing more paperwork—which will cost money in the form of payments to an accountant or his own time wasted when it could be better spent some other way.

Yes, these numbers may change dramatically. The lower your tax bracket, the lower the benefit. You may be paying more for medical insurance, or less, more for medical expenses, disability insurance, and life insurance, or less. Do the numbers, and see how it turns out. You may find that the money you save is barely enough to pay an accountant to run your corporation!

The S Corporation

The examples you've looked at so far relate to a full corporation—the C corporation, as it's sometimes known. But there's another, simpler, form of corporation: the subchapter S corporation (known simply as an *S corporation*). The nice thing about the S corporation is that it simplifies the way in which you pay taxes—in fact, there are no corporate taxes, because you treat all the corporation's income as personal income. There is no corporation or franchise tax, no double-taxation, and so on. The problem is that you also don't get all the advantages of a C corporation—no medical and disability deduction, no pension plan that you can borrow from, no free life insurance, and so on. So what's the point of an S corporation? Well, there's liability protection. The S corporation provides limited liability, without the complicated (and sometimes worthwhile) tax and benefits situation of the C corporation. But as you've seen before, liability protection may be illusory for a freelance writer. The other major advantage is that you may be able to pay yourself some of your income as dividends instead of salary, thus avoiding paying FICA on that income. But if you earn a lot of money you may be well over the limit at which most FICA stops, in which case you won't save much by diverting income to dividends. And if you don't make much money, the amount diverted to dividends may not be enough to make much difference anyway.

Should You Incorporate?

There seem to be three groups of writers as far as this incorporation question is concerned. There's a small group of people who have incorporated, and claim that everyone should do so. Then there's a large group that wonders whether it should incorporate. And finally, there's a small group, of which I'm a member, that believes that there's no reason for most writers to incorporate. Writers often get hung up on this issue. I attended a freelancer's meeting at a local writer's group recently, and several people wanting to become freelancers asked about incorporating. (They should be more worried about how to find customers!)

If you don't earn huge sums, and need to take everything that you earn in salary—the situation for most technical writers that I know—there may be little or no tax benefit in incorporating. You may actually end up paying more tax on the salary than you would if you weren't incorporated.

If you earn a lot of money but want to take it all out of the corporation, the IRS may say that you can't take it all as salary. For instance, suppose that you make $150,000 a year. There's a good chance that the IRS will *not* let you take this all as salary. How many technical writer employees do you know making that sort of money? If the IRS says that you can earn only $70,000, then $80,000 must be left in the corporation and taxed as corporate profit. If you want to take that money out, you'll have to take it as dividends—and pay tax on it again.

Even if you *do* want to leave money in the corporation, you can't continue leaving that amount of money there each year, year after year. You may reach the "accumulated taxable income" level, and the IRS will force you to take money out as dividends.

Here's a good reason for incorporating, though: You want to accumulate money that you can then invest in your business at a later date. For instance, if you plan to start a technical-writing agency you may want to buy or lease an office, and buy a lot of computer equipment. Suppose, for instance, that you want to accumulate $100,000 to start the business. If you are not incorporated you'll pay your personal taxes on everything you earn. If you are incorporated, though, you'll pay a much lower rate on the amount you accumulate, so you can reach that $100,000 level much sooner.

So should you incorporate or not? The answer depends on your situation. There are so many variables involved, so many things to consider, that there really is no simple answer—whatever the "incorporate quick and easy" books might suggest. The question has no simple solution. In fact there are so many problems with incorporation that I'm considering writing a book called *Don't Inc. Yourself!* For now, you'll have to figure it all out for yourself. Do some research, find out if the promised benefits are real or illusory—and if the benefits *are* real, figure out whether the disadvantages outweigh them. Talk with a tax accountant, and if the accountant says that you will benefit, ask for specifics—and ask about the problems, too. Whatever you do, don't rush into incorporation, or you may regret it.

Working Online

To err is human, but to really foul things up requires a computer.

Anonymous

I've written a number of books about the Internet and online services, but I'm not one who believes that everyone needs online access. However, if there's one group that really can benefit from having a connection to cyberspace, it's freelance technical writers. Here's why you need online access:

◆ *Communicating with clients.* I've been using online services to communicate with my clients for years, as have many other technical writers. And online communications are more widespread now than ever. With an Internet or major online service connection, you can send messages and review copies to your clients, and get software updates from them.

◆ *Contacting other technical writers.* You can communicate with other technical writers online. Got a question about a particular program or technique, want to know how much other writers charge for particular services or in a particular area? Go online and use the technical writers' discussion groups.

◆ *Networking.* E-mail provides another way to keep in touch with the other writers in your network.

◆ *Creating online products.* There's a whole new market out there. Technical writers are creating World Wide Web sites, and publishing documents in formats designed for the online world, such as Adobe Acrobat and ShockWave.

◆ *Finding job leads.* You can find thousands of job leads online. You can even join mailing lists that automatically forward job leads to your computer.

◆ *Getting product information.* Need a particular program or piece of hardware to get your job done? Go directly to the manufacturer's Web page and get information right away, or even download a program demo.

◆ *Doing general research.* It'll be a long time before the Internet can replace your public library, but you will find lots of very useful information online—zip-code tables, tax forms and publications, dictionaries, thesauri, and plenty more.

What Do You Need?

At the very least, you need an Internet connection of some kind. There are many ways to get online these days, and I don't have room to explain them all, so buy a good book about the subject (you might start with my own *Complete Idiot's Guide to the Internet* from Que). You may even want a couple of ways to access the Internet: one through a true Internet service provider (ISP), and another through one of the online services. You can have both fairly cheaply. If you have two services, you're more likely to be able to get online when you really need to.

Which online service should you use? I recommend CompuServe, because it is the oldest of the services. Many of your potential customers have been using CompuServe for years, longer than some of the other services have even existed. Many high-tech companies, programmers, and engineers are on CompuServe. For instance, if you go to the CompuServe WinHelp forum, you'll find it very busy and useful. The last time I looked at the equivalent area in America Online (AOL), I found a rather quiet discussion group, with not much going on. Of course you can try these services for free anyway, and decide which you prefer.

You may find that a local Internet service provider can give you a better connection to the Internet. Such a connection may be faster, and will often allow you to use software that the online services don't allow, or at least make it hard to configure. A local ISP's connection is usually cheaper, too. Local service providers vary greatly, though, from the absolutely awful to the incredibly helpful. There are thousands around these days, so ask local writers which ones they use and which one is the best.

What Will You Find?

Let's take a quick look at the different services you'll find on the Internet.

The World Wide Web

The World Wide Web is a giant hypertext system that links together documents from all over the world. You'll find documents on almost every conceivable subject, and many of specific interest to technical writers, including the following (note that you can find links to these pages at the Web page associated with this book, http://www.mcp.com/mgr/arco/techwr/):

ACM SIGDOC (The Association for Computing Machinery, Special Interest Group for Documentation)
> http://web.mit.edu/org/t/tps/www/NL/SIGDOC_WWW/ SIGDOC_home.html

Alliance for Computers and Writing
> http://english.ttu.edu/acw/

American Society of Indexers
> http://www.well.com/user/asi/

Association of Teachers of Technical Writing
> http://english.ttu.edu/ATTW/

COREComm's Worst-Technical-Writing-Sample-of-the-Month Contest
> http://www.corecomm.com/corecomm/worst.html

Gary Conroy's Technical Writing Page
   http://techwriting.miningco.com/m
IEEE Professional Communication Society
   http://www.ieee.org/pcs/pcsindex.html
Inkspot Resources for Writers
   http://www.inkspot.com/
Internet Links for Technical Communication
   http://miavx1.acs.muohio.edu/~mtsccwis/techcommlinks.html
Internet Resources for Technical Communicators (Cris Perez)
   http://www.rpi.edu/~perezc2/tc/
Internet Resources for Technical Communicators (Keith Soltys)
   http://www.interlog.com/~ksoltys/techcomm.html
John December Technical Communication Information Sources
   http://www.december.com/john/study/techcomm/info.html
John Hewitt's Writing Resource Center
   http://www.azstarnet.com/~poewar/writer/writer.html
Journal of Technical Writing and Communication
   http://literary.com/baywood/pages/TWE/index.html
National Writer's Union Technical Writers Code of Practice
   http://www.nwu.org/nwu/
Resources for Science and Technical Writers
   http://www.inkspot.com/genres/tech.html
Rhetoric and Technical Communication Resources
   http://rhetoric.agoff.umn.edu/Rhetoric/misc/links.html
Society for Technical Communication (STC)
   http://stc.org/
Software Resources for Technical Communicators
   http://www.in.net/~smschill/softcomm.htm
Stephen Schiller's Technical Communication Resources page
   http://www.in.net/~smschill/techcomm.html
Technical Communication at California Polytechnical
   http://www.calpoly.edu/~techcomm/
Technical Communications Resources (David Rand)
   http://www.cwcinc.com/davidr/techwr.html
Technical Communication Quarterly (TCQ)
   http://beauty.agoff.umn.edu/~tcq/
Technical Writing in India
   http://members.tripod.com/~Kamath/

Technical Writing Resources

> http://www.umsl.edu/~klein/TW_Resources.html

University of Southern Mississippi Resources for Science and Technical Writers

> http://ocean.st.usm.edu/~dshattls/tech.html

University of Southern Mississippi Technical Writing Project

> http://ocean.st.usm.edu/~dshattls/

Yahoo!'s Technical Writing Page

> http://www.yahoo.com/Business_and_Economy/Companies/
> Communications_and_Media_Services/Writing_and_Editing/
> Technical_Writing/

Is that enough for you? These Web sites contain so much useful information, it's pointless trying to summarize each one. Try visiting each in turn to see what's available. Check the STC site for links to local STC chapter pages, too.

Newsgroups and Mailing Lists

Newsgroups and mailing lists are discussion groups. The groups consist of anywhere from a handful of members to thousands; the largest technical writing group had about 2,000 members the last time I looked. Members exchange ideas, information, and the occasional insult.

A *newsgroup* is a discussion group to which your Internet service provider has to subscribe. Each day a newsgroup gets the latest messages and makes them available to you. You have to use a special newsreader program to read the messages.

A *mailing list* is a discussion group based on the e-mail system. You use your e-mail program to read the messages. When someone e-mails a message to the discussion group, a special program automatically sends a copy to everyone on the list.

Useful Mailing Lists

Here, then, are a few mailing lists that you might be interested in. You can find many more related lists at the Tile.Net (http://tile.net/lists/) and Publicly Accessible Mailing Lists (http://www.neosoft.com/internet/paml/) Web pages. You should also look at the enormous Liszt Searchable Directory of e-Mail Discussion Groups page (http://www.liszt.com/); this site has a directory of over 70,000 mailing lists. The Web pages previously listed also contain recommended lists.

After you've subscribed to a mailing list, read carefully the information you receive. It will explain how to stop receiving information from the list, how to read old, archived messages, how to receive one large message a day containing all the day's messages (known as a *digest*), and so on.

TECHWR-L

The largest technical writers list, TECHWR-L currently has about 2,000 members. To join the group, send an e-mail message to listserv@listserv.okstate.edu. Leave the subject line blank. In the body of the message, enter this:

sub techwr-l *yourfirstname yourlastname*

To participate in group discussions, send your e-mail messages to techwr-l@ listserv.okstate.edu. To correspond with the person in charge of the group, e-mail ejray@raycomm.com.

This mailing list is also available as a newsgroup: bit.listserv.techwr-l. In other words, the messages that go to the mailing list are automatically posted to the newsgroup (though not vice versa), so you can read messages in whichever form you prefer.

You can also get to the TECHWR-L archives, so that you can search for old messages. Go to http://www.cpub.com/techwrit/techwrit-l.htm, http://listserv.okstate.edu/ archives/techwr-l.html, or http://www.documentation.com/techwrit/techwrit-l.htm. You can also see who you're exchanging messages with at the Friendly Faces of Techwr-l Web page: http://www.azstarnet.com/~poewar/writer/pg/tech.html.

TECHCOMM

This small list is an outgrowth of techwr-l that's designed to allow a wider range of discussion subjects.

To join the group, send an e-mail message to list@user.itconsult.co.uk. In the body of the message enter this:

> join techcomm

To participate in group discussions, send your e-mail messages to techcomm@user.itconsult.co.uk.

For more information see the http://www.hairydog.clara.net/techcomm.html Web page.

To correspond with the person in charge of the group, e-mail tcadmin@hairydog.clara.net.

TEKCOM-L

A small Technical writing, technical communications, and World Wide Web publishing list.

To join the group, send an e-mail message to listserv@tamvm1.tamu.edu. In the body of the message enter this:

> sub TEKCOM-L *yourfirstname yourlastname*

To participate in group discussions, send your e-mail messages to tekcom-l@ tamvm1.tamu.edu.

To correspond with the person in charge of the group, e-mail tekcom-l-request@ tamvm1.tamu.edu.

STCCICSIG-L

This is the Society for Technical Communication's mailing list (it's currently rather quiet).

To subscribe to this list, send a message to majordomo@stc.org. In the body of the message enter this:

> SUBSCRIBE stccicsig-l *your-e-mailaddress*

To participate in group discussions, send your e-mail messages to stccicsig-l@stc.org.

To correspond with the person in charge of the group, e-mail owner-stccicsig-l@stc.org.

T-TELCOM

T-TELCOM is a mailing list for telecommuting and freelancing technical communicators. To join the group, send an e-mail message to listserv@twh.msn.sub.org. Leave the subject line blank, and in the body of the message, enter this:

> sub t-telcom *yourfirstname yourlastname*

To participate in group discussions, send your e-mail messages to t-telcom@twh.msn.sub.org. To correspond with the person in charge of the group, e-mail avobert@twh.msn.sub.org.

COPYEDITING-L

COPYEDITING-L is a mailing list related to copyediting, of course.

To join the group, send an e-mail message to listserv@cornell.edu. In the body of the message, enter this:

> sub COPYEDITING-L *yourfirstname yourlastname*

To participate in group discussions, send your e-mail messages to copyediting-l@cornell.edu.

ACW-L

The Alliance for Computers & Writing mailing list. To join the list send a message to listserv@unicorn.acs.ttu.edu. In the body of the message, enter this:

> sub ACW-L *your_first_name your_last_name*

To participate in group discussions, send your e-mail messages to acw-l@unicorn.acs.ttu.edu.

COMPOS01

A mailing list devoted to the study of computers and writing. To join the group, send an e-mail message to compos01@ulkyvx.louisville.edu. In the body of the message, enter this:

> sub COMPOS01 *yourfirstname yourlastname*

To participate in group discussions, send your e-mail messages to compos01@ulkyvx.louisville.edu.

PAGEMAKR

This newsgroup provides information about using PageMaker on the Mac or PC.

To join the group, send an e-mail message to listserv@miamiu.muohio.edu. In the body of the message, enter this:

> sub PAGEMAKR *yourfirstname yourlastname*

To participate in group discussions, send your e-mail messages to pagemakr@miamiu.muohio.edu.

WINHLP-L

WINHLP-L is a mailing list related to Windows Help authoring.

To join the group, send an e-mail message to listserv@admin.humberc.on.ca. In the body of the message, enter this:

> sub WINHLP-L *yourfirstname yourlastname*

To participate in group discussions, send your e-mail messages to winhlp-l@ admin.humberc.on.ca.

WORDPRO

WORDPRO is a mailing list about word processors in general.

To join the group, send an e-mail message to listserv@vm1.mcgill.ca. In the body of the message, enter this:

> sub WORDPRO *yourfirstname yourlastname*

To participate in group discussions, send your e-mail messages to wordpro@vm1.mcgill.ca.

WORD-MAC

This group is for users who run Microsoft Word on the Macintosh.

To join the group, send an e-mail message to mailserv@acc.haverford.edu.bitnet. In the body of the message, enter this:

> sub WORD-MAC *yourfirstname yourlastname*

To participate in group discussions, send your e-mail messages to word-mac@ acc.haverford.edu.bitnet.

WORD-PC

WORD-PC is all about running Microsoft Word on the PC.

To join the group, send an e-mail message to listserv@ufobi1.uni-forst.gwdg.de. In the body of the message, enter this:

> sub WORD-PC *yourfirstname yourlastname*

To participate in group discussions, send your e-mail messages to word-pc@ ufobi1.uni-forst.gwdg.de.

WP51-L

This newsgroup is all about WordPerfect 5.1 for DOS.

To join the group, send an e-mail message to listserv@acadvm1.uottawa.ca. In the body of the message, enter this:

> sub WP51-L *yourfirstname yourlastname*

To participate in group discussions, send your e-mail messages to wp51
l@acadvm1.uottawa.ca.

WPWIN-L

WPWIN-L is all about WordPerfect for Windows. To join the group, send an e-mail
message to listserv@ubvm.cc.buffalo.edu. In the body of the message, enter this:

> sub WPWIN-L *yourfirstname yourlastname*

To participate in group discussions, send your e-mail messages to wpwin-l@
ubvm.cc.buffalo.edu.

WRITERS

This newsgroup provides information for professional writers. To join the group, send
an e-mail message to listserv@mitvma.mit.edu. In the body of the message, enter this:

> sub WRITERS *yourfirstname yourlastname*

To participate in group discussions, send your e-mail messages to
writers@mitvma.mit.edu.

Useful Newsgroups

Now for a list of useful newsgroups. You can find more at Tile.Net (http://
www.tile.net/tile/news/) and Infinite Ink Finding News Groups (http://
www.jazzie.com/ii/internet/newsgroups.html). Note that you normally cannot read the
newsgroup unless your service provider subscribes to the group; if your ISP doesn't
subscribe to the group you want, ask it to. If the ISP won't, go to Yahoo!'s list of
public news servers (http://www.yahoo.com/News/Usenet/
Public_Access_Usenet_Sites/) to find a list of publicly accessible newsgroup sites.

There are thousands of newsgroups on the Internet—over 20,000 distributed interna-
tionally, many thousands more available only locally. Here are a few you might be
interested in (how you view a newsgroup depends on the type of software you are
using, so I haven't explained how to "subscribe"):

Newsgroup	Description
bit.listserv.techwr-l	A mailing list, in newsgroup form, for technical writers
alt.usage.english	The English language
comp.fonts	Computer fonts
comp.graphics	Computer graphics
comp.human-factors	Interaction between humans and computers
comp.infosystems.www.authoring.html	Web page creation
comp.multimedia	Multimedia
comp.os.ms-windows.programmer.winhelp	WinHelp authoring

comp.publish.cdrom.multimedia	CD-ROM multimedia publishing
comp.text	Desktop publishing
comp.text.frame	Desktop publishing with FrameMaker
comp.text.interleaf	Desktop publishing with Interleaf
comp.text.sgml	SGML publishing
misc.writing	Mainly creative writing, some technical writing
wpi.techwriting	A small technical writing newsgroup

Other Discussion Groups

If you get onto the Internet through an online service such as CompuServe or AOL, you may also find useful discussion groups within the service itself—that is, groups available only to subscribers of that online service, not to the Internet as a whole. These discussion groups have a variety of names (on CompuServe, they are known as *forums*; on Microsoft Network, they are known as *bulletin board services (BBSes)*; and so on).

CompuServe has the best selection of technical discussion groups, but all the services have at least something of interest. Spend a little while looking through the service's directory or index, searching on words such as *technical, writing, winhelp,* and *multimedia*.

Finding Job Leads

You can find loads of job leads on the Internet. You can even join mailing lists that will send job leads to you a few times a day. Here are a few ways to find these online job leads.

Newsgroup Leads

There are many newsgroups dedicated to job leads. For example, take a look at these:

Newsgroup	Description
misc.jobs	Job leads
misc.jobs.contract	Contract job leads
misc.jobs.misc	All sorts of job leads
misc.jobs.offered	More job leads!
misc.jobs.offered.entry	Entry-level job leads
misc.jobs.resumes	A newsgroup in which people post résumés

Also, go to theTile.Net News Web page (http://www.tile.net/tile/news/) and click the Search link. Enter the word *job* and click the Search button. In a moment or two you'll see a series of links to other documents, listing a variety of newsgroups by newsgroup name and by subject. You'll see entries such as these:

Jobs in Atlanta, Georgia

Jobs offered and wanted in Nevada

Job postings in the bay area

Jobs needed or offered in the Memphis area

Jobs offered and wanted in North Carolina

Jobs offered and wanted

Jobs wanted and available at the University of Arkansas

Jobs available and wanted in Ohio

Jobs and internships for Computer Science students

Job announcements at the University of Texas Computer Science Department

Another great place to look is in the newsgroups related to your area of interest. Technical-writing jobs are often posted to bit.listserv.techwr-l, Windows help authoring jobs in the comp.os.ms-windows.programmer.winhelp newsgroup, multi-media openings in the multimedia groups, and so on.

Mailing Lists

There are also many job-lead mailing lists. For instance, go to the Tile.Net/Lists Web page (http://tile.net/lists) and, as you did for newsgroups, search for the word *job*. Here's what I found when I did this:

ABLE-JOB: St. John's University Job Opportunity List

CAATJE-L: CAAT Job Evaluation List

ECOLOG-L: Ecological Society of America: grants, jobs, news

FEDJOBS: Federal Job Bulletin Board

GUM-NCC: Orsay, France (gumncc.earn.net)

JOB-LIST: Job offers from EARN Institute members

JOBPLACE: JobPlace (self-directed job search techniques and job placement issues)

JOB-TECH: Technology and Employment Conference

JTPA-L: Job Training Partnership Act Administrator's List

LIBJOBS: Library and Information Science jobs mailing list

SIG-14: RESNA Special Interest Group-14 on Job Accommodation

SWJOBS: AD&A Software Jobs Weekly

TESLJB-L: Jobs and Employment Issues (TESL-L sublist)

As with the newsgroups, you'll also often find job leads in the related mailing lists. The TECHWR-L mailing list often has technical-writing leads, for instance.

Professional Organizations

You'll find that many professional organizations have online job leads. They may set up a Web site with job leads available, either publicly or perhaps viewable only with a password. Such organizations are more likely to set up a mailing list, though, as it's very easy to do so and has the benefit of automatically mailing job leads directly to the people who need them (because those on the list need not check a Web site for daily updates). Check with your local STC chapter, local writing organizations, computer-consulting groups, and so on, to find out if any organizations in your area provide a mailing list.

Selling Your Services Online

Finding job leads online is all very well, but these are usually simply another way to distribute information about jobs; they are online classifieds. Most of the jobs being offered are "onsite" jobs, situations in which the client wants to hire a full-time employee, or perhaps a contract employee who will work at the client office. But how about finding work you can deliver in cyberspace? You can work for companies far from you—on the other side of the country, continent, or even the world. And how about more aggressive online marketing, tracking down companies online who might be able to use your services?

Although you can find such leads online, it's not necessarily easy. I've worked for Amgen, a big drug company in California, and for MasterCard in New York. I live in Denver, so how did I find this work?

In the first case I just happened to see a message from a programmer in the CompuServe CONSULT forum. He was looking for someone who could create a Windows help file for him. A couple of people responded, but he liked my WinHelp résumé best, so I got the job. This is a simple way to find a job, but pretty much like following a job lead.

In the second case I decided to market my services online. I put a few messages in the CONSULT forum, basically asking whether anyone needed any help with WinHelp. Before long, a programmer e-mailed me, and, within a couple of weeks I had a contract with MasterCard. I believe I could easily have found more work in this way if I'd spent more time looking, and if I'd used a multitude of mailing lists, newsgroups, and forums. But I had more work than I needed anyway, so didn't spend more time looking.

Now, it's important to note that you can't simply go out onto the Internet, tell people in newsgroups and mailing lists that you're a writer available for work, and expect floods of job offers. For all the talk about telecommuting, and about how the Internet makes geography unimportant, the fact is that, all things being equal, a client will prefer to work with someone down the road than across the nation. And that's quite understandable. It *is* better if you can come in and meet the client, it *is* better if you can meet the product developers.

So how do you sell at a distance? You've got to provide clients with something they're having trouble finding locally. Perhaps you have a particular skill that they can't find, or a reputation that's hard to beat. In my case I was selling Windows help authoring, something that few writers at the time understood. In one case my client already had a technical writer working on paper documents, but when asked if he could do the Windows help files, he simply said "no." Out he went, and in I came; I did both paper and online.

I'm sure that the Internet is making it easier to work at a distance, that it's bringing down the skill- or reputation-level required to convince a client to do business with you. People are getting used to the idea of working online, used to the idea of working with people over a wide geographic area. It's probably easier to find work in cyber-space now than when I sought clients on CompuServe. Still, you need to be more than a generic technical writer to make this work.

The most unusual situation I know of is that of Ian MacDonald. This Canadian writer is currently living in Malaysia, yet his technical-writing clients are in North America, Europe, and South Africa. It wasn't easy to set up this situation, I'm sure, but it just goes to show what can be done. The great thing about cyberspace is that it provides a way for writers to stay plugged into a good job market even when they live miles from anywhere. This is easier for experienced writers to do, of course, but it's quite possible to build toward a situation in which you can live where you want, yet still work profitable technical-writing projects.

Writing Magazine

Articles and Books

I never write "metropolis" for seven cents because I can get the same price for "city."

Mark Twain

For a number of reasons, you should take a look at the technical book and magazine-article market. Writing for corporate clients, documenting their products, can be very lucrative. But you can make money writing for the computer press (computer magazines and newspapers) and for computer-book publishers, too, and also use your published writing to boost your contracting or consulting income. Here are a few good reasons to sell your writing for publication:

◆ *Satisfaction.* It simply "feels good" to see your work in a magazine, or find your book at the local bookstore.

◆ *Setting yourself apart from the crowd.* As I've mentioned before, many of your potential corporate clients have a low opinion of technical writers. If you've been published, though, you set yourself apart from the average writer—you are now a *writer*, not simply a technical writer. They'll think of you a little differently, as a professional writer rather than someone who simply writes for a day job.

◆ *Name recognition.* The more work you have published, the better known your name will become in your area. Other writers will remember you, and clients will be more likely to hear about you.

◆ *Job leads.* Now and again someone will see something you've written and call you. You probably won't be flooded with leads directly from your writing, but I've had a few leads this way.

◆ *Great interview tools.* How can you impress clients during an interview? Sure, you can show them the last user manual you wrote, though it probably won't have your name on it, and the client won't know for sure that you wrote it or how much of it you wrote. But place a series of articles or several books in front of clients, and they'll sit up and take interest.

◆ *Improving your "conversion" rate.* If you write for publication, you'll find your interview-to-job conversion rate improves, because your potential clients will have a higher opinion of you. While most writers cannot expect to convert most interviews into signed contracts (in any sales job, you sell only to a minority of your potential clients), I've found that in recent years I get most of the jobs I go after. I'm sure that to a great degree this is thanks to the impression that my published work gives my clients.

♦ *A great additional income.* You're not going to be writing magazine articles and books for free, of course. You'll get paid for your work (at least, in most cases).

♦ *Perhaps your primary income.* If you are lucky, writing for publication can become your primary source of income. It's ironic that many journalists become technical writers because they're tired of the poverty in which most journalists live. But there are ways to make good money while writing for publication, as you'll learn later in this chapter.

♦ *Adding a little of variety to your writing.* Sometimes it's nice to write something a little different. I've done a piece on snow running for Denver's *Metropolitan Ski Times*, a piece on paragliding which I eventually sold to *Men's Journal*, and various pieces on tax and employment law issues. And I wrote the book *The Best Sex of Your Life* with Dr. James White.

Don't underestimate the impact that getting published can have on your business. Even if you never do more than a couple of books and a dozen or so magazine articles, you can use this work to give your consulting career a real boost.

I recently spoke with a well-known consultant and author in the multimedia field. He's published several books, but he admitted to me that the books had never made him much money and he probably won't be writing more. Still, it was well worth doing the books, he said: "I can get $500 a day more from my clients because I've written those books."

Magazine Writing

It's really quite easy to get started writing magazine articles (honestly!). There are opportunities all around you. Here's how I got started. Someone at the company at which I was contracting showed me a copy of *PD News* (now *Technical Employment News*—see Appendix B). This is a job-shopper's publication, heavy on job listings but light on editorial (at least at that time, back in 1989).

I noticed that the publication had a few articles that had been pulled from syndicated news feeds, and a few pieces written by *PD News* readers—mainly engineers of various types. I figured that if these readers can get published and paid, so could I. So I sent a piece about taxes, which *PD News* promptly published and paid for. Then I sent them another piece, which the editors also published and paid for. So I asked if they wanted a regular column; they said yes, and I became a columnist, with my photo on the front page of *PD News* every two weeks.

Now, they weren't paying much, only 10 cents a word. Still, my average take was $90 per article, and some of the articles I wrote in 90 minutes or two hours. (A few I wrote in less than an hour. For one or two, I had to do some research, so they took quite a bit longer, but I've also reused them in this book.)

That was my start in writing, something I could put on my résumé and list of publications. About the same time I started writing books, too (which I'll discuss in a moment). I also looked around for other publications, and did a few small pieces. Then I started contacting the big computer magazines—*Windows Magazine* and *Windows User*, for instance. I just called up and offered them my services; I think my first suggestion was for a review of Microsoft Money.

However, I don't do a lot of magazine work anymore, apart from my "Geek News" column. I'll admit that I don't particularly like magazine writing. Or rather, I like the writing, I don't like the business so much. There seem to be plenty of minor irritations, such as these:

- Each sale you make is small. You make a few hundred, maybe a couple of thousand, dollars. Then you have to make another sale. You have to find a regular column with a good magazine to make it work.

- Editors can be very inconsiderate, promising to get back to you about an article soon but never responding.

- Editors are sometimes difficult to work with. One editor e-mailed me instructions about the article she wanted on the day that the article was due, just as I was putting the finishing touches to it.

- Editors sometimes promise more than they deliver. For instance, I once had a magazine offer to buy an article from me "on spec." (*On spec* means, "If we like it, we'll buy it," not, "If you write it, we'll think about it and check to see if it fits.") When I submitted the article, the editors then told me they'd already done something on that subject, so they didn't want it!

- Magazine publishing is a fairly unstable business. On two occasions I've written articles for publications that went out of business before publishing my article.

- You'll often find your work modified at the last moment, to make it fit the available space. A reasonably eloquent finish to an article, for instance, may be truncated and end up sounding quite ridiculous. And some periodicals like to add spelling mistakes.

You can make magazine writing pay, though. My primary ambition has been to write books, so I haven't concentrated on magazines. However, if I did want to do magazine work, I'd try to find a regular piece—a column for one or two of the big computer or online magazines, or a regular product-review job. (Look at the names of the people doing product reviews for the computer magazines; you'll often see the same name several times in the same issue, and month after month, too.)

I *have* gone out of my way to do magazine work now and again. Initially I did it to add things to my résumé. Sometimes I do it for the money (some of my work has been quite well paid; I did an article about World Wide Web browsers for a major computer publication that netted me about $300 an hour). Sometimes I've written things just because I thought it might be fun. And the work is surprisingly easy to get. I don't want to suggest the work will simply fall into your lap, but if you prepare properly, and are persistent, you *will* get magazine work.

How *You* Can Start

If you'd like to try writing for magazines, start by reading books on writing query letters (a query letter is the letter you send to a periodical suggesting ideas) and a couple of books on how to write articles. You might even subscribe to a writer's magazine, such as *Writer's Digest*. Then start looking for work. Check with local periodicals; I have a friend who got a regular column with a small monthly business paper in Colorado simply by suggesting that it needed information about the online world. Many small papers and magazines are desperate for good writing. They may not pay much, but they are a good way to get started.

But don't write too many query letters. I know that all the writer's advice books and magazines say you should always contact an editor in writing, not to bother them in person, but I've found that you can often get through to editors directly. (Maybe that's particular to the computer business.) Or perhaps you can contact them via e-mail. You'll often find the names of the editors in a magazine's masthead. There's often an editorial telephone number, too, and sometimes each editor's e-mail address. Don't be too pushy, and don't waste their time. Get to the point and offer them an article, and you'll often get a reasonably polite reception.

Writing Computer Books

Getting started in the computer-book business is also surprisingly easy (assuming you can write and are persistent, that is). Unlike the trade-book or fiction business, computer-book publishers often actively seek new writers. I've seen computer-book publishers place messages in CompuServe forums and Internet mailings lists asking for writers to contact them. These publishers are *always* looking for good writers.

While writing this section, I checked my e-mail. Here's what I found in one of the job mailing lists I subscribe to (see Chapter 24):

> Subject: WRITERS> Ventana Press Search
>
> Computer Writers & Editors Wanted
>
> Ventana Press, a major computer book publisher, is actively seeking fresh authors, technical editors, and ideas for a wide variety of computer-related books.
>
> If you have a great idea for a book you'd like to write or are interested in performing a technical review, please write to talent@vmedia.com.

When I first started writing computer books I made a big mistake. I assumed that it would be hard to work for the big computer-book publishers, that I'd have to work my way up. So when I heard the owner of a small publishing company say, at a Society for Technical Communications meeting, that he needed writers, I jumped at the chance. I called him, and went to meet him. He asked me to write a sample chapter, to make sure I could actually write, then asked me to write a book about a program called Enable/OA. And so I did, and have regretted it ever since. It was a 600-page book, took about 600 hours to write, and paid me a total of around $600 (6-6-6—it must have been cursed from the start).

Once I'd written this book, I offered my services to the big computer-book publishers. What I didn't realize at the time was that I could have gone directly to those big publishers in the first place, and bypassed this doomed project. So here's what I'd do if I could go back and do it again.

First, I'd go to my local bookstore and take a look at books published by the major publishers—the publishers that seem to have a whole lot of books on the shelves such as Que, Sybex, New Riders, Peachpit, Sams, Sams.net, Ventana, and IDG. I'd look near the front and back of the books and note the contact information. You'll find postal addresses, Web URLs, and e-mail addresses. (You can also find much of this information on the Internet, as I'll discuss later in this chapter.)

Then I'd start contacting people. I would Contact *everyone*, not just a few and not just one person at each publisher; if I found the e-mail addresses of two or three editors at one publisher, I'd e-mail all of them. After all, e-mail one and that editor may have quit or may simply not respond; e-mail all three and you're more likely to get somewhere.

I would e-mail and write letters, offering my services writing computer books. What would I say? That I'm a good writer, that I have several years experience in technical writing, and so on. I'd describe my experience, the types of software and hardware that I'd worked with. And I might also include an idea for a book, though that's not essential.

Next I'd go online and visit all the publishers' Web sites. Virtually all of them have Web sites these days. I'd look for more e-mail addresses, and perhaps even "if you want to be a writer" links.

Will you get a response if you use this method? Absolutely. You may hear from some saying you've contacted the wrong person, though they'll probably give you another person to contact. In some cases you may get a phone call. When I first contacted Sybex suggesting that they do a book on Peachtree Accounting (and that I write the book, of course), I got a call from an editor almost as soon as she'd received the letter (this was back in the days when few people were using e-mail). I never did do a book about Peachtree Accounting, but a few months later Sybex asked me to write *Mastering Micrografx Designer*. (I ended up writing five books for Sybex.)

It's more likely that you'll hear from someone asking if you would write a chapter or two in a book. Some publishers use teams of writers to create books; a 25-chapter book may have 10 or 15 writers working on it, each one paid a set fee. Publishers do this partly because they can create books very quickly this way (though I hate working on these teams, as it seems an awful way to put a book together), and partly as a way to "test" writers. Write a chapter or two for them and do a lousy job, and that's the last work you'll do for them. Do a good job, though, and they'll offer you more, and perhaps offer you a book. (Don't wait to be asked, though; it's up to you to ask *them*. Remember, the squeaky wheel gets the grease—and the persistent author gets the book.)

When you start writing for a publisher, don't assume you can ease up on your marketing. Get to know the editors, and make it quite clear that you want to write complete books for royalties. They may need reminding now and again that you are there and available. Call and ask them what books are coming up, and what might be suitable for you. And keep talking with the other publishers, too. It's common for computer-book authors to write for more than one publisher.

If I Had to Do It Again

I made a number of mistakes in my magazine- and book-writing career. I think I could have moved further and faster if I'd known then what I know now. Here are some of the things I did wrong:

◆ *I should have started sooner.* If I'd started before we had children, my wife and I could easily have lived off her salary and the advances I'd get for my books. I could have done 12 books in the first couple of years, really getting my book career moving very quickly. However, I didn't decide to become a writer until a few months before my first son was born; we'd already decided that my wife would stop working to look after the kids, so I had to worry about short-term income, not long-term goals.

◆ *I picked a small computer-book publisher.* As I've already mentioned, the first book I wrote was a big mistake. I was so eager to get into print that I took a contract from a small publisher instead of going straight to one of the big computer-book publishers. I would have earned an advance (the small publisher didn't pay one), the chance of the book making money would have been much greater, and my royalty rate would have been higher.

◆ *I took any book offered to me.* I wrote my second book for Sybex, at the time one of the two biggest computer-book publishers. After that book, I took any project that Sybex offered to me, without considering the project's potential. I should have thought more about whether the project would be a viable one. I was simply happy to be writing books.

◆ *I should have switched publishers sooner.* I should have looked for publishers who would value my skills more than Sybex. When I moved to other publishers who spent more effort to cultivate their best writers, I was offered better projects. (Sybex is still a good publisher to work with, by the way, and has since changed the way in which they handle writers.)

◆ *I should have found an agent sooner.* My agent brought me some excellent projects, books that I wouldn't have been able to get without an agent. He looked for projects that had a good chance of doing well, books that would advance my career. Within two years of signing with an agent I had a best-seller.

How to Pick a Book That Sells

When you first start writing computer books, don't worry too much about whether the book you are about to write will turn into a best-seller; it probably won't. Later, though, you might want to be more picky. Here are a few (gross) generalizations about what makes a best-selling book:

◆ *PC books sell more than Mac books.* Let's face it, there are many more PC users than Macintosh users. A book about the PC version of Netscape will sell many times more copies than a book about the Mac version.

◆ *Basic user books sell more than bigger, more detailed and advanced books.* I avoid the really big, very detailed books. For instance, Que has a Using series and a Special Edition series. The Using series provides the basic information about a product, and I've done a few of these. At times Que's editors have suggested Special Editions, but these books contain a great deal of detail, and are very big—600 pages or so. They'll sell fewer copies, though; there are more people who will buy *Using Netscape* than *Using Netscape Special Edition.* I regard all computer books as a gamble. If I do a Special Edition, I have to do twice as much work. My wager is twice what I'd wager when doing a Using book, yet the payoff is generally less. Why bother?

◆ *Bigger, more advanced books often do very well!* On the other hand, some Special Editions have sold extremely well, and as they are priced much higher, they pay a higher royalty—and thus are often very lucrative. Figure this one out for yourselves. I still haven't managed to decide which is the best bet—the smaller, introductory books or the bigger, advanced books.

◆ *Utility books don't sell well.* Books about utility programs usually don't do particularly well. I was once offered a book about Microsoft Plus! and, I'm glad to say, turned it down. Books on products such as Norton Desktop, Microsoft Schedule, and Adobe Type Manager probably won't sell well. While a lot of people buy these products, they don't usually buy books about them, often because the products are very simple, and because these are the sorts of programs that you get into, do your job, then get out—not the sorts of programs that you work with for eight hours a day.

◆ *The program can't be too easy to use.* If a program is very easy to use, why buy a book about it? That's probably why my book on Microsoft Money didn't sell well; Money is simply too easy to work with.

◆ *The heavier the competition, the greater the risk.* The more people using a program, the larger the potential market. However, in some cases there are so many people using a program that every publisher is writing a dozen books on the subject! Windows 3.1 and Windows 95 are examples. In such cases, there are so many books that most aren't making money. (Of course some are doing *very* well.)

◆ *Timely or early publication is critical to a book's success.* Computer books must be on time, released when the software is available. That means that you must write such books based on beta (pre-release) software. Of course the earlier a book comes out, the longer it can sell, too.

◆ *You want to find books that the publisher has high expectations for.* Many publishers classify their books as being in one of three levels: A, B, or C. I'll explain these levels later in this chapter, but basically publishers produce books that they expect to do very well (the A-list), books that they expect to do okay (the B-list), and books that they don't really expect to do a whole lot (the C-list). You want to avoid the C-list books and do only A- or B-list books, and preferably stick with the A-list books.

◆ *All the preceding could be wrong.* These are all generalizations. For instance, there are Mac books that have become best-sellers, some big, advanced books that make their authors very rich, and some books in very competitive markets that make huge sums of money.

I've made enough mistakes, so I want to try to avoid more. In the end, it's all a gamble, though. But I think I can exclude some books that I'm *sure* won't be profitable. Unfortunately I don't have a magic formula for picking a best-seller, and so most of my books *haven't* been best-sellers. (Luckily, several have.)

It's Not Always Easy

In the early days of the computer-book business, $50,000 advances were not uncommon. Some $1 million advances were paid, too. These days the business is much harder, and much more competitive. I think it's probably easier for a good writer to make $100,000 in corporate technical writing than in computer books. However, it's easier for a good writer to make $250,000, $350,000, or more writing computer books than in corporate technical writing. In other words, there are limits to how much a freelancer can make in the corporate technical-writing field, but the potential is much higher in computer books. (Of course only a few writers make those sorts of sums.)

I don't want to make it all sound too easy. It's pretty easy to get started, but it can be hard work to keep going. You can do it if you persevere, but for many people the question is, "Is it all worth it?" For instance, I know three people who tried writing books, but gave up after a couple of books because they found that it wasn't profitable. However, all three have thriving businesses—one runs a technical-writing agency, one a multimedia company, and one an online-services business. For these people writing books was not a great ambition, it was something they tried a few times and then they moved on to other things.

But for me it was my ambition, so I plugged away for a few years. My first book was a disaster. My second and third made reasonable money, probably around $35 for every hour I put in. I had a couple of other very poorly paid projects, then a couple of projects with big advances (which, again, worked out around $35 an hour). It wasn't until my 11th book that I had a best-seller, and even after that, I had several that did pretty poorly. One friend and colleague who has written a few computer books said recently, "You did it the right way; if you are going to write computer books, you have to set it up like a factory, just keep churning a book out every couple of months." Write enough books, and some will work and more than pay for the ones that don't.

Now I feel more secure; I have some books that are doing very well, but it took a while to get here. I could have done it in less time, if I'd made the right moves; maybe some of the advice I've given here will help someone do what I did, only faster. But be ready to work hard, and accept that you probably won't get a best-selling book right away! (On the other hand, maybe you will; I know a couple of people lucky enough to get best-sellers on their first books. Just don't count on it.)

If You Decide to Write Computer Books

Here are a few things you should be aware of if you do decide to write computer books.

A-, B-, and C-List Books

Many computer-book publishers consider their books as falling into one of three categories: A-, B-, or C-list books. A-list books are those that are expected to sell very well, and possibly turn into best-sellers (perhaps selling 50,000 copies and up). B-list books are expected to do reasonably well, make a little money, but probably never become best-sellers. C-list books probably won't do much at all, and may not sell enough copies to pay for the author's advance—we'll be discussing advances in a moment. (One sales manager told me that what he regarded as a C-list book was one that was projected to sell around 7,500 copies, though they often sell much fewer, too.)

Thousands of computer books are published each year. Of course most of these books are C-list books. Most C-list books actually represent a *loss* for the publisher. So why do publishers bother doing C-list books? For a couple of reasons. First, you never know when a C-list book will do well, and turn into a B- or even an A-list book. Publishing is, to some degree, a gambling business; you are never sure which book is going to hit, so you increase your odds by doing lots of them. The second reason is that the bookstore buyers expect to see C- and B-list books, as well as A-list books. A publisher can't go to a bookstore buyer and tell them that *all* their titles are A-list titles! The bookstore buyers want to know which books will do really well, which will do reasonably well, and which will just sell a few copies here and there.

So, the question for you is, should you do a C-list book? Yes, maybe one or two, but you don't want to make a habit of it. You *can't* make a decent living writing C-list books. Most C-list books are written by people who will never write more than one or two books, or by writers on their way up. C-list books may sell 7,500 copies, perhaps many less. You may average $5,000 to $6,000 per book, if that. Do six or seven of these a year, and you'll gross maybe $30,000 to $40,000. Subtract your business expenses, medical expenses, Self Employment tax, and so on, and you are earning a pittance.

So it's okay to do C-list books at the start, but you *must* move into the B-list and, you hope, the A-list in order to make your writing career profitable. And to do this you must be able to work quickly and produce good books. (By the way, A-list books sometimes end up being B-list or C-list books. It's just the luck of the game.)

What Makes a Best-Seller?

A computer book does not become a best-seller solely because of the quality of the book. It becomes a best-seller through a combination of factors, from being the first on the market to being published by a big publisher that can afford to push the book.

I can think of lousy books that have done very well, and excellent books that have died. After I wrote *Peter Norton's Windows NT: Tips and Tricks*, a reviewer in *PC Magazine* described it as "an excellent choice." It sold very badly, though, because by the time it came on the market the bookstores had more NT books than they knew what to do with. Windows NT didn't sell well in the first year or two of its life, despite the presales hype. Bookstores had stocked up on NT books, expecting a bonanza, and the last thing they wanted was *another* NT book.

On the other hand, I could name a best-selling computer book that clearly didn't deserve success, a book that purported to provide software and instructions that would allow the reader get onto the Internet within a few minutes. Unfortunately most readers could not use the software because the author omitted some critical information. The book became a best-seller, though, because it was published by a well-respected publisher with good distribution, and because it was published right at the beginning of the Internet boom.

There's a lot more to creating a best-selling computer book than writing a good book. I have written several best-selling computer books. I think they are good books, but I also know that however good they are, that's *not* the reason they became best-sellers!

It is possible for a bad writer to make money; if a writer's first book is a best-seller, that writer's going to make money. However, the writer may have the book taken away and given to another writer when the time comes to write the revision.

Learn More About Contracts

Before you sign a publishing contract, read a book about contracts. When I first started in the business, I read *How to Write and Negotiate a Book Contract or Magazine Agreement* by Richard Balkin (Writer's Digest Press), which was very handy (note, however, that it is based on the trade-book business, and the computer-book business is a little different). There's a lot to know about contracts, and I've only mentioned a few salient points here. You might also consider getting an agent, or showing your contracts to a publishing-business lawyer before you sign. (Make sure you use a lawyer who's familiar with publishing; others probably won't be able to assess the contract effectively.)

Royalties Are Based on Net

Unlike the "trade"-book publishers—the companies that publish nonfiction and fiction books sold by bookstores—computer-book publishers pay royalties based on the amount of money they are paid for the book, not the price of the book on the book's cover. For instance, most novels earn royalties expressed as a percentage of the book's price; a $20 hardback book paying a 10 percent royalty will earn the author $2 per book. But a $20 computer book earning a 10 percent royalty will earn only around $1 a book, because the royalty is based on the *net*, the amount of money the bookstores and wholesalers pay the publisher for the book. On average, the publisher is paid about 50 percent of the book's value.

Royalties Will Be Less Than You Think

When you first sign a contract, it's tempting to figure out the royalty per book. But don't forget that some of those books will be sold at a very high discount. Most contracts have a special clause stating that if a book is sold at a high discount—perhaps 55 percent or 60 percent—your royalty rate will be halved. For instance, suppose you've written a book that will sell for $20. Your royalty rate is 8 percent net. So, if the publisher sells the book at a 40 percent discount—for $12—you'll get 96 cents, 8 percent of $12. If the publisher sells the book for a 50 percent discount, you'll get 80 cents, 8 percent of $10. But what if the book sells for a 60 percent discount, for $8 (many books are sold to discount stores at discounts as high as this)? You might think you'd get 8 percent of $8, or 64 cents. But you won't, you'll only get 32 cents, because of a clause in the contract that reduces the royalty rate by half for books sold at discounts of 60 percent or more.

One publisher has recently tried changing this clause, invoking the royalty cut at discounts of only *50 percent*. This is such a low discount that if you allow this clause in your contract, you will find dramatic reductions in your royalties. Many books are sold at a 50 or 55 percent discount. This clause should be for 60 percent discounts or more. If you find your contract has the breakpoint at 50 percent, try to get it changed to 55 percent or better still to 60 percent. You might not be able to, but at least try.

The Advance Against Royalties

You'll be paid an *advance*, which really means "advance against royalty." In other words, the publisher pays you some money up front (maybe $5,000 to $10,000, sometimes much more). Later, when the book begins making money, the royalties earned are used to pay off this advance. It's not until the entire advance has been paid off that you begin earning more money.

Remove the Options Clause

Many contracts contain a clause that gives the publisher the right to see an outline for your next book, and to decide whether to buy the book, before you show the outline to another publisher. Remove this clause; few publishers will complain if you do (simply say that you plan to make your living writing books, and that this clause is too restrictive for a full-time writer). It has absolutely no benefit to you, and can make it difficult to sell an idea to another publisher.

What Will You Give the Publisher?

When you contract to do a book with a publisher, what are you expected to provide? First, you'll have to give the publisher the text, your writing. This will probably be in Microsoft Word format, maybe WordPerfect. You may have to "code" some of the text, by adding some kind of "tag" before the text—(a) to indicate a first-level heading, (b) to indicate a second-level heading, and so on. These days you're more likely to be using the word processor's styles to format text.

One thing you'll almost certainly *not* have to do is the final layout of the book. That will be done by the publisher's own design staff. There are a few projects in which the writer does the layout, but these are rare, more rare now than a few years ago.

You'll also have to provide pictures, usually screenshots of the program you were writing about. You'll use a special screenshot program, which saves the pictures as .PCX, .BMP, or .TIF images (.PICT if you are working with a Macintosh program). You'll put a note in your text telling the publisher where to place the snapshots.

You'll have to deliver your text on a multipart schedule; 25 percent, 50 percent, 75 percent, and 100 percent, perhaps, or maybe a couple of chapters a week. These books often have to be written very quickly—somewhere between 5 and 10 weeks, sometimes even less. In rare cases you may have six months or longer. The writers with agreements to do Windows 95 books, for instance, ended up with *far* more time than they originally expected, often a year or more, though that's very unusual (the time was so long because of delays in the release of Windows 95).

Author Reviews

Soon after you've finished your book, you'll start to get your author reviews back. These are the edited pages or files. (In some cases you'll get author reviews for the early chapters back before you've finished the later chapters.) Your author reviews will probably be electronic; you'll get the word processing files back with the editorial changes made. You have to read through and make sure the meaning has not been changed, and answer any questions that the editor and technical reviewer may have posed. (Most books are reviewed by someone who knows the subject that you are writing about, to make sure you don't screw up.)

In most cases, you won't have to create an index. The publisher will do that at the very end of the process. Some computer-book contracts call for you to pay for the indexing, or perhaps pay for half the indexing.

On the Way to the Bookstore

Once the book is finished, how long will it take to reach the bookstores? My first book took 10 months, a disaster in the computer-book business. My first best-seller was very fast, though. I sent in the last chapters of *The Complete Idiot's Guide to the Internet* around December 10, 1993. I still had to do the author reviews, yet the book was back from the printers, ready to ship to the bookstores, by late January.

The book then finds its way to the bookstore. When do you get paid? Maybe never. You've already been paid an *advance*, of course, but if the book never sells enough—if it never *earns out* the advance—you'll never see any more money. (If you wrote a C-level book, there's a good chance you'll never see more money.)

Suppose that the book does earn more in royalties than you've been paid in advance. When do you get the money? You may have a long wait. Most publishers pay royalties twice a year. You may have to wait six months, perhaps even longer. For instance, let's say your book hits the bookstores in February. The end of June may be the end of the royalty period, with the actual royalty payment arriving a month later, the end of July. But perhaps your book hasn't earned out the advance yet, so you get nothing. It's not until the next royalty-payment date, six months later, at the end of January of the next year—10 or 11 months after the book hit the bookstores—that you finally get any money (assuming that the advance has been earned out).

A few publishers try to make life easier. The Macmillan Publishing imprints (including Que, Sams, Sams.net, New Riders, ZDNet, Hayden, and Brady) pay monthly royalties. Three months after your book is published, you start to get monthly royalty checks. Because the two-payments-a-year system can make it so hard for a new writer to get started, Macmillan figures that providing monthly checks helps writers establish themselves in the business. IDG also pays monthly, but there's a six-month waiting period first.

Sell In Versus Sell Through

You'll hear these two terms in the book business: *sell in* and *sell through*. *Sell in* refers to books being sold to the bookstores. If your book sells in well, it's a really good sign, of course. But sometimes the bookstore buyers are wrong, they have more faith in a book than the book-buying public does. So the book doesn't *sell through* as well as it sold in. In other words, the bookstores only sell a relatively small portion of the books they bought from the publisher. Eventually the bookstores send back the rest, and the publisher reduces the money your account had been credited for those sales accordingly. So if your first book sells in well, don't run out and spend your royalties, because you may not receive it all!

Don't Be Too Pushy

Don't make yourself hard to work with by demanding too much on your contracts. In other words, don't act the prima donna, especially when you are new to the business. I've seen computer-book writers give really lousy advice to new writers, advising that they not accept a contract unless it contains a particular clause, that they demand this or that concession. However, if you push too hard, you'll lose the contract.

For instance, I once heard a computer-book writer advise a new writer to accept a contract only if royalties were paid on list price, not net. Nice idea, except that the chances of an established computer-book publisher giving such a contract are practically nil for a new writer. (Such a contract *might* be possible for a big name.) What this experienced writer didn't say was that all his contracts had paid royalties on net, not list price. Another writer gave advice in a newsgroup about negotiating contracts—without explaining that he was so difficult to work with and so combative about his contracts that he'd had a lucrative book taken away from him on the second edition, and was now finding it hard to get book contracts. As a publishing insider told me, "He's probably lost a couple of hundred thousand dollars through being difficult to work with."

Be careful when experienced writers start telling you to demand this or that. Often they are talking from a position of strength and experience, and advising an ideal contract that even they don't get. It may take you time to work your way up, so don't be too pushy on the way. If you're not sure how to negotiate contracts, get an agent at the first opportunity.

Three Tips to Success

Here's how to succeed in the computer-book business.

- ◆ Write quickly; computer books often have to be produced in a very short time.
- ◆ Write good books. There are a lot of books that are little more than rehashed user's manuals. Write a good book, though, and the publisher is more likely to give you more work, and less likely to take a successful book away from you on the second edition.
- ◆ Finally, deliver when you are supposed to deliver. Publishers have serious problems trying to get their authors to deliver on time; late delivery is probably the norm rather than the exception. In fact some publishers now add clauses to their contracts allowing them to penalize writers who deliver as little as a week late. So, before leaving this subject, here are just a few reasons writers have given for not delivering on time—given to me by an editor at a major computer-book publisher:

I missed the Federal Express pickup time.

Fedex lost my shipment . . . for the *sixth* time! (And I *still* can't seem to find the tracking number.)

I was in an earthquake.

My computer was hit by lightning.

My _____ (fill in family member) died.

My _____ (fill in family member) is sick.

My dog got hit by a car.

My cat is throwing up blood.

I have hemorrhoids, and cannot sit down to work at my computer.

My neck has gone numb from deadline stress.

My electricity lines went down when a car ran into a light pole near my house.

My hard disk crashed.

I moved.

I am being evicted, and I have to pack.

My floppy disk drive is broken, so the manuscript is all on my hard drive, but I can't send it to you.

A virus has corrupted all the manuscript files.

I'm going on vacation.

I started a new job, and no longer have time to write.

Writing is harder work than I expected it to be.

I'm finishing up a book for another publisher.

You mean the disk I sent you was blank? I wonder how that happened.

I don't have the documentation.

My voice mail/answering machine must have lost your messages.

I accidentally deleted your last e-mail message before reading it.

I'm having a friend read it before I turn it in, and he's _____. (Fill in an excuse, such as sick, vacationing, slow, tired, stupid, or dead).

Editors understand that things happen that really *do* stop you from delivering. It just seems that awful things happen to writers *all the time*. If you can make sure such awful things don't happen to you too often, your editors will be very grateful—and will reward you with more book projects.

Information on the Internet

You can find useful information about computer-book publishing on the Internet. The single best source of information is the StudioB Web site and mailing list (http://www.studiob.com/). The mailing list has 650 members—writers, agents, editors, and publishers. You'll find some big-name authors and publishers on this list, so there's good advice to be had. And another advantage to this mailing list is that the list owners send out e-mail advertisements periodically. The ads are from authors looking for coauthors, publishers looking for editors and authors, and so on. To subscribe to the mailing list, send an e-mail message to list@studiob.com. In the subject line, enter the word *subscribe*.

The Web site has an archive of all the mailing list messages. You might want to spend a few hours digging through this archive to see what you can find. It also has weekly articles about the business, with advice from editors and successful authors.

Another place that might be useful is the Resources for Computer Book Authors site at http://www.bdt.com/home/cackerman/authors.htm. This site contains a list of computer-book publishers and computer-book agents, though it's currently a little out of date. There are also a few articles about getting into computer-book writing, developing proposals, and royalties. There's also the Publisher's Catalogues Page (http://www.lights.com/publisher/), a list of thousands of publishers of all kinds (not just computer-book publishers), all around the world.

You might also want to check out the Waterside Productions Web site at http://www.waterside.com/. Waterside is the largest agency in the business, and it also hosts an annual conference for the computer-book business in San Diego. The Web site also has links to a few dozen publishers' Web sites.

Epilogue

> What we call luck is the inner man externalized.
>
> We make things happen to us.
>
> Canadian novelist Robertson Davies

After I wrote the first edition of this book—then called *The Technical Writer's Freelancing Guide*—I was very happy to discover just how useful other writers found the book. People wrote to tell me how much the book had helped them. When the original publisher let the book go out of print, a local writers' group asked for permission to photocopy the book, because so many people wanted a copy.

Still, I know I've missed a lot, things that would be useful to know that I haven't told you. How do I know I've missed stuff? Because every time I "lurk" in a tech-writer's mailing list or forum, or listen to freelancers talk at a local meeting, I hear great advice, really useful techniques that other writers have used in their careers. Each writer's experiences are different, so each has something unique to provide, and none knows every little technique. That's why it's so important for new freelancers to keep in contact with other, more experienced, freelancers. Spend time in the online discussion groups, in Society for Technical Communication (STC) chapter meetings, and in other small writers' groups.

Finally, I want to stress that the program I've outlined in this book, the system for financial success in technical writing, *does* work! I know it works because I've made it work, and other writers have too. Some will meet this system with skepticism, while others quietly smile. After a discussion about this subject in the techwr-l mailing list, one writer sent me private e-mail, telling me that her income was currently "in six figures," and that she knew "several writers who are also doing this today." But she won't talk publicly about this: "Clients get miffed when they realize you are probably earning twice what they do, so I just keep quiet and drive a small car."

She ended her message with the comment that success in freelance technical writing "is a matter of tenacity and market know-how." I couldn't agree more. Learn the ropes, understand your market, and be persistent, and you can successfully sell your services in the freelance technical-writing field. Let me know how you do; you can contact me at techsuccess@mcp.com.

A

Contractor's

Checklist

Use the first part of this checklist before you begin looking for work. Make copies of the "Negotiating with the Agencies" and "On the Road" sections of the checklist and use them to take notes when you talk to the agencies.

Before Looking for Work

Have you calculated how much you earn per hour?	❑
Dollars per hour	$

(Remember that this is an estimate only. How much you "earn" is a relative number, depending on the cost of replacing your benefits; see Chapter 13.)

Have you selected a medical insurance policy?	❑
Have you selected a long-term disability policy?	❑
Have you selected a life insurance policy?	❑

Using the Agencies

Have you made a list of all the agencies?	❑
Check:	
Appendix C	❑
Colleagues	❑
Yellow Pages	❑
Contractors' publications	❑
Classified ads	❑

continues

247

Using the Agencies   *Continued*

Internet mailing lists and newsgroups	❑
Have you written your cover letter and résumé?	❑
Have you printed your mailing labels?	❑

Negotiating with the Agencies

Before accepting a contract, you must know the answers to these questions. Remember to ask both the agency and company, where applicable:

Is the job a permanent position or a contract?	Yes ❑	No ❑
Is the agency looking for contractors or employees?	Yes ❑	No ❑
What industry is the job in?		
What type of work?		
How long is the contract?	months	
How much is the agency paying?	$ /hour	
Who is the client?		
Where is the contract?		
How much overtime is available?	hours/week	
How much overtime is expected?	hours/week	
Is overtime paid at time-and-a-half?	Yes ❑	No ❑
Does the agency have a medical insurance policy?	Yes ❑	No ❑
How much is the policy? (single, married, children)		$
How much is the deductible?	$	
How much are the out-of-pocket payments?	$	
What percentage does it pay after the deductible? (Eighty percent is common.)	%	
Does it include dental?	Yes ❑	No ❑
Does it include vision?	Yes ❑	No ❑
Does the agency have a long-term disability policy?	Yes ❑	No ❑
Is it included with the medical?	Yes ❑	No ❑
If not, how much is it?	$	

continues

How much coverage does it provide?	\$	
What is the waiting period?	days	
Does the agency pay for vacations?	Yes ❏	No ❏
Does the agency pay for sick leave?	Yes ❏	No ❏
How long do you have to work before getting paid leave?	days	
What is the ratio of work days to free days (for example, if you work 130 days, you get 6 days off)?	:	
Are paid-leave days ever vested (that is, if you work for nine months, will the agency pay all free days or only those earned in the first six months)?	Yes ❏	No ❏
Does the agency pay a mileage/travel allowance?	Yes ❏	No ❏
How much?	\$	
Does the agency have a 401(k) pension plan?	Yes ❏	No ❏
How long must you be employed to be eligible?	months	

Personal:

Is there a dress code?	Yes ❏	No ❏
Is smoking allowed or banned?	Allowed ❏	Banned ❏
Is there a company cafeteria?	Yes ❏	No ❏
Other:		
Other:		
Other:		
Other:		

On the Road

Does the job pay a per diem?	Yes ❏	No ❏
How much per week?	\$	
Is there a state or local income tax?	Yes ❏	No ❏
How much?	%	
How much more will general living expenses be?	\$	
How much will accommodation cost?	\$	
Will the agency pay any moving expenses?	Yes ❏	No ❏

continues

On the Road   *Continued*

How much? $

Anything else?(Add your own special requirements here.)

Looking for Independent Contracts

Have you called your "key" contacts?   ❑

Have you called local professional-society
job banks?   ❑

Have you checked the newspaper classified ads?   ❑

Have you talked with other department heads
at your current contract?   ❑

Have you called all the members of your
network (friends, colleagues, and so on)?   ❑

Have you checked discussion groups on
the Internet and online services?   ❑

Have you "advertised" your services
on the Internet?   ❑

Have you called old employers?   ❑

Have you called old colleagues?   ❑

Have you cold-called your list of peers?   ❑

Have you been to any local job fairs?   ❑

Have you called the list of companies
you've found from old classified ads?   ❑

Have you checked your card file or database
and called everyone you haven't called so far?   ❑

Have you cold-called a list of companies that
can use your services?   ❑

Contractors'

Publications

There are several publications targeted at contractors. Two in particular are of special help to road-shoppers, contractors who travel around the country working on different contracts. These magazines contain agency ads and listings of contracts, and several other services that may be useful.

Many people use these magazines to road-shop successfully, and so can you. ("I have been lucratively employed for the past nine years; this is a direct result of your efforts," one job-shopper wrote to *Technical Employment Weekly*.) Others just use the magazines to keep in touch with what is going on in contracting and to use their special services.

Technical Employment Weekly (originally PD News)

Publications and Communications, Inc.
12416 Hymeadow Drive
Austin, TX 78750
(512) 250-9023
FAX: (512) 331-3900
E-mail: editors@pcinews.com
Web: http://www.pcinews.com/pci/ (publisher's main page)
http://www.pcinews.com/pci/ten/ (The *Technical Employment Weekly* page)

This was the U.S.'s first publication serving the contract-employment industry. It's a weekly publication with display ads and listings of contracts throughout the nation. However, you don't have to subscribe to view these listings, as you can get to them on the World Wide Web for free (for the moment, at least). You can also view a directory of technical service agencies.

Technical Employment News (*TEN*) includes articles on subjects of interest to "job shoppers." It's currently 16-pages long with about 70 listings each week.

A one-year subscription varies from $55 (within the U.S.) to $175 (Japan, Australia, and New Zealand). You can get a single issue for $6. The publisher also produces a directory of technical-service agencies, which is free with a one-year subscription or $39.95 without a subscription.

Contract Employment Weekly (C.E. Weekly)

CCN Publications
P.O. Box 97000
Kirkland, WA 98083-9700
(206) 823-2222
FAX: (206) 821-0942
E-mail: publisher@ceweekly.wa.com, (Prodigy: WGGH23A Compuserve: 71052,2415)
Web: http://www.ceweekly.wa.com
Gopher: gopher.ceweekly.wa.com

This is a weekly publication with hundreds of listings of contracts and display ads. Each issue is about 80-pages long. One-year subscriptions are $65 (you can also order 12 issues for $30, and single issues for $8). *C.E. Weekly* also has a Web site, though you'll have to enter a password—which you are given when you subscribe—to access the job listings. The site has some useful links to other job resources on a public page, though.

C.E. Weekly also has a lot of services useful to job shoppers: a directory of agencies (around 1,000 agencies); a bulletin board service (BBS) for people who don't have Internet access; résumé-mailing and résumé-faxing services; a hot list sent to agencies; an address-change notification sent to 1,100 agencies; agency mailing labels; résumé typing and printing; a mail-forwarding service; and more.

Computer Consultants' and Contractors' Newsletter and Job Express

Corry Publishing
2840 W. 21st St.
Erie, Pa 16506
(814)838-0025
FAX: (814)836-9605
E-mail: corrypub@corrypub.com
Web site: http://www.corrypub.com/

These publications mainly list contracts in Maine, New York, New Jersey, Connecticut, and Pennsylvania. *Job Express* is a 12-page newsletter that is published twice a month (except August), listing consulting jobs and carrying subscribers' ads. Many of the listings—probably most—are from agencies.

The *Computer Consultants' and Contractors' Newsletter* is published once a month (except August). It's 12 pages long, half of which is filled with business-card-size ads from agencies and services. The rest contains short articles on consulting—interviews with people in the business, local news, contracting-law updates, book reviews, and so on—and a few ads.

The same company also publishes *The Consultant's Ye**ow Pages*, a directory listing over 6,000 agencies. The entries are firms and government agencies that use data-processing personnel, and include a contact name and telephone number.

A one-year subscription to both *Job Express* and *The Computer Consultants' and Contractors' Newsletter* is $79.95. A six-month subscription is $49.50. *The Consultant's Ye**ow Pages* is $42.95, on paper or floppy disk.

Technical

Service Firms

This appendix lists the names and telephone numbers of a few technical writing companies and large technical service firms. You should build your own list of agencies in the area in which you want to work (see Chapter 8), but you can use this list to make initial contacts and get a feel for the market.

You can also find useful lists of agencies at the following Web pages:

John Hewitt's Technical Writing Center:
http://www.azstarnet.com/~poewar/writer/pg/tech.html

Technical Communicators Recruitment Pages - UK:
http://www.hairydog.clara.net/tclnkjobuk.html

Technical Communicators Recruitment Pages - US:
http://www.hairydog.clara.net/tclnkjobus.html

You can also find more technical-writing agencies at **Yahoo!'s Technical Writing page:**

http://www.yahoo.com/Business_and_Economy/Companies/
Communications_and_Media_Services/Writing_and_Editing/
Technical_Writing/

Technical Writing Agencies

Author Services Technical

4 Icknield Way
Letchworth
Herts. SG6 1EX United Kingdom
(01462) 481144
Fax: (01462) 483480

Comtech

710 Kipling St. #400
Denver, CO 80215
(303) 232-0659
Fax: (303) 232-0659

1798 Technology Drive
Suite 236
San Jose, CA 95110
(408) 451 3110
Fax: (408) 451 9340
E-mail: info@comtech-serv.com
Web: http://www.comtech-serv.com/

COREComm

5151 San Felipe, Suite 801
Houston, TX 77056
(713) 624-2485
Fax: (713) 624-2486
E-mail: corecomm@corecomm.com
Web: http://www.corecomm.com/
corecomm/welcome.html

Dashe & Thompson

205 South Scoville
Oak Park, IL 60302
(708) 445-0150
Fax: (708) 383-9722

401 North 3rd Street, Suite 500
Minneapolis, MN 55401
(612) 338-4911
Fax: (612) 338-4920
E-mail: hr@dashe.com
Web: http://www.dashe.com/

Knowledge Transfer International (KTI)

747 Third Avenue
New York, NY 10017
(212) 355-8080
Fax: (212) 355-7266
E-mail: ross_squire@ktic.com
Web: http://www.ktic.com/

125 Cambridge Park Drive
Cambridge, MA 02140
(617) 864-7300
Fax: (617) 864-9545
E-mail: tim_brown@ktic.com

Kudos

9/10 Westminster Court
Hipley Street, Woking
Surrey, GU22 9LQ, UK
(1483) 747227
Fax: (1483) 747337

3 Sandyford Office Park
Blackthorn Avenue
Dublin 18
(1) 294 0960
Fax (1) 294-0953
E-mail: 71612.1545@compuserve.com
Web: http://www.kudos.co.uk/

Manual 3, Inc.

10 South Third Street, Fourth Floor
San Jose, CA 95113
(408) 293-9654
Fax: (408) 293-0241
E-mail: info@manual3.com
Web: http://www.manual3.com/

NIVA

500-1145 Hunt Club Road
Ottawa, Ontario K1V 0Y3
Canada
(613) 737-6000
Fax: (613) 737-5868
E-mail: niva@magi.com
Web: http://www.magi.com/~niva/
index.html

ProSoft Publishing

1617, Avenue de la Salle
Bureau 5
Montréal, Québec H1V 2J7
Canada
(514) 253-1085
Fax: (514) 253-5835

SK Writers

20430 Town Center Lane, Suite 5E1
Cupertino, CA 95014
(408) 252-4818
Fax: (408) 252-2101
E-mail: shirley@skwriters.com

SkuppSearch, Inc.

580 Sylvan Avenue
Englewood Cliffs, NJ 07632
(201) 894-1824
Fax: (201) 894-1120

Technical Standards

1720 Seely Ct.
San Marcos, CA 92069
(619) 471-1819
Fax: (619) 471-1879
E-mail: tecstdjd@ix.netcom.com
Web: http://www.tecstandards.com/

Techwrights, Inc.

540 Route 10 West, Suite 314
Randolph, NJ 07869
(201) 786-7244

TMS Computer Authors, Ltd.

Hambledown House
Catteshall Lane
Godalming, Surrey, GU17 1JJ
United Kingdom
(1483) 419717

Words & Images

10 Luss St.
Moggill, Queensland, Australia 4070.
(+61) 7 3202-7573
Fax: (+61) 7 3202-7514
E-mail: ian@wordsimages.com
http://www.wordsimages.com/

Technical Service Agencies

ADIA Technical Services

100 Redwood Shores Parkway
Redwood City, CA 94065
(415) 610-1096
Fax: (415) 610-1249

Aerotek

4144C Innslake Drive
Glen Allen, VA 23060
(800) 792-7208
(804) 346-0588
Fax: (804) 747-4969

AiDE, Inc. Design Services

P.O. Box 6746
Greenville, SC 29606
(803) 244-6123
Fax: (803) 322-1040

B & M Associates

199 Cambridge Road
Woburn, MA 01801
(800) 487-2967
(617) 938-9120
Fax: (617) 932-3930

Belcan Technical Services

P.O. Box 429138
Cincinnati, OH 45242
(800) 945-1900
(513) 489-4300
Fax: (513) 489-0830

Butler Service Group

110 Summit Avenue
Montvale, NJ 07645
(800) 526-0320
(201) 573-1113

CDI Corporation

1717 Arch St., 35th Floor
Philadelphia, PA 19103-2768
(800) 562-5463
(215) 569-2200
Fax: (215) 569-1750

Consultants and Designers, Inc.

360 West 31st Street
New York, NY 10001
(212) 563-8400

Ewing Technical Design

40 South Street
P.O. Box 10479
West Hartford, CT 06110
(203) 249-6311

The Franklin Company

600 Reed Road
Broomall, PA 19008
(800) 523-4948
(215) 356-1010
Fax: (610) 353-5764

General Devices, Inc.

207 East Main Street
P.O. Box 667
Norristown, PA 19404
(215) 272-4477

Gonzer Associates, L.J.

1225 Raymond Boulevard
Newark, NJ 07102-2919
(201) 624-5600
(800) 631-4218

International Technical Services

141 Central Avenue
P.O. Box 239
Farmingdale, NY 11735
(516) 694-4433
(800) JOB-TIME (562-8463)

Kirk Mayer, Inc.

11801 Mississippi Avenue
Los Angeles, CA 90025
(310) 479-7794
Fax: (310) 479-7223

Lehigh Design

14120 McCormick Drive
Tampa, FL 33626
(813) 855-9411

MiniSystems

124 West Figueroa Street
Santa Barbara, CA 93101
(805) 963-9660
(800) 445-5506 (outside California)

Nelson, Coulson and Associates, Inc.

333 West Hampden, $NO507
Englewood, CO 80110
(303) 761-7680

Nesco Design Group

14120 McCormick Drive
Tampa, FL 33626
(813) 855-9411

Oxford and Associates, Inc.

75 Pearl Street
Reading, MA 01867
(617) 944-6200
(800) 426-9196

PDS Technical Services

P.O. Box 619820
Dallas, TX 75261
(214) 621-8080
(800) 777-9372

Peak Technical Services, Inc.

3424 William Penn Highway
Pittsburgh, PA 15235
(412) 825-3900
(800) 284-2841

Pollack and Skan, Inc.

120 West Center Court
Schaumberg, IL 60195
(312) 359-4949
(800) 544-7817 (outside Illinois)

Quantum Resources

P.O. Box 35630
Richmond, VA 23235-0630
(804) 320-4800

Ray Rashkin Associates, Inc.

1930 South Alma School Road
$NOD107
Mesa, AZ 85210
(602) 897-2479
(800) 543-6076

Salem Technical Services

1333 Butterfield Road
Downers Grove, IL 60515
(312) 990-8800
(800) 323-7200

S&W Technical Services, Inc.

8122 Datapoint Drive $NO930
San Antonio, TX 78229
(512) 699-1080

SEI Technical Services

7725 Little Avenue
Charlotte, NC 28226
(704) 542-7100
(800) 331-1618

Superior Design

250 International Drive
P.O. Box 9057
Williamsville, NY 14231-9057
(716) 631-8310

TAD Technical Services Corp.

639 Massachusetts Avenue
Cambridge, MA 02139
(800) 225-5776 (outside Massachusetts)
(800) 842-1417 (Massachusetts only)

Tech/Aid

P.O. Box 128
Needham Heights, MA 02194
(617) 449-6632
(800) 225-8956

TRS, Inc.

P.O. Box 26147
Greenville, SC 29616
(803) 297-3110
(800) 522-5627

Volt Technical Services

101 Park Avenue
New York, NY 10178
(212) 309-0300
(800) 367-8658

Western Technical Services

301 Lennon Lane
Walnut Creek, CA 94598-9280
(415) 930-5300

Yoh Company, H.L.

1818 Market Street
Philadelphia, PA 19103
(215) 299-8400
(800) 523-0786, extension 8400

International Listings
Butler Service Group

JL Gegerkalong Lebak N0. 18
Dandung 40153 Indonesia
(22) 212445
Fax (22) 214487

Digitext

15 High Street
Thame
Oxfordshire, OX9 2BZ, UK
(1844) 214690

D

Associations

There are several organizations for technical writers. The most significant is the Society for Technical Communication (STC). It has 144 chapters—mostly in North America—with almost 20,000 members, 15 to 20 percent of whom are freelancers. The STC is by no means the only organization for technical writers, though. This appendix provides information about the STC, and contact information for a variety of other writers' organizations.

You could also track down other local organizations; for example, if you work in telecommunications, you may want to join a society related to that industry. These associations can be an excellent source of leads. Go to your library and ask whether it has a directory of local associations. You can also check the following books:

◆ *Consultants and Consulting Organizations Directory*, Gale Research Company

◆ *The Encyclopedia of Associations*, Gale Research Company

◆ *The National Trade and Professional Associations of the United States*, Columbia Books

If you still can't find an organization related to your profession, maybe you should start one. It may even be possible to start one as a profit-making venture; see Howard Shenson's book *The Complete Guide to Consulting Success* for a discussion of starting a professional association.

The Society for Technical Communication

The STC is "devoted to the advancement and the theory and practice of technical communication," but it's also a great way to meet technical writers in your area. Most chapters have monthly meetings, and many have annual seminars and competitions and publish local newsletters. The national organization itself publishes a quarterly journal (*Technical Communication*), a newsletter that appears 10 times a year (*Intercom*), and a quarterly newsletter for student members (*Interchange*). It also publishes a variety of books and manuals.

The STC holds an annual conference, awards scholarships, and offers research grants. You can also buy insurance at a discount through Mutual of Omaha if you are an STC member.

The STC can even help you find work. Just meeting your colleagues is an important way to find job leads, of course, but many local chapters also maintain a "job bank" that lists local jobs and contracts. The STC publications often carry ads for jobs, and the STC's computer bulletin board system includes a nationwide list of jobs. The STC now has a World Wide Web site, too, with links to local chapters' Web sites.

Each year the STC publishes a national membership directory which is sent to members at no additional cost. (Some chapters publish a local directory.) There is a Consulting and Independent Contracting Professional Interest Committee that publishes a quarterly newsletter, *The Independent Perspective*, has a Consulting Forum on the STC's bulletin board, conducts regional conferences, and is planning to publish "kits" such as a "useful contracts" kit and one about setting rates.

You can contact the STC as follows:

901 North Stuart Street
Arlington, VA 22203
Telephone: (703) 522-4114
Fax: (703) 522-2075
BBS: (703) 522-3299
E-mail: stc@tmn.com
Web: http://stc.org/
FTP: ftp.clark.net/pub/stc

Other Technical Writers' Organizations

SIGDOC (Special Interest Group for Documentation) of the ACM (Association for Computing Machinery)

c/o ACM
P.O. Box 12115
Church Street Station
New York, NY 10249
Telephone: (212) 626-0500
Fax: (212) 944-1318
E-mail: acmhelp@acm.org
Web: SIGDOC—http://www.acm.org/sigdoc/
Web: ACM—http://info.acm.org/

IEEE-PCS (Institute of Electrical and Electronic Engineers/Professional Communication Society)

IEEE Service Center
P.O. Box 1331
Piscataway, NJ 088555
Telephone: (908) 562-5501
Web: http://www.ieee.org/pcs/pcsindex.html

Society of Documentation Professionals

Renee Pauley
Membership Director
Clear Point Consultants
3 Centennial Drive,
Peabody, MA 01960,
Telephone: (508) 532-6400
E-mail: rpauley@clearpnt.com
http://www.sdpro.org/

Alliance for Computers and Writing

Fred Kemp
Department of English
Texas Tech University
Lubbock, TX 79409-43091
Telephone: (202) 651-5494
E-mail: ykfaq@ttacs.ttu.edu or alliance@ttacs.ttu.edu
Web: http://english.ttu.edu/acw/

Association of Teachers of Technical Writing

Billie J. Wahlstrom, ATTW
Department of Rhetoric
201 Haecker Hall
1364 Eckles Avenue
University of Minnesota
St. Paul, MN 55108-6122
E-mail: ATTW-L@ttu.edu or
ditsd@ttacs.ttu.edu
Web: http://english.ttu.edu/ATTW/

American Society of Indexers

P.O. Box 48267
Seattle, WA 98148-0267
Telephone: (206) 241-9196
Fax: (206) 727-6430
E-mail: asi@well.com
Web: http://www.well.com/user/asi/
Web: http://www.well.com/user/asi/

Outside the U.S.

INTECOM (International Council of Technical Communication)

INTECOM is an umbrella society for technical-communication societies. Member associations include the STC (U.S.), IEEE-PCS (U.S.), ISTC (U.K.), tekom (Germany and Austria), CRT (France), STIC/QTD (The Netherlands), Dantecom (Denmark), FTI (Sweden), NFTI (Norway), ASTC (Australia), ETTY (Israel), TECOM-Schweiz (Switzerland), and ITCSA (South Africa).

Brigitte Beuttenmüller
Markelstr. 34
70193 Stuttgart, Germany
E-mail: tek-b.beutte@geod.geonet.de
(President, 1997: Brigitte Beuttenmuller)
Web: http://www.nts.mh.se/~fti/Intecom.htm

ASTC (Australian Society For Technical Communication)

Julie Fisher
68 Holmes Road
AUS Moonee Ponds, 3039
Victoria
Australia
Telephone: +61 3365 2272
Fax: +61 3365 2292
E-mail: JulieFisher@vut.edu.au
Web: http://yarra.vicnet.net.au/~astc/ or
http://www.uts.edu.au/fac/hss/astc/

CRT (Conseil des Rédacteurs Techniques)

Jean-Paul Bardez
5, villa des Carrières
94120 Fontenay-sous-Bois
France
Telephone: +33 1 48756633
Fax: +33 1 48756566
E-mail: 100423.1635@compuserve.com
Web: http://www.iut.univ-paris8.fr/~crt
or http://khety.iut.univ-paris8.fr/~crt/

DANTEKOM (Danish Society for Technical Communikation)

Thomas O'Connor
Solbakken 1
Snostrup
Frederikssund 3600
Danemark
Telephone: +45 42 263366
Fax: +45 42 269322

ETTY

Julian Zelenko
8, Spinoza St.
Apt. 3
Ra'anana
43588 Israel
E-mail: zelenko@shani.net

FTI (Föreningen Teknisk Information)

Johan Näsström
Gladsax 28
S-272 94 SIMRIMSHAMM

Sweden
Telephone: +46 70 7652542
Fax: +46 414 21157
Web: http://www.nts.mh.se/~fti/

Irish Society of Technical Communicators

Eoin O'Riain
P.O. Box 3516
Shankill
County Dublin, Ireland.
E-mail: readout@iol.ie
Web: http://www.maths.tcd.ie/
~pmoloney/istc/index.html

ISTC (Institute of Scientific and Technical Communicators)

Gerry D. Gentle
Strathmore
12 Hitchin Road
Letchworth
Herts SG6 3LL
Great Britain
Telephone: +44 1462 484367
Fax: +44 1462 483480
E-mail: istc@istc.org.uk
Web: http://www.istc.org.uk/istc/ and
http://dspace.dial.pipex.com/town/
plaza/jk49/

ITCSA (Institute of Technical Communicators of South Africa)

Jan Roodbol
P.O. Box 30544
SA-0132 Sunnyside
South Africa
Telephone: +27 12 831553
Fax: +27 12 831553

NFTI (Norsk Forening for Teknisk Information)

Tove qstberg
Maridalsun 272B
0872 Oslo
Norway
Telephone: +47 22 182610
Fax: +47 22 180958
E-mail: jery@sni.no

STIC (Studiekring voor Technische Informatie & Kommunikatie)

Rob Punselie
Vonderweg 11
5600 Eindhoven
The Netherlands
Telephone: +31 40 2757670
Fax: +31 40 2757710
E-mail: punseli@IAEhv.nl

TECOM-Schweiz

Walter Krein
Kirchbergstr. 30
5024 Kuettigen
Switzerland
Telephone: +41 62 8273454
Fax: +41 62 8273454
E-mail: wkrein@swissonline.ch

tekom (Gesellschaft für technische Kommunikation e.V.)

Brigitte Beutenmüller
Markelstr. 34
70193 Stuttgart 1
Germany
Telephone: +49 711 6572595
Fax: +49 711 6574013
E-mail: tek-b.beutte@geod.goenet.de
Web: http://www.tekom.de/

Other Writers' Organizations

American Medical Writers Association

9650 Rockville Place
Bethesda, MD 20814-3998
Telephone: (310) 493-0003
Fax: 493-6384
E-mail: tscom005@dunx1.ocs.drexel.edu

Associated Business Writers of America

1450 South Havana, Suite 424
Aurora, CO 80012
Telephone: (303) 751-7844
Fax: 751-8593

Association for Business Communication

University of North Texas
College of Business
Department of Management
Denton, TX 76203
Telephone: (817) 565-4423
Fax: (817) 565-4930

Association of Earth Science Editors

781 Northwest Drive
Morgantown, WV 26505
Telephone: (304) 599-2865
Telephone: (304) 285-4679
Fax: 599-8904

Association of Railway Communicators

Association of American Railroads
50 F Street NW
Washington, DC 20001
Telephone: (202) 639-2562
Fax: (202) 639-2558

Aviation and Space Writers Association

17 South High Street, Suite 1200
Columbus, OH 43215
Telephone: (614) 221-1900
Fax: (614) 221-1989

Computer Press Association

3661 West 4th Avenue, No. 8
Vancouver, BC, Canada V6R 1P2
Telephone: (604) 733-5596
Fax: (604) 732-4280

Construction Writers Association

P.O. Box 30
Aldie, VA 22001
Telephone: (703) 771-4133
Telephone: (202) 393-2040

Council of Biology Editors

11 LaSalle, No. 1400
Chicago, IL 60603-1210
Telephone: (312) 201-0101
Fax: (312) 201-0214
E-mail: tscom005@dunx1.ocs.drexel.edu

Editorial Freelancers Association

71 West 23rd Street, Suite 1504
New York, NY 10010
Telephone: (212) 929-5400
Fax: (212) 929-5439

Freelance Editorial Association

P.O. Box 380835
Cambridge, MA 02238-0835
Telephone: (619) 729-8164

National Association of Science Writers

P.O. Box 294
Greenlawn, NY 11740
Telephone: (516) 757-5664
Fax: (516) 757-0069

National Writers Union

873 Broadway, Suite 203
New York, NY 10003-1209
Telephone: (212) 254-0279
Fax: (212) 254-0673

Optometric Editors Association

11365 Sunset Hills Road
Reston, VA 22090
Telephone: (703) 471-5872

Small Business Associations

Small business associations can provide support for small businesses, such as insurance coverage, business discounts, and newsletters.

Home Business Institute

The Home Business Institute offers a variety of services for small businesses, including liability insurance.

138 Hillair Circle
White Plains, NY 10605
Telephone: (914) 946-6600
Fax: (914) 946-6694

National Association of the Self-Employed (NASE)

This 300,000-member association offers a wide range of services, including health and disability insurance. Call for information. (Note, however, that there have been serious complaints about NASE's health policy. See *Home Office Computing*, January 1992.)

2328 Gravel Road
Fort Worth, TX 76118-6950
Telephone: (800) 232-6273

National Association of Private Enterprise

P.O. Box 612147
Dallas, TX 75261-2147
Telephone: (800) 223-6273
Fax: (817) 332-4525

National Business Association

5025 Arapaho, Suite 515
Dallas, TX 75248
Telephone: (214) 458-0900
Telephone: (800) 456-0440
Fax: (214) 960-9149

Consulting Associations

American Consultants League

1290 Palm Avenue
Sarasota, FL 34236
Telephone: (813) 952-9290
Fax: (813) 925-3670

American Consulting Engineers Council

1015 15th Street NW
Washington, DC 20005
Telephone: (202) 347-7474

Association for Computing Machinery (ACM)

P.O. Box 12115
Church Street Station
New York, NY 10249 USA
Telephone: (212) 626-0500
Fax: (212) 944-1318
E-mail: acmhelp@acm.org
Web: ACM—http://info.acm.org/

Association of Computer Professionals

9 Forest Drive
Plainview, NY 11803
Telephone: (516) 938-8223

Association of Independent Information Professionals

245 5th Avenue, Suite 2103
New York, NY 10016
Telephone: (212) 779-1855
Fax: (212) 481-3071

Fastbreak Syndicate, Inc.

An organization for writers, illustrators, artists, and so on.

P.O. Box 1626
Orem, UT 84059
Telephone: (801) 785-1300

Independent Computer Consultants' Association

933 Gardenview Office Parkway
St. Louis, MO 63141
Telephone: (314) 997-4633

Professional and Technical Consultants Association

P.O. Box 4143
Mountain View, CA 94040
Telephone: (415) 903-8305

Correspondence

Courses,

Training Courses,

and Seminars

This appendix contains information about technical writing education. Also check the associated Web site at http://www.mcp.com/mgr/arco/techwr/.

Correspondence Courses

These organizations have technical-writing and associated correspondence courses. Also check with your local library, which may have a listing of courses (for instance, in the U.S., there's a book called *The Macmillan Guide to Correspondence Study*).

College of Technical Authorship

Correspondence courses providing City and Guilds certification (a British certification recognized in many parts of the world).

P.O. Box 7
Cheadle
Cheshire SK8 3BT, England
Telephone: (0161) 437-4235 (if calling from the U.S., dial 011-44-161-437-4235)
Fax: (0161) 437-4235
E-mail: crossley@coltecha.u-net.com
Web: http://www.coltecha.u-net.com/

Distance Education Office of the University of Waterloo

Technical Writing on the World Wide Web course.

Telephone: (519) 888-4567, ext. 6034
E-mail: mjones@corr1.uwaterloo.ca or pdbeam@watarts.uwaterloo.ca
Web: http://itrc.uwaterloo.ca/~engl210e/

McGraw-Hill Continuing Education Center/NRI Schools

This organization doesn't have technical writing courses, but has related courses, such as desktop publishing and multimedia programming.

4401 Connecticut Avenue
Washington, DC 20008
Telephone: (202) 244-9815
Telephone: (202) 244-9792
E-mail: info@mhcec.com
Web: http://www.mhcec.com/

Ohio University Independent Study

Ohio University
Tupper Hall 302
Athens, OH 45701-2979
Telephone: (800) 444-2910
Telephone: (614) 593-2910
Fax: (614) 593-2901
E-mail: indstudy@ouvaxa.cats.ohiou.edu
Web: http://www.cats.ohiou.edu/
~liflear/

Oklahoma State University

Independent and Correspondence Study
001H Classroom Building
Oklahoma State University
Stillwater, OK 74078-0404
Telephone: (800) 522-4002 (toll-free in
Oklahoma)
Telephone: (405) 744-6390
Fax: (405) 744-7793
Web: Try http://www.okstate.edu/
education/inc.html or http://
www.okstate.edu/

University of California Extension

University of California
Berkeley, CA 94720
Telephone: (510) 642-8245

University of Iowa

Division of Continuing Education
Center for Credit Programs
Guided Correspondence Study
International Center
Iowa City, IA 52242
Telephone: (319) 353-2575
Telephone: (800) 272-6430 (within
Iowa)
Telephone: (800) 553-6380 (bordering
Iowa)

University of Massachusetts Dartmouth Division of Continuing Education—CyberEd

This organization runs a Technical and
Business Writing course over the World
Wide Web.

UMass Dartmouth, CyberEd
Division of Continuing Education
University of Massachusetts Dartmouth
North Dartmouth, MA 02747
Telephone: (508) 999-9129
Fax: (508) 999-8621
Web: http://www.umassd.edu/cybered/
distlearninghome.html

U.S. Department of Agriculture

The USDA has a variety of courses that
may be of interest to technical writers—
technical editing, writing for business,
indexing, writing for professionals,
report writing, and so on.

The Graduate School, USDA
Correspondence Program
Ag Box 9911
Room 1112, South Agriculture Building
14th Street and Independence Avenue
S.W.
Washington, D.C. 20250-9911
Telephone: (202) 720-7123
TDD: (202) 690-1516
Fax: (202) 720-3603
E-mail: correspond@grad.usda.gov
Web: http://grad.usda.gov/corres/
corpro.html

The Writing Center

A variety of writing courses.

303 South High Street
West Chester, PA 19382
Phone: 610-436-4600
Fax: 610-344-0950
Email: WritingCtr@aol.com
Web: http://www.tregistry.com/ttr/
write.htm

More on the Internet

There are many sources of information about technical-writing education on the Internet. Take a look at the following pages.

ATTW Academic Programs (good list of college courses): http://english.ttu.edu/ATTW/programs.html

Business Issues and Practices in Technical Communication: http://www.mercer.edu/~tco635/

Coventry University, BA in Technical Communication http://www.gold.net/petecom/coventry.htm

Dakota State University—ENGL 405, Technical Report Writing http://www.dsu.edu/departments/liberal/english/techwrit/

Education and Training Courses in the UK Web: http://www.istc.org.uk/istc/educate.htm and http://dspace.dial.pipex.com/town/plaza/jk49/educate.htm

English Technical Writing University of Waterloo: http://itrc.uwaterloo.ca/~engl210e/

Internet Technical Writing Course: http://uu-gna.mit.edu:8001/uu-gna/text/wamt/acchtml/acctoc.html

Masters in Technical and Scientific Communication (Miami): http://miavx1.acs.muohio.edu/~mtsccwis/

Mercer University—Master of Science Technical Communication Management: http://www.mercer.edu/~mstco/index.html

O'Conner's Tech Writing E161: http://www.missouri.edu/~c359452/E161/frame.html

OmniScribe Consulting Technical Writing Course: http://goofy.iafrica.com/~rexm/write.htm

Introduction to Technical Communication, Austin Community College: http://www.io.com/~hcexres/tcm1603/tcmmain.html

Peterborough Technical Communication: http://www.gold.net/petecom/

Purdue University On-line Writing Lab (OWL): http://owl.english.purdue.edu/

Rensselaer—Language, Literature, and Communication: http://www.rpi.edu/dept/llc/wwwllc/index.html

Roane State Community College Online Writing Lab: http://fur.rscc.cc.tn.us/OWL/OWL.html

Schools with Technical Communication Programs http://luigi.calpoly.edu/Techcomm/Other_TCPrograms/Other_TCPrograms.html

Sheffield Hallam University—Technical Authorship: http://www.shu.ac.uk/schools/cs/pgrad/mata.htm

South Bank University in London: http://www.scism.sbu.ac.uk/About/

STC's Academic Programs in Technical Communication: http://www.stc-va.org/Academics/school.html

STC's main pages: http://www.stc-va.org/ and http://www.stc.org/

Technical Communication at California Polytechnic State University: http://www.calpoly.edu/~techcomm/

Technical Writer Program at Algonquin College: http://www.cst.algonquinc.on.ca/techwriter/twframes.htm

Technical Writing Homepage, Texas Christian University: http://delta.is.tcu.edu/~marek1/wri/tech.html

Utah State University Tech Writing Course: http://www.usu.edu/~english/tech/tech.html

Writer's Conference Web Site (Course 9602: Freelance Technical Communications): http://www.writersconf.com/

Writing in Professional Cultures Using the World Wide Web: http://web.syr.edu/~cfsmith/courses/wrt405/general/homepage.html

Writing the Information Superhighway: http://www.lsa.umich.edu/ecb/infohighway.html

WRT405 Professional and Technical Writing: http://wrt.syr.edu/wrt/classes/405/gr/engcoop95.html

Seminars

These organizations do seminars in technical writing and associated skills.

Dashe & Thompson

205 South Scoville
Oak Park, IL 60302
Telephone: (708) 445-0150
Fax: (708) 383-9722
E-mail: seminars@dashe.com
Web: http://www.dashe.com/

Dashe & Thompson

Minneapolis
401 North 3rd Street, Suite 500
Minneapolis, MN 55401
Telephone: (612) 338-4911
Fax: (612) 338-4920

HELP University

Courses on WinHelp authoring.

Alec Sonenthal
c/o Greenbrook Technical
Communications

10809 Chestnut Ridge Road
Austin, TX 78726
Telephone: (800) 801-HELP
Fax: (214) 902-9049
E-mail: info@helpuniversity.com
Web: http://www.helpuniversity.com/

Information Mapping

300 Third Avenue
Waltham, MA 02154
Telephone: (617) 890-7003
Fax: (617) 890-1339
E-mail: custserv@infomap.com
Web: http://www.infomap.com/

Presenting Data and Information

Graphics Press
P.O. Box 430
Cheshire, CT 06410
Telephone: (800) 822-2454
Telephone: (203) 272-9187
Fax: (203) 272-8600

Pubsnet Inc. Seminars

34 Chelmsford Street
Chelmsford, MA 01824
Telephone: (508) 244-0272
(Massachusetts)
Fax: (508) 256-0365
E-mail: info@pubsnet.com
Web: http://www.pubsnet.com/

Seminars in Usable Design

710 Kipling Street, Suite 400
Denver, CO 80215
Telephone: (303) 234-0123
E-mail: bill.hackos@comtech-serv.com
Web: http://www.usabledesign.com/

SOLUTIONS

274 Main Street
Reading, MA 01867
Telephone: (800) 448-4230
Telephone: (617) 942-1610
Fax: (617) 942-1616
E-mail: solutions@sol-sems.com.
Web: http://www.sol-sems.com/

F

Other Resources

Co-op America

See Chapter 13's discussion of insurance programs.

2100 M Street, NW
Washington, DC 20063
Telephone: (202) 872-5307
Telephone: (800) 424-2667

Copyright Office

Library of Congress
Washington, DC 20559-6000
Telephone: (202) 707-3000
Web: http://lcweb.loc.gov/copyright/
Gopher: marvel.loc.gov
Telnet: marvel.loc.gov (login as marvel)
Telnet: Locis.loc.gov

Nolo Press Self-Help Law Center

See Chapter 6's discussion of suing clients for unpaid monies.

950 Parker Street
Berkeley, CA 94710
Telephone: (510) 549-1976
Telephone: (800) 992-6656 (outside the 510 area code)
Fax: (800) 645-0895
E-mail: noloinfo@nolopress.com
Web: http://www.nolo.com/

Safeware

See Chapter 13's discussion of computer insurance.

5760 North High Street
P.O. Box 656
Columbus, OH 43085
Telephone: (800) 800-1492

SelectQuote Insurance Services

See Chapter 13's discussion of insurance programs.

140 Second Street
San Francisco, CA 94105
Telephone: (800) 343-1985

Small Claims Court Citizens Legal Manual

See Chapter 6's discussion of suing clients for unpaid monies.

HALT, Inc.

201 Massachusetts Avenue, NE, Suite 319
Washington, DC 20002

Workers Trust

See Chapter 13's discussion of insurance programs.

P.O. Box 11618
Eugene, OR 97440
Telephone: (503) 683-8176
Telephone: (800) 447-2345

Bibliography

This bibliography contains a list of books that you might find useful. Some I've found useful in my career, others have been recommended to me by other technical writers.

Books About Technical Writing

Clear Technical Writing. John A. Brogan (McGraw-Hill). Excellent; you have to get this one.

The Complete Guide to Writing Software User Manuals. Brad M. McGehee (Writer's Digest Books). A good primer on writing computer user guides.

The Craft of Research. Wayne C. Booth, Gregory C. Colomb, and Joseph M. William, editors (University of Chicago Press).

The Elements of Style. William Strunk, Jr., and E. B. White (Macmillan Publishing Co.). A good, quick way to brush up your grammar skills.

The Elements of Technical Writing. Gary Blake & Robert Bly, Macmillan, 0-02-013085-6.

How to Manage a Successful Software Project: Methodologies, Techniques, Tools. Sanjiv Purba, David Sawh, and Bharat Shah (John Wiley and Sons).

How to Write a Computer Manual. Jonathan Price (Benjamin/Cummings Publishing Co.). Covers writing, testing, revising your work, and recommending software changes. Very good.

How to Write a Usable User Manual. Edmond H. Weiss (ISI Press). Stodgy, but a good overview of the process . Some companies use this book as their tech-writing bible.

Inteviewing Practices for Technical Writers. Earl McDowell (Baywood Publishing Company, Inc.).

Managing Your Documentation Projects. JoAnn Hackos (John Wiley and Sons). Hackos is the owner of a technical writing agency (Comtech), and a well-known lecturer and seminar leader, as well as a prominent member of the Society of Technical Communication (STC). This book was recommended to me; it reportedly walks you through the procedures needed to set up and manage documentation projects. It also includes information on estimating project length, which could be very useful for pricing.

Science and Technical Writing: a Manual of Style. Philip Rubens (A Henry Holt Reference Book). This one was recommended as a replacement for *The Elements of Style*.

The Technical Writer's Handbook. Matt Young (University Science Books). A humorous dictionary of terms and misuse.

Technical Writing: a Reader-Centered Approach. Paul V. Anderson (Harcourt Brace Jovanovich). A big book that seems to cover everything from grammar to page layout.

Technical Writing for Business and Industry. Patricia Williams and Pamela Beason (Scott, Foresman, & Co.).

Technical Writing for Technicians: How to Build a Career As a Hardware Technical Writer. Warren R. Freeman, Contemax Publishers, 0-9644739-0-9.

The Technical Writing Game. Janet Van Wicklen (Facts on File). Another writer recommended this one to me saying that the book offers a useful (although not comprehensive) look at the logistics of getting work and dealing with subject matter experts—that is, the people you have to pry the information out of before you can write.

Techniques for Technical Communicators. Carol Barnum and Saul Carliner, editors (Prentice Hall).

Writing Effective Software Documentation. Patricia Williams and Pamela Beason (Scott, Foresman, & Co.). Lots of examples of page layout.

Writing for the Corporate Market. George Sorenson (Mid-List Press).

Society for Technical Communication Publications

The STC publishes a number of books and guides on a variety of subjects, from Basic Technical Writing to Technical Editing (see Appendix D for its address). I haven't used any of these, so I can't recommend them, but I'm sure they are useful. You can find more information—and place orders—at the STC World Wide Web site at http://www.stc-va.org/.

Getting Started in Consulting & Independent Contracting

This is an "electronic" book that you can read on the World Wide Web. Articles on various subjects from experienced freelancers (members of the STC's Consultants & Independent Contractors Special Interest Group): http://english.ttu.edu/cicsig/gscic.htm

Books About the Business of Writing and Consulting

Cash Copy. Dr. Jeffrey Lant (JLA Publications, 50 Follen Street, Suite 507, Cambridge, MA 02138, (617)547-6372). Don't waste money on advertising or direct mail until you have read this book from the self-promotion guru. Buy directly from him and you'll never get off his mailing list, but you might find some other interesting books.

Complete Guide to Consulting Success. Howard Shenson (Enterprise Publishing, Inc., 725 North Market Street, Wilmington, DE 19801). An excellent overview of consulting. This book has a one-year, "no questions asked" guarantee.

The Consultant's Kit: Establishing and Operating Your Successful Consulting Business. Dr. Jeffrey L. Lant (JLA Publications, 50 Follen Street, Suite 507, Cambridge, MA 02138, (617)547-6372).

Consulting: the Complete Guide to a Profitable Career. Robert E. Kelley (Charles Scribner's Sons).

Freelancing—the First 30 Days. Bill Coan (Coan & Company, 606 Kessler Drive, Neenah, WI 54956). An excellent guide to the "nuts and bolts" of finding contract work. This book has a money-back guarantee.

Going Freelance: a Guide for Professionals. Robert Laurance (John Wiley and Sons).

The New Freelancer's Handbook: Successful Self-Employment. Marietta Whittlesley (Simon & Schuster). Although written for freelancers working in the arts (writers, actors, dancers, and so on), this is an interesting book covering everything from coping with job-related stress to getting onto a TV game show.

The Psychology of Call Reluctance: How to Overcome the Fear of Self-Promotion. George Dudley and Shannon Goodson (Behavioral Science Research Press). Teaches you to overcome any reluctance to sell yourself; especially useful if you really hate cold-calling.

Secrets of a Freelance Writer: How to Make $85,000 a Year. Robert W. Bly (Dodd, Mead & Company). Lots of good ideas about selling your services.

Taxes, Insurance, and General Business Information

The Complete Guide to Health Insurance.. Kathleen Hogue (Walker & Co.).

Health Insurance Made Easy—Finally. Sharon Stark (S. L. Stark, 7525 Norwood, Prairie Village, KS 66208, (913) 383-9039). Stark used to be a benefit approver and customer service representative for a medical insurance company. This is a detailed description of all the medical insurance benefits and exclusions, and what to look for when buying a policy.

How Do I Pay for My Long Term Health Care? Maya Altman (Berkeley Planning Association). This is aimed at retirees and preretirees.

How to Keep Your Hard-Earned Money: the Tax Saving Handbook for the Self-Employed. Henry Aiy'm Fellman (Solutions Press, Inc., (800) 211-0544, ISBN 0-9648715-05-5). A general introduction into the things you can do to cut your tax bill. Covers the pros and cons of deducting home-office expenses, hiring family members, setting up retirement plans, and so on.

Insuring Your Business. Sean Mooney, (I.I.I. Press). Free from the Insurance Information Institute, 110 William Street, New York, NY 10038. You can call the institute at (212) 669-9200.

J. K. Lasser's Your 19xx Income Tax. The J. K. Lasser Institute (Simon & Schuster). Reissued toward the end of each year. This is a good guide to your taxes. Includes a special year-end supplement, mailed to your home, providing last-minute tax updates and a telephone hot line with taped information on over 50 subjects.

The Only Other Investment Guide You'll Ever Need. Andrew Tobias (Bantam). The sequel to *Still the Only Investment Guide You'll Ever Need.* A good way to make sure you use your newfound wealth wisely.

Payment Refused. William Shernoff (Richardson & Steirman). If you are interested in some of the dirty tricks that insurance companies use to avoid paying your claims, read this. It gives a little information on protecting your rights, also.

Shopping for Health Care in Confusing Times. Henry Berman and Louise Rose (Consumer Reports).

Small-Time Operator. Bernard Kamoroff (Bell Springs). This best-seller is a clear, concise guide to keeping your accounts and paying taxes.

Still the Only Investment Guide You'll Ever Need. Andrew Tobias (Bantam). A good way to figure out what to do with all the extra money you are going to earn, and a useful discussion about life insurance. You may also want to read *The Only Other Investment Guide You'll Ever Need.*

What's Wrong With Your Life Insurance? Norman F. Dacey (Macmillan Publishing Co.).

Winning the Insurance Game. Ralph Nader and Wesley Smith (Knightsbridge Publishing). Misnamed; it should have been *Trying to Win the Insurance Game.* The way the insurance industry has the odds stacked against you, there's not much chance of actually winning. You're going to need all the help you can get. This book's a good one.

The Writer's Pocket Tax Guide. You can find this on the World Wide Web: http://www.nyx.net/~dcypser/home.html

Much, Much, More

For information about many more technical-writing related books, go to these sites on the World Wide Web:

John Renish's Booklist (available in various locations, in several formats):

Viewable in your Web browser: http://www.interlog.com/~ksoltys/twritres.html or http://stc.org/pics/idsig/booklist/

Downloadable Microsoft Word and text files: http://pip.dknet.dk/~pip323/ufm/books.htm, http://www.raycomm.com/techwr-l.html, and ftp://listserv.okstate.edu/techwr-l/

Thomas Warren's "Graphics in Technical Communication" list:

Downloadable Microsoft Word files and text files: http://pip.dknet.dk/~pip323/ufm/books.htm, http://www.raycomm.com/techwr-l.html, and ftp://listserv.okstate.edu/techwr-l/

Index

A

Accommodations, cost of, 87
Accountants, 149
Active voice, 27–28
ACW-L mailing list, 224
Advantages of freelancing, 43–48
  easier to find new work, 45
  easier to leave a bad job, 45
  happiness with freelancing lifestyle,
    48
  job security, 46–47
  money, 44
  more balanced view of life, 44–45
  no background checks, 47–48
  no office politics, 47
  opportunity to move, 46
  referral fees, 48
  speaking your mind, 48
  a stepping-stone to other endeavors,
    46
  time off, 44
  travel, 46
  variety, 43
Agencies (technical writing or technical
  service agencies), 32
  companies that only use, 145–46
  contracts with, 33–34, 103–4
  finding, 71–80
    all agencies, reasons to contact, 72–74
    asking colleagues, 75–76
    building a list with other writers, 76
    contractors' publications, 77
    in newspapers, 77–78
    mailing, preparing a, 78–79
    one agency, working with, 74–75
    the Internet, 78
    Yellow Pages, 76–77
  insurance offered by, 59–60
  keeping in touch with contacts in, 135
  list of, 253–57
  pseudo-salaried employees of, 34

  questions to ask, 81–90
    company offering the contract, 84
    contractors or employees, 82
    401(k) plans, 86
    industry the job is in, 82
    length of contract, 83
    long-term disability policy, 85
    medical insurance, 84–85
    mileage allowance, 86
    miscellaneous personal considerations,
      86
    moving expenses, 88
    out-of-town contracts, 86–88
    overtime, 84
    per diems, 87
    permanent position or contract, 82
    rates of pay, 83–84
    state and local taxes, 87
    type of work, 82
    vacations and sick leave, 85–86
    where the job is, 84
  starting your own, 168
  true salaried employees of, 34–35
  unethical behavior that hurts clients,
    91–97
    competition among agencies, 93–94
    less qualified persons, encouraging
      clients to take, 95
    many good contractors do not work
      with agencies, 94
    percentage of the pay kept by agencies,
      94
    reasons companies should avoid
      agencies, 92
    references, checking of, 92–93
    rehiring the contractor not allowed,
      95
    unknowingly getting independents,
      95–96
Amortization, 160
Anderson, Paul V., 25
Appearance, 119–20

B

Background checks, 47–48
Bad-contract cycle, 74
Bankruptcy, incorporation and, 214
Behavioral control, independent-
  contractor status and, 164–65
Benefits, 105–16
  credit unions, 115
  lack of, as disadvantage of freelancing,
    49–50
  medical insurance. *See* Medical insurance
  pension plans. *See* Pension plans
  value of, 57
Benson, Pamela, 25
Books
  on technical writing, 24–25
  writing. *See* Computer books, writing
Brogan, John, 25
Business cards, saving, 138
Business expenses. *See also* **Tax deductions (deductible expenses)**
  estimating excessive, 68
  exaggerated, 66–68
  incorporation and, 208, 209
  unreimbursed, 154–55
Business insurance, 115–16

C

Cafeteria, company, 61
Calls to or from agencies, 80
Capital, savings as, 50
Card file, 134, 135, 143
Center for Mobility Resource's Relocation
  Salary Calculator, 87
Change, ability to handle, 41
Classified ads, 136–37, 142, 143
Clothes, 119–20
COBRA (Consolidated Omnibus Budget
  Reconciliation Act), 106–7
Cold calling, 143–45
College courses in technical writing, 23–24
Command tables, 30
Commuting expenses, 150–51
Competition among agencies, clients hurt
  by, 93–94
COMPOS01 mailing list, 224
CompuServe, 220
Computer books, writing, 231–44
  A-, B-, and C-list books, 237–39
  author reviews, 241
  best-selling books, 236–39
  contracts, 240–41
  income from, 7

Internet resources, 244
  mistakes to avoid in, 235–36
  relations with publisher, 242–43
  royalties, 240–42
  time to reach bookstores, 241–42
  tips for success, 243–44
*Computer Consultants' and Contractors'
  Newsletter*, 252
Conciseness, 26–27
Connections, looking for, 26
Consultants (consulting), 32–33, 167,
  185–96
  associations of, 263
  building a reputation, 193
  charging by the project, 186
  definition of, 186
  estimating projects, 187–89
  explaining the price to clients, 190
  extensions and, 189–90
  finding a niche, 194–95
  finding contracts, 195–96
  juggling projects, 192–93
  just-in-time learning approach, 193
  making contacts, 196
  quality of work and, 192
  time-saving tips, 191
CONSULT forum (CompuServe), 229
Consulting firms, 32
Contacts. *See also* **Networking**
  keeping records of, 138–39
*Contract Employment Weekly
  (C.E. Weekly)*, 80, 252
Contractors. *See* **Independent contractors**
Contracts, 171–81
  book and magazine, 240–41
  client responsibilities provisions, 178
  copyright provisions, 179–81
  document review provisions, 176–77
  extension provisions, 177
  factors to consider in signing, 175–76
  fixed-fee, 174–75
  letter of agreement, 172–73
  more information on, 181
  overtime provisions, 177
  payment terms, 171–74
  restrictive covenants in, 103–4
  technical accuracy provisions, 176
  with technical service agencies, 33–34
COPYEDITING-L mailing list, 224
Copyright
  contract provisions on, 179–81
  registering a, 180
Corporation. *See also* **Incorporation**
  getting money out of, 213
Correspondence courses, 264–67
"Country club" atmosphere, 119

Courses, 264–67
  technical writing, 23
Cover letter for agencies, 79
Credit unions, 115
Cross-references, 29

D

Day care, 62
Death benefits, incorporation and, 213
Deen, Roger L., 3
Dental insurance, 59
Depreciation, 160
Direct mail, finding work via, 195–96
Disability insurance, 60, 112–13
  incorporation and, 212, 216
  of agencies, 85
Disadvantages of freelancing, 49–55
  long-term work relationships, lack of, 50
  management positions not available, 53
  mentor or guide, lack of, 50
  no benefits, 49–50
  not getting paid, 54
  office politics, no opportunity to get involved in, 50–51
  pension plans, 51
  savings, need for more, 50
  sell yourself, need to, 51
  time spent job hunting, 52
  training not available, 53
  uncertainty and insecurity, feelings of, 51–52
  vacations, not getting, 52
  Workers' Compensation insurance not available, 53
Discounts, employee, 62
Discussion groups, 227. *See also* Mailing lists; Newsgroups
Dividends, 213
Double-taxation, 209, 211–13
Dragging a job out, 120

E

Earnings. *See* Income
Earnings of technical writers, 4–7
Editors, professional, 30
Education. *See also* Training
  company-paid, 61
  self-, 131
Eighth-grade reading level, 28
E-mail, contacting agencies via, 80

Employee benefits. *See* Benefits
Employee discounts, 62
Employees
  of technical service agencies
    pseudo-salaried, 34
    true salaried, 34–35
  status as, for tax purposes, 163–69
  talking money with, 121
  temporary, 31, 33
Expenses. *See also* Business expenses
  contract provisions on, 178
  deductible. *See* Tax deductions
Experience
  needed by contractors, 36
  wide range of, 45

F

401(k) plans, 60
  agencies and, 86
Faxes, contacting agencies via, 80
Feature tables, 30
Fellman, Henry Aiy'm, 214–15
FICA (Social Security tax), 159
  calculating your income and, 62–64
  incorporation and, 207
Figures, 28–29
Financial control, independent-contractor status and, 164, 165
Finding work. *See* Job hunting
Fixed-fee contracts, 174–75
Fixed fees, payment schedules for, 54
Fog Index, Gunning's, 28
Form 4562, 160
Freelancing (freelance writers), 31–42. *See also* Independent contractors (independent freelancers; sole proprietors)
  advantages of, 43–48
    easier to find new work, 45
    easier to leave a bad job, 45
    happiness with freelancing lifestyle, 48
    job security, 46–47
    money, 44
    more balanced view of life, 44–45
    no background checks, 47–48
    no office politics, 47
    opportunity to move, 46
    referral fees, 48
    speaking your mind, 48
    a stepping-stone to other endeavors, 46
    time off, 44
    travel, 46
    variety, 43
  definitions of, 31

Freelancing (freelance writers), *(continued)*
disadvantages of, 49–55
long-term work relationships, lack of,
50
management positions not available,
53
mentor or guide, lack of, 50
no benefits, 49–50
not getting paid, 54
office politics, no opportunity to get
involved in, 50–51
pension plans, 51
savings, need for more, 50
sell yourself, need to, 51
time spent job hunting, 52
training not available, 53
uncertainty and insecurity, feelings of,
51–52
vacations, not getting, 52
Workers' Compensation insurance not
available, 53
income of, 5–7
skills needed for, 38–42
change, ability to handle, 41
get on well with people, ability to, 42
gossip, inclination to, 40–41
learn quickly, ability to, 41–42
money-handling ability, 38–39
reputation for being good at what you
do, 41
self-motivation, 41
sell yourself, ability to, 39–40
uncertainty, ability to handle, 39
three-step method of, 36–37
types of, 33–35
Fringe benefits. *See* **Benefits**

G

Gender gap, in income of technical writers,
8–9
Geographical location
of agency jobs, 84
of technical writers, 9
income and, 5
Getting on well with people, 42
Gunning's Fog Index, 28

H

Headings, 28
Health club, 61
Health insurance. *See* **Medical insurance**
Health Insurance Portability and Account-
ability Act of 1996 (Kennedy-Kassebaum
bill), 107–8, 110

Health Maintenance Organizations
(HMOs), 59, 108–9
Helping people, networking and, 138
Home office, tax deductions for, 153–54
Hourly rate, 5–7, 129. *See also* **Income**
(earnings)
at permanent job, calculating, 57
when to make calculations, 58
negotiating with agencies and, 83–84
percentage kept by agencies, 94
Hours worked per year, 64
HTML, creating Web pages with, 194

I

Income (earnings). *See also* **Hourly rate;**
Salary
as advantage of freelancing, 44
from permanent job, calculating,
57–68
cafeteria, company, 61
day care, 62
deducting expenses, 67–68
disability insurance, 60
discounts, 62
educational courses, 61
employer contributions to pension
plans and tax-free savings plans,
61
expenses, job-related, 66
expenses that are not business-related,
67
FICA (Social Security tax), 62–64
health club membership, 61
hours worked per year, 64
medical, dental, and vision insurance,
59–60
miscellaneous benefits, 64
pension plans, 67
tax-free savings plans, 60–61
term life insurance, 60
vacations, 67
when to make calculations, 58–59
worksheet for, 64–66
too much, freelancers spoiled by, 53–54
unemployment pay, 53
vacation pay, 52
Income of technical writers, 4–9
gender gap in, 8–9
Incorporation, 168, 207–18
advantages of, 212–13
business expenses and, 208, 209
deducting medical expenses and,
159
disadvantages of, 213–14
do-it-yourself books on, 211

marketing and, 204–5
misconceptions about, 207
saving money by, 215–17
Independent contractors (independent freelancers; sole proprietors), 34. *See also* **Freelancing**
checklist for, 247
definition of, 31
experience needed by, 36
fee basis, 33
hourly rate, 33
publications targeted at, 251–52
reasons companies use, 35–36
savings to clients, 96–97
status as, for tax purposes, 163–69
behavioral control, 164–65
financial control, 164, 165
information on, 169
marketing and, 204–5
safe harbor, 166
taxes and, 157–62
Indexes, 29, 241
Information Mapping, 28
Insecurity, as disadvantage of freelancing, 51–52
Insurance
business, 115–16
disability, 60, 112–13, 216
life, 60, 113, 216
medical. *See* Medical insurance
Internet, the, 22
computer-book publishing resources, 244
finding agencies through, 78
Internet service providers (ISPs), 220
Interviews
networking and, 136, 137
with clients, 99–101
IRAs (Individual Retirement Accounts), 60, 61, 114

J

Jargon, 27
Java and JavaScript, 194
Job banks, 136, 142
Job Express, **252**
Job fairs, 137, 143
Job hunting (finding work), 45, 141–47. *See also* **Agencies, finding**
consulting work, 195–96
need to spend more time, 52
not-so-cold calling, 143–45
online, 219
online resources, 227–29
published writings and, 231–32
steps to, 141–43

Job offers, from agencies, 72–74
Job satisfaction, 37–38
Job security, 46–47
Job shops, 32
Joint employment, 96
Just-in-time learning approach, 193

K

Kelley, Robert E., 175
Kennedy-Kassebaum bill, 107–8, 110
Keogh plans, 61, 114–15

L

Lant, Jeffrey, 135
Learning. *See also* **Training**
quickly, 41–42
Letter of agreement, 172–73
Library research, 143
Life insurance
incorporation and, 212, 216
term, 60, 113
Limited liability, 214
Liquidation, 213
Living costs, out-of-town contracts and, 87
Loans, from your corporation, 213
Location, geographical
of agency jobs, 84
of technical writers, 9
income and, 5
Long-term disability insurance. *See* **Disability insurance**
Long-term work relationships, lack of, 50
Lunches, business, 137

M

McGehee, Brad M., 25
Magazine articles, writing, 231–34
mistakes to avoid in, 235–36
Mailing, preparing a, 78–79
Mailing labels, for agencies, 78
Mailing lists, 222
job leads, 228
Management positions not available to freelancers, 53
Maternity insurance, 59
Medical expenses
deducting, 159
incorporation and, 212, 216
Medical insurance, 59–60, 105–12
COBRA (Consolidated Omnibus Budget Reconciliation Act) and, 106–7

Medical insurance, *(continued)*
  deducting from your taxes, 112, 159,
    215–16
  finding your own, 106
  group policies, 109–10
  Health Maintenance Organizations
    (HMOs), 108–9
  individual policies, 109
  Kennedy-Kassebaum bill and, 107–8, 110
  of agencies, 84–85
  reducing the cost of, 111
  spouse's, 108
  tax deductions for, 60
Medical Savings Accounts (MSAs), 110
Mentor, lack of, 50
Mileage allowance, agencies and, 86
Money. *See also* **Income (earnings)**
  ability to handle, 38–39
**Moving, choice of, as advantage of
  freelancing,** 46
Moving expenses, 88, 157
Multimedia authoring, 195

N

Nader, Ralph, 106
Networking, 133–39, 219
  information needed for, 133–34
  tips for building a network, 134–38
Newsgroups, 222, 226–28
  job leads, 227–28
Newspapers, finding agencies in, 77–78
Nonwords, 27

O

Office politics, 47
  no opportunity to get involved in, 50–51
Online access. *See also* **Internet, the**
  need for, 219
On-the-job training, 24
Organizations for technical writers, 258–63
Overtime, 84, 121–25
  contract provisions, 177
  joint employment and, 96
"Overtime, Once Again," 123–25

P

PAGEMAKR mailing list, 224
Parties, 137
Payments (getting paid), 44
  not getting paid, 54
  timely, contract provisions on, 177
Payment terms, 171–74

Pension plans, 51, 60–61
  employer contributions to, 61
  exaggerating the cost of, 67
  incorporation and, 212
  SEP, 61, 114
Per diems, 87, 151–53
Permanent jobs
  agency's clients kept from offering, 95
  calculating income from, 57–68
    cafeteria, company, 61
    day care, 62
    deducting expenses, 67–68
    disability insurance, 60
    discounts, 62
    educational courses, 61
    *employer contributions to pension
      plans and tax-free savings plans,
      61*
    expenses, job-related, 66
    *expenses that are not business-related,
      67*
    FICA (Social Security tax), 62–64
    health club membership, 61
    hours worked per year, 64
    *medical, dental, and vision insurance,
      59–60*
    miscellaneous benefits, 64
    pension plans, 67
    tax-free savings plans, 60–61
    term life insurance, 60
    vacations, 67
    when to make calculations, 58–59
    worksheet for, 64–66
Price, Jonathan, 25
Profession, technical writing as a, 13–14
Professional associations, 135–36, 258–63
  online job leads, 229
Profit, deducting, 68
Promptness, 119
Proofreading, 30
Pseudo-salaries, 34
Publications. *See also specific publications*
  contractors', finding agencies in, 77

R

Readers, 26
Reading level, 28
Recruiters, 137
Redundancies, 27
References, checking of, by agencies,
  92
Referral fees, 48
Rehiring contractors, by clients, 95
**Relocation Salary Calculator, Center for
  Mobility Resource's,** 87

Reputation
building a, as a consultant, 193
for being good at what you do, 41
Research, online, 219
Restrictive covenants, 103–4
Résumés
for agencies, 79, 80
updating your, 21–22
Royalties, 240–42

S

Sabbaticals, 44
Salary, 4–5, 213. *See also* **Hourly rate;**
Income (earnings)
pseudo-, 34
Sales (marketing), 197–205
always look for, 198
asking for a high hourly rate and, 203
assuming, 200
bringing objections of client into the open,
201
familiarity with programs and, 199–200
incorporation and, 204–5
of solutions, not skills, 202
online, 229–30
positive approach, 199
practicing, 204
promises and verbal agreements not
enough, 198
self-confidence and, 200
setting yourself apart from other writers,
200–201
the more leads the better, 197–98
Sales taxes, 87
Savings, as business capital, 50, 130–31
Savings plans, tax-free, 60–61, 113–15
Schedule C, 158–59
S corporation, 217
Self-confidence, sales and, 200
Self Employment tax, 66, 157–59
Self-motivation, 41
Selling yourself, 39–40
Sell in *versus* sell through, 242
Seminars, 267
Seminars, technical-writing, 24
SEP (Simplified Employee Pension) plans,
61, 114
Shenson, Howard, 174
Sick leave, agencies and, 85–86
Skills needed for freelancing, 38–42
change, ability to handle, 41
get on well with people, ability to, 42
gossip, inclination to, 40–41
learn quickly, ability to, 41–42
money-handling ability, 38–39

reputation for being good at what you do,
41
self-motivation, 41
sell yourself, ability to, 39–40
uncertainty, ability to handle, 39
Small business associations, 262–63
Small Claims courts, 54
Smith, Wesley, 106
Social Security tax. *See* **FICA**
Society for Technical Communication
(STC), 4, 24, 25, 258–59
getting started as a technical writer and,
20–21
medical insurance, 110
Software testing, 195
Sole proprietors, 34. *See also* **Independent**
contractors (independent freelancers;
sole proprietors)
Solutions, selling, 202
State and local taxes, 87
STCCICSIG-L mailing list, 223
Stock profits, incorporation and, 212–13
Subheadings, 28
Success, chances of, 54–55

T

Table of contents, 29
Tables, 28–29
feature, 30
Tautology, avoiding, 26
Tax credits, for day care, 62
Tax deductions (deductible expenses), 150
for business expenses, 67
home office, 153–54
insurance and medical costs, 159
mileage, 150–51
moving expenses, 157
not business-related
67
per diems, 151–53
travel expenses, 151–53
Taxes, 149–62
books and publications, 161–62
filing, 154–57
forms you need, 160
incorporation and, 209–14
independent freelancers (sole proprietors)
and, 157–62
miscalculating, calculating expense of
being a freelancer and, 66
of freelance "employees" of agencies, 154
out-of-town contracts and, 87
per diem and, 87
preparing your own returns, 149–50
sales, 87

Tax-free savings plans, 60–61,
  113–15
   employer contributions to, 61
Tax preparers, 149
Tax Reform Act of 1986, 166
TECHCOMM mailing list, 223
Technical Employment Weekly
  (originally *PD News*), 80, 251
Technical-service agencies, 32
Technical writers
   job of, 4
   typical backgrounds of, 14–15
Technical writing
   as profession or trade, 13–14
   drawbacks of, 9–10
TECHWR-L mailing list, 222–23
TEKCOM-L mailing list, 223
Temporary employees, 31, 33
Term life insurance, 60, 113
Time off, 44
Training, 21
   not available to freelancers,
     53
   on-the-job, 24
Training courses, 264–67
Travel, as advantage of freelancing,
  46
Travel expenses, 151–53
T-TELCOM mailing list, 224

U

Uncertainty
   ability to handle, 39
   as disadvantage of freelancing,
     51–52
Unemployment pay, 53
Unreimbursed business expenses,
  154–55

V

Vacation pay, 52
Vacations, 44, 52
   agencies and, 85–86
   assigning a value to, 67
Variety, as advantage of freelancing, 43
Veterans, medical services for, 106
Vision insurance, 59

W

"We Always Pay Time-and-a-Half for
  Overtime," 121–23
Weiss, Edmond, 28
What Is a "Fair" Rate?, 89
Williams, Patricia, 25
Windows Help files, 194
WINHLP-L mailing list, 225
Winning the Insurance Game (Nader and
  Smith), 106, 109
WORD-MAC mailing list, 225
WORD-PC mailing list, 225
WORDPRO mailing list, 225
Words, short vs. long, 27
Workers' Compensation insurance, 53
Work for hire, 179, 181
   avoiding all mention of, 180
Work habits, 117–21
World Wide Web (the Web), 220–22
WP51-L mailing list, 225–26
WPWIN-L mailing list, 226
WRITERS mailing list, 226

Y

Yellow Pages, finding agencies in, 76–77
Young, Matt, 25